# The Devadasi

### The Life and Times of Ban

Sriram. V

**EastWest**

Venkat Towers, 165, P.H. Road, Maduravoyal, Chennai 600 095
No. 38/10 (New No.5), Raghava Nagar, New Timber Yard Layout, Bangalore 560 026
Survey No. A - 9, II Floor, Moula Ali Industrial Area, Moula Ali, Hyderabad 500 040
23/181, Anand Nagar, Nehru Road, Santacruz East, Mumbai 400 055
4322/3, Ansari Road, Daryaganj, New Delhi 110 002

*Copy Editor:* Rukmini Amirapu

ISBN: 978-81-88661-70-1

*Cover design:* Art Works, Chennai

*Typeset in* BakerSignet

*Printed at*
Repro India Ltd. Navi Mumbai

# Contents

Dedicated
to the memory of
Banni Bai
whose dearest wish it was that the
story of Bangalore Nagarathnamma be told

# Foreword

Sriram.V. has an established reputation as a social historian concentrating on Carnatic music, heritage in general, and environmental issues. His book 'Carnatic Summer' has received great welcome as a volume of biographies of some towering figures of Carnatic music, biographies that bring the subjects before us, warts and all, and not hagiographies. He has now come out with the biography of an extraordinary lady, Bangalore Nagarathnammal whose name will be remembered as long as Tyagaraja's name is remembered.

Nagarathnammal was a doughty feminist at a time when feminism was just beginning to make its way in the West and was almost unheard of in India. Her achievements are all the greater for the fact that she came from a community that was generally looked down upon. She grew up in near poverty but competence and determination enabled her to establish herself in life as a musician and dancer and to command the respect of fellow artists, including the most famous. The story of how she fought for the right of women to perform at the annual Tyagaraja *aradhana* in the teeth of opposition from prominent figures who were running it is told by Sriram in detail. So are the stories of her determination to get an authentic version of the book *Radhika Santwanamu* published and distributed resulting in the book being banned by the Government of Madras and her part in fighting the *Anti-Nautch* movement that sent most of the Devadasi community into penury and threatened to destroy the legacy of *Sadir, padams* and *javalis*.

But it is for her role in building a *Mandapam* round the Samadhi of the great composer Tyagaraja that she will be remembered. She stepped in when two different groups were conducting the *Aradhana* without doing anything practical in the matter and spent the fortune she had earned in constructing the *Mandapam* and ensuring that the Samadhi was an attractive memorial to the saint-composer. She spent the last part of her life in Tiruvayyaru looking after the proper upkeep of the memorial.

Nagarathnammal played an important part in bringing together the two rival factions celebrating the *Aradhana*, though ultimately, she was "no longer the prime mover of the *Aradhana* " as Sriram puts it. But truly she was a Dasi in the temple of Tyagaraja. She is present today in Tiruvayyaru through a life size stone image in a sitting posture with folded hands facing the Samadhi. She would have wished for no more.

All this and more are brought out by Sriram in the book. The trouble he has taken to get his facts is obvious in the narrative. If one may be pardoned for using a hoary cliché he has left no stone unturned. Interestingly, the archives of the Government of Madras\Tamilnadu have proved a rich source of material. Sriram has woven a skilful narrative in this volume which I commend to all lovers of Carnatic Music and devotees of Tyagaraja.

**K.V.Ramanathan**
*Editor-in-Chief*
*Sruti,*
*October 2007*

# Introduction

*"O Ladies! See how sweet is His speech as He discusses with Tyagaraja the merits of the dance and the music of the celestial women and dancing girls, adept in handling Sringara Rasa"* (Tyagaraja in "Paluku Kandachakkarenu", raga Navarasa Kannada, tala Deshadi)[1]

~

Classical Indian music is today divided into two distinct streams, the North Indian Hindustani and the South Indian Carnatic. This book deals with the second art form. However, this is not a book on music appreciation nor is it on the rules that govern music. It is simply the chronicle of a woman's life, a woman who was a practising Carnatic musician and more importantly a Devadasi – a term that meant handmaiden of God, at one time respectable and regarded as the custodian of the arts. It later came to be equated with prostitution.

The concept of dedicating women to temples or places of worship is as old as civilisation. The custom existed in Greek, Roman, Egyptian and other ancient cultures. Indian cultures were no exception and the system was well developed in South India in particular, from very early on. There was a rigid hierarchy among these women, based on the duties they performed at the temple, which varied from washing vessels and sweeping the floor, to stringing garlands of flowers, preparing sandal paste and at the highest level of sophistication, singing and dancing before the deity. Such women were considered to be married to the deity and were recognised as respectable members of society. There was no particular caste from which women could be drawn for dedication and there are instances in the legends of princesses and girls from priestly classes becoming handmaidens of God.[2] The Devadasis thus formed an occupational group rather than a caste.[3] Those who sang and danced were trained rigorously in the performing arts and were hence considered custodians of tradition and of the arts.

There were women dedicated to the arts outside the ambit of the temple too. Some were attached to kings and others to rich patrons, while another group entertained the public through music and dance especially during celebrations and social occasions. While there was a clear distinction between the various categories, over a period of time, especially with the arrival of the British, these boundaries faded and the term Devadasi came to encompass all such women. They were referred to in local parlance by various terms such as *Kalavanth*, *Sani*, *Sule* and *Devar Adiyal*.

Being married to a deity meant an escape from widowhood for Devadasis and when they passed away, the deity of the temple underwent a ritual period of mourning. The Devadasis had certain other privileges as well. Most of them were literate, some were very highly learned and all of them had absolute right to the properties bequeathed to them by the temple in return for their services. Chastity was not a parameter in their line of work and they could take on patrons. They were never considered to be prostitutes.

Given the rather unique status that Devadasi women enjoyed as compared to the lot of women in other castes and strata of society, girls were the preferred progeny. This too contrasted with the commonly held notion in India that boys meant social security and an assured future while girl children only meant lifelong expenditure and trouble.

Property held by Devadasis passed on from mother to daughter, a unique matriarchal system in a predominantly male-dominated society. Adoption of girls was therefore common among Devadasis and as late as the early years of the 20th century, even poor Brahmin families gave away their daughters in adoption to well-to-do Devadasis.

The history of the Devadasis and the history of the development of South Indian music and dance are intertwined. Both depended on patronage which in turn depended on peace and prosperity. The South Indian kingdoms were largely spared from frequent invasions and it is no wonder that music and dance flourished and so did the Devadasi system.

The lands near the rivers Krishna, Godavari and the Kaveri, owing to regular deposits of silt were fertile. Prosperity therefore reigned in these regions. Kings and the wealthy could indulge in pursuits such as patronising and nurturing the arts. The Cholas whose ascendancy began in 850 AD with the capture of Tanjavur were active patrons of the arts. During the reign of Raja Raja Chola from 985 to 1013 AD, the construction of the Brihadeeswarar Temple was undertaken and he appointed musicians, singers and dancers for service in various temples in Tanjavur and granted them lands and houses as remuneration. An inscription in the shrine (referred to as Sri Rajarajeswaram), states that as many as 400 dancing girls were appointed for temple service. Most importantly, this inscription identifies the women as belonging to the Lord. The inscription also decrees that the land given to these women be passed on after their death to those among their descendants who were qualified and fit to carry on the same services. The relevant section is reproduced below:

"The Lord Sri Rajaraja Deva had... transferred temple women from (other) temple establishments of the Chola country as temple women of the Lord of the Sri Rajarajesvara (temple). To (these persons) shares were allotted as allowance. The (value) of each share which consisted of the produce of (one) *veli* of land was to be one hundred *kalam* of paddy (measured by the *marakkal* called Adavallan, which is equal to a Rajakesari). Instead of those among these shareholders, who would die or emigrate, the nearest relations of such persons were to receive that allowance and do the work. If the nearest relations were not qualified themselves, (they) were to select (other) qualified persons, to let (these) do the work and to receive (the allowance). If there were no other near relations, the (other) incumbents of such appointments were to select qualified persons from those fit for such appointments, and the person selected was to receive the allowance."[4]

It would be fair to assume that the same practice existed in other temples as well. When the king was powerful and able, as Rajaraja and his son Rajendra were, the system worked well. But with the weakening of the empire, temple administration was neglected and many of the women did not receive their dues. Subsistence necessitated taking on a patron and the progeny that came from such a liaison took to the arts. The girls were trained in music and dance and the men became dance teachers and instrumentalists. Thus what started off as a professional guild crystallised into a caste.

The Cholas were defeated by the Pandyas of Madurai in 1279 AD and there followed a hundred years of confusion, with wars being fought between the Pandyas and the Hoysalas in the south and the Kakatiyas and the Yadavas in the north. In 1310 AD, Malik Kafur invaded from the north and in 1318 AD the short-lived sultanate of Madurai came into being. The Vijayanagar rulers overthrew this in 1378 AD and the south came under that empire.

Under the Vijayanagar kings, art once again flourished and reached its zenith during the reign of King Krishnadeva Raya who ruled from 1509 to 1529 AD. This period saw the emergence of the Carnatic tradition of music, with composers such as Tallapaka Annamacharya (1408-1503 AD) and Purandara Dasa (1484-1564 AD), leaving their imprint on the art form. There are records of dancing and singing women being attached to temples and a parallel group being attached to the palace with women of both strains being accorded great respect by the ruler and the common people. Kannada and Telugu were the state languages, along with Sanskrit which was preferred by the Brahmins who occupied high posts. The Devadasis settled in many parts of South India and during the process of expanding their repertoire of songs, became polyglots.

When the Vijayanagar Empire splintered following the battle of Tallikota in 1565 AD, the local viceroys, titled Nayaks, declared themselves independent. The remnants of the Vijayanagar dynasty set up court in Chandragiri, but the Nayaks of Tanjavur, Madurai and Gingee became the real powers. The Nayak kingdom of Tanjavur emerged stable and prosperous, thanks to a series of enlightened rulers and the proximity of the river Kaveri and its numerous tributaries which ensured plenty of agricultural produce and therefore wealth. The rulers were also munificent patrons of the arts and many of them were musicologists and practising musicians. It also helped that Govinda Dikshita the musicologist, scholar and administrator was chief minister during the reigns of two kings namely Achyutappa Nayak (1572-1614 AD) and Raghunatha Nayak (1600-1634 AD). The modern-day veena was perfected during the reign of Raghunatha Nayak, which also saw the writing of several important treatises on music. The third ruler, Vijayaraghava Nayak (1633-1673 AD) had as his minister Govinda Dikshita's son Venkatamakhi who wrote the *Chaturdandi Prakasika*, a monumental treatise on music. Scholars, musicians and artistes came from far and wide, seeking their patronage. Among these were several Brahmin families from the Andhra region who were gifted lands in the Kaveri delta for sustenance. Telugu being the lingua franca, also became the language of choice for musical compositions. A further fillip to the Carnatic repertoire came in the form of Kshetrayya, a 17th century composer who left behind a large corpus of love poems mostly with the signature of Muvva Gopala. These songs, classified as *Padams* ideally suited the *abhinaya* art of the Devadasis and soon other composers of the *padam* emerged, some of them in Tamil as well. The *javali*, yet another form of love song emerged around the same time and also became completely identified with the Devadasi repertoire.

The status of performing women artistes remained high during the reign of the Nayak kings. Devadasis being almost the sole category of women who could aspire to education, were greatly honoured in the Nayak court. Two women artistes of Raghunatha Nayak's reign were Ramabhadramba and Madhuravani. Ramabhadramba was attached to the ruler himself and wrote the *Raghunatha Nayakabhyudayamu*, a fine Telugu work in his praise. The last ruler, Vijayaraghava too maintained a court which boasted of some very erudite and scholarly women artistes. The court poet Chengalvakalakavi in his Telugu work *Rajagopala Vilasamu* names several women who were experts in different types of dance. Among the court's poets were three women, Rangajamma, Krishnamamba and Lilavati, of whom the first was the ruler's concubine. Her work *Usha Parinayamu* refers to several musical instruments and ragas. Though there is evidence of her having been a composer of *padam*s and verses, these have not surfaced. Rangajamma also composed the *Mannarudasa Vilasamu* which is dedicated to her beloved ruler.[5]

The Nayak reign ended abruptly in 1673 AD due to a war with the Madurai Nayaks which saw the death of Vijayaraghava. A brief interlude followed during which the arts were the first casualty. However in 1676 AD, the son of Vijayaraghava Nayak sought the help of the Marathas in regaining his throne. Ekoji, half brother of the great Maratha chieftain Sivaji, arrived and liked the area so much that he declared himself the ruler, thereby ushering in the Maratha rule in Tanjavur, which was to last till 1799 AD.

The arts received great encouragement under the Marathas. The rulers appreciated the beauty of Telugu and Sanskrit and these languages continued to hold sway over the region. Rulers such as Sahaji (1684-1712 AD), Tulaja I (1728-1736 AD), Ekoji II (1736-1739 AD) and Sarabhoji II (1798-1799 AD) were composers in these languages as well.[6] The court teemed with scholarly activity and creative output. However it was also with the arrival of the Marathas that the role of women became subordinate in court and scholarly matters. Among the few exceptions was Muddupalani, concubine of the ruler Pratapasimha (1739-1763 AD), whose erotic work *Radhika Santvanamu* was the subject of a key episode in Bangalore Nagarathnammal's life as we shall see later in this book. Women continued to be active in the arts, but more as performers and not as scholars who created operas, songs or plays. However, they benefited from the ever increasing repertoire of songs. The Maratha rulers and their court poets created several operas for performance in temples during festivals and these were handed over to the Devadasis. Soon these pieces became family heirlooms and were handed down from mother to daughter.

The smooth fabric of life in Tanjavur began to slowly unravel with repeated invasions by neighbouring rulers such as Hyder Ali, his son Tipu Sultan and the Nawabs of Arcot. The English, who had set up factories and later forts in Madras and Cuddalore began to play an important role in the area by the time of Tulaja II (1763-1787 AD), the penultimate ruler of Maratha Tanjavur. Tulaja's rule witnessed not only upheavals in political terms but also in the field of Carnatic music and therefore in the larger sphere of the arts. The arrival of three major composers, collectively referred to as the Carnatic Trinity, revolutionised the world of music. There were several common features in all three lives. All of them were born in the temple town of Tiruvarur at around the same time, all three were taught music by near mythical personalities and they all eschewed royal patronage, even while dedicating their lives to music.

Syama Sastri (1762-1827 AD) was born into a family that officiated at the shrine of Bangaru Kamakshi in Tanjavur. In time, he became the chief priest there and dedicated most of his small corpus of songs to this deity. The youngest among the trio was Muttuswami Dikshitar (1776-1835 AD), who hailing from a strongly musical family adopted a peripatetic lifestyle that revolved around temples. He composed largely in Sanskrit and despite being a scholar and a practitioner of the esoteric *Sri Vidya* cult, taught his songs to a number of *nagaswaram* artistes, dance masters, drummers and at least two Devadasis. Dikshitar's songs, associated as they were with temples, were kept alive by Devadasis despite they being largely religious in content.

It was however the second of the Carnatic Trinity who was destined to become most famous. This was Tyagaraja (1767-1847 AD). Although born in Tiruvarur, Tyagaraja grew up immersed in an atmosphere of devotion to Rama in Tiruvayyaru. The composer took to worshipping his idol with music and in time there grew a great corpus of songs created in a brilliant new idiom in which day to day happenings and a wealth of emotions were incorporated. Tyagaraja experimented with new ragas, composed in a variety of metres and also experimented with the opera in which category two of his works have survived. He had a large retinue of disciples, all men, who began spreading the songs far and wide. In time, the songs of Tyagaraja became the mainstay of the Carnatic platform. Significantly, Tyagaraja's songs were not very popular with the Devadasi tradition. Most of his disciples were Brahmins and his songs emphasised the devotional element rather than eroticism, which was the mainstay of songs sung by the Devadasis.

During the lifetime of the Trinity, Sarabhoji, the last ruler of the Maratha dynasty ascended the throne in 1798. The very next year he voluntarily gave away his kingdom to the British, preferring to be their pensioner. With plenty of time on his hands, Sarabhoji became a great patron of the arts attracting several composers and artistes to his court. He spent his energies in renovating and enhancing the great Saraswathi Mahal library which even today remains a treasure house of manuscripts on music and much more. The British influence also became palpable. The violin came into Carnatic music and the Devadasi ensemble and so did the clarinet.[7] It became fashionable for singers and dancers to learn some English songs for the entertainment of the foreigners who became visible at dance performances organised by wealthy natives. The *manipravalam* genre, which comprised songs that had more than one language, saw the addition of English as well.[8]

Though Sarabhoji and after him, his son Sivaji II (d 1855) kept up the patronage to various temples and ensured that Devadasis were protected, the palace artistes began seeking greener pastures and this was the city of Madras where several rich businessmen, *dubashes* and *nabobs* were living. The *Sarva Deva Vilasa*, a manuscript that describes the fledgling city of Madras in the 18th century, speaks of several rich patrons and courtesans attached to their retinue. With the decline of the Maratha court in the 19th century, Madras became the centre of power and soon many Devadasis settled there. The princely states of Mysore, Pudukottah, Travancore and the principalities of Ramanathapuram, Sivaganga, Pithapuram, Bobbili, Vizianagaram and Venkatagiri emerged as centres of patronage as well and many Devadasis moved to these areas.[9] This meant abandoning the temples to which they had originally been attached. But by then these shrines had ceased to be a source of income and it became clear that the temporal patron held the key to a comfortable existence. The divisions between the various types of performing women completely vanished and a majority of them took to performing for the rich and mighty businessmen, government officials and ruling princes. Duties in the temples too became less well defined except in the larger shrines such as Tiruvarur, xviii The Devadasi and The Saint

Srirangam and Tiruttani where the responsibilities of the Devadasis were strictly codified. In time most temples required the Devadasis to be present only during the main *puja* hour when it was the dancing girl's responsibility to offer the *kumbha harati* (later corrupted to *kumbharati*). At the end of the worship it involved waving a camphor flame kept on a brass pot and she performed this ritual to the accompaniment of her ensemble. The *kumbharati* became synonymous with the Devadasi system in the early 20th century. If there were many women attached to a temple, they took turns to perform this rite. Devadasis also had specific roles to perform during temple processions, such as warding away the evil eye from the deity. This involved dance performances and also the *kumbharati*.

Dance continued to remain the chief occupation of the women. As they grew older and found it difficult to dance they took to singing and even then they mimed the emotions depicted in the song, as they sang sitting down.

Abbe J. A. Dubois, who had visited India early in the 19th century wrote about Devadasis in his 'Hindu Manners, Customs and Ceremonies'.[10] The work offers a European point of view about the system as it existed at the time of the Carnatic Trinity.

"Courtesans, whose business in life is to dance in the temples and at public ceremonies, and prostitutes are the only women who are allowed to learn to read, sing, or dance. It would be thought a disgrace to a respectable woman to learn to read; and even if she had learnt she would be ashamed to own it. As for dancing, it is left absolutely to courtesans; even if they never dance with men.

The courtesans or dancing girls attached to each temple – are called devdasis (servants or slaves of the gods), but the public call them by the more vulgar name of prostitutes. And in fact they are bound by their profession to grant their favours, if such they be, to anybody demanding them in return for ready money. It appears that at first they were reserved exclusively for the enjoyment of the Brahmins. And these lewd women, who make a public traffic of their charms, are consecrated in a special manner to the worship of the divinities of India. Every temple of any importance has in its service a band of eight, twelve or more. Their official duties consist in dancing and singing within the temple twice a day, morning and evening, and also at public ceremonies. The first they execute with sufficient grace, although their attitudes are lascivious and their gestures indecorous. As regards their singing, it is almost always confined to obscene verses describing some licentious episode in the history of their gods."

It would appear that by the time Dubois visited South India, the public demands on the Devadasis had begun to increase. For he goes on to write:

"Their duties however, are not always confined to religious ceremonies. Ordinary politeness requires that when persons of any distinction make formal visits to each other they must be accompanied by a certain number of these courtesans. To dispense with them would show a want of respect towards the persons visited, whether the visit was one of duty or politeness. These women are also present at marriages and other solemn family meetings."

The practice of drawing girls from various communities for the role of Devadasi appears to have continued even during the visit of Dubois. He writes:

"(They) are recruited from various castes, some among them belonging to respectable families. It is not unusual for pregnant women, with the object of obtaining a safe delivery, to make a vow, with the consent of their husbands, to devote the child that they carry in their womb, if it should turn out a girl, to the temple service. They are far from thinking that this infamous vow offends in any way the laws of decency, or is contrary to the duties of motherhood. In fact no shame whatever is attached to parents whose daughters adopt this career."

Dubois also notes that Devadasis were essentially women of grace and refinement. He notes:

"They employ all the resources and artifices of coquetry. Perfumes, elegant costumes, coiffures best suited to set off the beauty of their hair, which they entwine with sweet scented flowers; a profusion of jewels worn with much taste on different parts of the body; graceful and voluptuous attitudes...

...the quiet seductions which Hindu prostitutes know how to exercise with so much skill resemble in no way the disgraceful methods of the wretched beings who give themselves up to a similar profession in Europe...

. Of all the women in India it is courtesans, and especially those attached to the temples, who are the most decently clothed. Indeed they are particularly careful not to expose any part of the body. Experience has no doubt taught them that for woman to display her charms damps sensual ardour instead of exciting it, and that the imagination is more easily captivated than the eye.

The most shameless prostitute would never dare to stop a man in the streets; and she in turn would indignantly repulse any man who ventured to take any indecent liberty with her."

The fall in temple patronage and the consequent drop in earnings were however forcing the women to sell themselves at the time of Dubois' visit. He writes:

"The Devadasis receive a fixed salary for the religious duties which they perform; but as the amount is small they supplement it by selling their favours in as profitable a manner as possible.

All the time which they have to spare in the intervals of the various ceremonies is devoted to infinitely more shameful practices; and it is not an uncommon thing to see even sacred temples converted into mere brothels."[11]

Dubois' thinking was clearly influenced by his occidental approach. Western-educated Indians thought no differently. The Indian concept of *shringara* or eroticism was considered something to be ashamed of when compared to high-minded Victorian idealism. The concept of a free woman entitled to choose her partners and with absolute right to property and access to education was anathema to this band of people. Such a woman by the very nature of her life was considered immoral and branded as a whore.

The Devadasi system too, witnessed a steep decline in standards of learning. Though it is fashionable today to think of all Devadasis in highly romantic terms, they were in reality a community of women who were exploited by men and then abandoned when they were no longer of any use. Most of them lived in near-poverty, their hereditary links with temples cut off, thanks to changing times. By the turn of the 20th century most depended on wealthy patrons for their upkeep and some took to performing in public as well. Life was especially tough for the older ones who could not attract patrons and many of them often had large families to support. There was also the continuous problem of what to do with the less talented and less good-looking girls. These had no option but to either marry the men of the community or take to a life of prostitution. Ironically, the very community which was meant to give freedom to women was harsh on those who were not gifted with an aptitude for the arts. The menfolk of the community invariably presented many problems with only a few becoming talented musicians, mainly instrumentalists, and dance masters. Those men who were not talented had perforce to become procuring agents for women. Finding patrons for their daughters was the main occupation for many Devadasis and most of them were considered to be hard-nosed grabbers who were out to milk their patrons, bringing untold sorrow to the legitimate wives and families. Addiction to tobacco and alcohol was common and disease due to unhealthy living conditions was rampant. And yet, by a strange quirk of fate, they were also custodians of the arts.

It was a strange situation. On the one hand the community was the storehouse of arts. On the other it was the repository of all evil and every conceivable vice. Opinion was therefore sharply divided. On top of all this was the western mode of education and the relentless pressure from Christian preachers and proselytisers who condemned the entire system as vile. Having never experienced the existence of such a community in their own lands, these people had no hesitation in condemning all Devadasis as prostitutes and their art as sinful.

The orthodox among the Brahmins were of the same view. Tyagaraja, being one of them, abhorred the system though there are unsubstantiated tales that he once witnessed a dance by Muttuswami Dikshitar's Devadasi disciple Kamalam and blessed her. Given such a background and his puritanism, none could have imagined that the life of a Devadasi would become intertwined with the history of his Samadhi. As the Devadasi system declined and was stamped out, this woman alone swam against the tide and made a name for herself, all the while never allowing anyone to forget that she was a Devadasi and proud of it. This was Bangalore Nagarathnamma, a true Devadasi.

### References

[1] Ramanujachari, C; The Spiritual Heritage of Tyagaraja; Ramakrishna Mission; Madras; 1958; hereinafter referred to as Ramanujachari, C; p 567.

[2] Ramesh, MS Miss; 108 Vaishnavite Divya Desams Volume II; TT Devasthanams, Tirupati, 1994.

[3] Jordan, Kay K; From Sacred Servent to Profane Prostitute, A History of the Changing Legal Status of the Devadasis of India, 1857-1947; Manohar Publishers and Distributors, Delhi, 2003, hereinafter referred to as Jordan, Kay K; p 43.

[4] Pandither, Rao Sahib Abraham M; Karunamirtha Sagaram, Book 1; Karunanithi Medical Hall, Tanjore; 1917.

[5] Seetha, S; Tanjore As A Seat Of Music; University of Madras; 2001, hereinafter referred to as Seetha, S; p 34-36.

[6] Ibid; p 64-121.

[7] Seetha, S p111.

[8] Menon, Indira; The Madras Quartet; Roli Books; New Delhi; 1999; hereinafter referred to as Menon, Indira; p 37.

[9] Ibid;

[10] Dubois, Abbe JA; Hindu Manners, Customs and Ceremonies; Oxford; Third Edition Reprinted 1943.

[11] Ibid; p 585-587.

৵৽

# Chapter 1

*"From my very birth, you have blessed me with true devotion*
*and protected me, helping me to lead a respectable life"*
(Tyagaraja in "Pattividuva Raadu", raga Manjari, tala Adi)[1]

~

The birth of a girl child was always a happy occasion for a Devadasi. Putta Lakshmiammal Vaishnavi of Heggade Devanna Kotha[2], a village of considerable antiquity tracing its history to the Pandavas[3] had every reason therefore to be delighted. Her daughter was born on 3rd November 1878, which as per the Indian calendar was the ninth day of the waxing phase of the moon in the month of *Karthikai* (November/ December) in the *Bahudhanya* year.[4] The asterism *Shravishta* was in the ascendant, which augured well for the girl. She would be rich and famous.

Putta Lakshmi then twenty one, was a Devadasi attached to the Sri Kanteswaram Temple of Nanjangud. Strangely enough, for a Devadasi, her mother's name is not recorded, but we do know that her father was one Subbanna, a prosperous Brahmin of Mysore.[5] Putta Lakshmi's patron was M Subba Rao, a *vakil*, of Mysore.[6] Income from temple duties was next to nothing and Putta Lakshmi depended on Subba Rao's munificence to live.

When Nagarathnam was around a year and a half old, Putta Lakshmi fell out with Subba Rao.[7] The parting was painful and the mother and child were stripped of all their possessions, beaten and paraded on the streets.[8] A new patron had to be found.

Mysore was then a veritable crucible of the arts, for under the benign patronage of successive rulers, artistes of various disciplines thrived. After the death of Tipu Sultan in 1799, under the rule of the Wodeyars, temples were built on a lavish scale and earlier ones were renovated and extensively added to in size. Musicians were employed at all the Murzai or palace controlled temples to perform at specific times of the day and on special occasions.

The palace itself had several musicians and dancers on its rolls and they were all housed in Chamarajnagar, a locality that came up specifically for palace employees.[9] When Nagarathnam and her mother arrived in the city, the ruler was Chamaraja Wodeyar X, who had succeeded to the throne in 1868. His reign saw several musical greats visiting the court and performing there.[10] The king was also a trained violinist and often paired up with court musician Seshanna on the veena or as accompanist to singers Chikka Subba Rao and Subbanna. Several compositions were dedicated to him.[11] Drama was yet another of the ruler's passions and plays were regularly staged for his benefit. Putta Lakshmi found a patron for herself in Giribhatta Thimayya a Sanskrit scholar, musician and instructor at the Shakuntala Nataka Sabha, a troupe set up by the Maharajah to stage plays at the palace.[12] He had been decorated with the title of *Sangita Sahitya Kavita Visarada* by the Palace[13] and was a powerful presence in court.

All went well till 1886. Despite being the head of a large family[14], Giribhatta Thimmayya took the mother and daughter under his wing and provided them with food and clothing and most importantly, began teaching Nagarathnam. In her he found a quick learner. Beginning when she was five, the girl learnt music and Sanskrit poetry from him. He laid down a sound foundation of Sanskrit grammar and took pains to ensure that her diction was perfect. Within a short while she had learnt three sections of *Amarakosha*, the Sanskrit thesaurus. In a few more years she became proficient in and could recite sections from the *Jaimini Bharata*, the *Rajasekhara Vilasa* and the *Kumara Vyasa Bharata*.[15] Among the various senior disciples of Giribhatta Thimmayya was Bidaram Krishnappa, son of Viswanathiah, leader of the Mysore Palace troupe of *Yakshagana* artistes.[16] He was entrusted with the task of training Nagarathnam in music.[17] The girl was also made to learn Kannada, Telugu and some English.[18]

It appeared to many of those witnessing her rapid development that soon there would be very little left for Giribhatta Thimmayya to teach her. There were comparisons with the relatively slow progress made by another girl, Chandrarekha. Certain jealous people poisoned the mind of the learned scholar sufficiently enough for him to feel threatened by young Nagarathnam. His enthusiasm waned considerably and by the time Nagarathnam was nine, he broke off all relations with Putta Lakshmi and her daughter. His parting shot was that Nagarathnam was destined to collect cow dung in the streets of Mysore.[19]

It must have been with a sense of déjà vu that Putta Lakshmi assessed the future. The scenario was bleak, for none would have dared to come to the support of a woman at loggerheads with a powerful court poet. There was no option other than to leave Mysore. But not before Putta Lakshmi had sworn to herself that she would never return to the city until her daughter was invited by the Maharajah himself. In response to Giribhatta Thimmayya's comment, she responded that she would ensure that the hands that he predicted were destined to collect cow dung would be presented with gold bangles in appreciation by the Maharajah himself.[20] If she failed, she and her daughter would commit suicide. The two set out with their meagre possessions to distant Kancheepuram. The famed Dhanakoti sisters of that town were good friends of Putta Lakshmi and it was her earnest hope that the elder of the two, Dhanakoti Ammal would consent to becoming Nagarathnam's guru.

The community of performing women pointed at Dhanakoti with pride. She was the undoubted star of their firmament. She and her formidable sisters Kamakshi and Palani Ammal all took pride in being disciples of the Syama Sastri lineage with Kachi Sastri, the grandson-in-law of the great composer having taught their mother. Their grandmother, also a Kamakshi was a renowned performer of her times and was referred to as 'Mettu' Kamakshi owing to her residence in Kancheepuram's Putteri Road, close to the Kacchapeshwara Temple being on a medu or mound.

Dhanakoti was the real celebrity of the family. She teamed up with her sister Kamakshi as the Dhanakoti Sisters and had a successful career as a singer. Her repertoire was extensive, comprising besides Syama Sastri kritis, several songs from Arunchala Kavi's Rama Natakam, Puliyur Doraiswami Iyer's songs, padams of Muthuthandavar and Subbarama Iyer, Palani Andavar kritis and several verses from the Tiruppugazh. Defying convention which said that women could not attempt pallavi singing, she learnt the intricacies and became the first female artiste to sing them. She had a particularly large fan following in Telugu-speaking areas such as Kakinada, Eluru and Rajamundry. Being childless, she showered her affection on all her disciples and kept open house, feeding many and often housing invalids who were treated at her expense. However, Dhanakoti herself was not in the best of health, having been diagnosed with dropsy a few years previously.[21]

When the weary and footsore Putta Lakshmi and Nagarathnam reached Kancheepuram, they would have had no difficulty in finding Dhanakoti's house, for it was known for the generosity of its inhabitants, musical and otherwise. But though the welcome was warm, a bitter disappointment awaited them, as Dhanakoti, owing to worsening health was turning away hopeful disciples. All of Putta Lakshmi's entreaties were of no avail. Dhanakoti recommended the mother and daughter approach a renowned violinist in Srirangam for lessons, but Putta Lakshmi had exhausted whatever financial resources she possessed. Travelling further south on what might be a fruitless visit was impossible and after enjoying the famed Dhanakoti hospitality for sometime, the mother and daughter duo left for Bangalore where Putta Lakshmi's brother Venkitasamappa was a violinist of some repute.

Bangalore, the city whose name would in future get prefixed to Nagarathnam's, was then essentially a cantonment town, rather western in layout and character and very dissimilar to Mysore. The Civil and Military Station was separated by a great swathe of greenery, (later named the Cubbon Park), from the native quarter, the old locality of Pette, dominated by a central fort, then in the process of being dismantled by the British.[22] Nagarathnam's uncle lived in Nagarathpet, one of the great bazaars of the old town. His must have been a modest dwelling, one of the first floor residences above the shops, overlooking a narrow street close to the Kalikamba temple.[23] The temple itself must have seemed a far cry from the vast Srikanteswara shrine to which Nagarathnam and her mother were accustomed, for this was a small structure with the deity visible to everyone on the street, with hardly any space for circumambulation. The homes too were small and the streets were invariably spaces that were "left after the houses had been built".[24] The meanness of space when compared to Mysore must have created a sense of claustrophobia in the mother and daughter but there was no time to think of all this. Like a woman possessed, Putta Lakshmi set to work on her daughter's education.

Getting her daughter to become a court dancer was Putta Lakshmi's ambition and she knew that this was no easy task. The palace had high standards and a panel of court musicians and dancers usually evaluated an aspirant. The process involved checking out the interviewee's knowledge of music and dance, her proficiency in several languages and also her physical beauty and deportment. Scholars would ask tough questions, challenge a posture or gesture that the dancer had used and ask her to respond. Some would compose verses on the spot and ask the dancer to mime the gestures appropriate to its meaning, extempore. All this required an appreciation of literature and verse and profound knowledge of *puranic* lore.[25] Methodically, Putta Lakshmi began getting her trained in all these departments.

For a brief while, Uncle Venkitasamappa taught Nagarathnamma the violin and when she had attained a certain standard, she was apprenticed under Hyderabad Munuswamappa,[26] a well known violinist, who belonged to the lineage of Tyagaraja's disciples.[27] The tutelage was apparently in vocal music, for within a short while Nagarathnam was pairing off brilliantly as a singer with Munuswamappa's niece Chandravadana.[28]

All this was however not enough for Putta Lakshmi. Nagarathnam was made to study languages as well, including Telugu and English. She was also taught dance by Bangalore Kittanna, while Madras Tiruvenkatachar taught her the art of *abhinaya*, an important element in dance. The money for so many lessons was hard to find and Putta Lakshmi sacrificed whatever she had in order to put together the forty rupees that were needed each year for all this.[29]

The mother appears to have become increasingly impatient as time passed and was merciless with her daughter, once even going to the extent of branding her with a hot iron ladle when she felt that the girl was not progressing in her studies.[30] Nagarathnam however never harboured any ill will towards her mother, for later in life she would always speak emotionally about the sacrifices the latter made for her education. Developments in Bangalore probably continuously reminded the mother of her oath. In 1887, the Maharajah purchased land and began construction of the city palace in Bangalore, styled largely on

Windsor Castle, England. The proximity of Mysore royalty must have spurred Putta Lakshmi on. In 1889, Prince Albert Victor, son of the Prince of Wales and grandson of Queen Victoria visited Bangalore and welcoming him was a large illuminated float on the waters of the Dharmambudhi tank. A special feature of the event was the dance of Devadasis on the float.[31] If Putta Lakshmi and Nagarathnam were among the vast crowds that thronged the banks of the tank, they would have been reminded of their mission, to get back to Mysore, but only as invitees of the ruler himself.

The stresses and strains of life, especially the immense sacrifices she had made towards bringing up her daughter soon sapped Putta Lakshmi's constitution. In 1891 she was diagnosed with tuberculosis[32] and it was clear that she did not have long to live. The dying Putta Lakshmi must have critically assessed her daughter. The girl was not a beauty in the conventional sense. Short in stature and with a tendency to run to fat, Nagarathnam had a strikingly flawless skin and was of a fair complexion, always an asset in India. Masses of curly hair framed the forehead providing a contrast in setting to the ivory skin. Her eyes were her greatest assets; they shone brightly with all her native intelligence coming through. She was proficient in many languages, a good conversationalist and a talented singer and dancer. Even as life's breath ebbed away, Putta Lakshmi must have felt content that she had done all that was in her power and that the girl had proved worthy of the sacrifice. In her last moments she informed Munuswamappa of her oath and that he would now have to shoulder the responsibility of getting a royal invitation for Nagarathnam.

Munuswamappa appears to have become *in loco parentis* to the girl after Putta Lakshmi's passing. This was necessary, for apparently Nagarathnam's uncle Venkitasamappa had some other plans for her, which going by the hint that Nagarathnam gave much later in an account of her life, amounted to commercial exploitation. There was added trouble from a member of the Royal Family too. This man had helped Putta Lakshmi in her dark days, perhaps looking upon it as an investment which would provide returns in future.[33] The guru protected Nagarathnam and successfully "evaded these two planets".[34] He must have assiduously promoted his disciple and soon she was giving dance performances and attracting the attention of affluent personalities. Munuswamappa then pulled off a coup of sorts – an opportunity to perform at the residence of 'Veena' Seshanna, the senior-most musician of Mysore.

Seshanna was a legend in his own lifetime. Even the musicians of Tanjavur not given to praising the Mysore style spoke warmly of him.[35] Though he came from a great musical lineage, claiming Pacchaimiriyam Adiyappaiah, the composer of the immortal 'Viribhoni' *varnam* as one of his ancestors, Seshanna's initial years were full of hardship rather similar to Nagarathnam's. In time he had worked his way up to success. Seshanna was adept not only on the veena with which his name is inextricably linked, but also on the piano, the violin and the *swarabath* and it is said that he taught himself to play the *jalatarangam* in one day.[36] As is typical of someone who has come up the hard way, Seshanna was a hard taskmaster and a disciplinarian and drawing praise from him was not easy. It must have therefore been with some trepidation that Nagarathnam and Munuswamappa prepared themselves for the performance. The invitation itself was too important to refuse and so Munuswamappa and Nagarathnam appear to have bent the oath of Putta Lakshmi a little. They travelled to Mysore, not at the invitation of the palace, but on that of a palace artiste.

Mysore Vasudevachar, in his reminiscences has penned an account of how Nagarathnam carried herself before senior artistes and it may be a good indication of the kind of impression she made on her first appearance:

"It was at Veene Seshanna's house that I first met Nagarathnamma. The manner in which she conducted herself in the presence of elders like Seshanna, Subbanna and Bidaram Krishnappa attracted my attention. She stood before them respectfully, her head modestly turned down, as though she had come to offer worship at their feet. Her voice was sweet but she spoke little. When she did speak, her words were delicate and graceful. Her very bearing engendered a sense of respect for her."[37]

It is not clear if Nagarathnam sang or danced or perhaps did some of both at Seshanna's house. Whatever the nature of the performance, it was greatly appreciated by all the *vidwans* and art lovers present and soon word got around to the palace about a new find. The performance at Seshanna's house would have been witnessed by other palace artistes as well and on the basis of this, Nagarathnam was invited to perform at the Amba Vilasa Palace in 1893 during the coming of age celebrations for Princess Jayalakshmammani. Seated in the audience was Giribhatta Thimmayya Sastri and he was magnanimous enough to bury the hatchet and bless Nagarathnam with all success.[38] Putta Lakshmi's oath had been fulfilled.

The "benign gaze of the ruler"[39] had fallen on Nagarathnam, and with his grace, in her own words; she "was able to lead an independent life in Mysore, acquiring fame and fortune."[40] She resumed lessons under Bidaram Krishnappa. The eminent Harikatha artiste Tanjavur Krishna Bhagavatar visited the palace during the annual Dasara festival and having heard Nagarathnam perform, prophesied that she would attain unimaginable heights.[41] However, within a year Chamarajendra Wodeyar was dead and his 10-year-old son Krishnarajendra succeeded him, with the widowed queen acting as regent during the minority of the prince.[42] A wave of Victorian morality was then sweeping through the higher echelons of the state and the Government began taking steps to phase out the Devadasi system. The practice of offering dance services at the Muzrai or state-controlled temples was first targeted and in 1895, an order was passed to drive out dancing girls attached to temples and by 1898 temple authorities stopped recruitment of women for dance offerings. '*Tafe*', as the dance of the Devadasi was known in Mysore began to be frowned upon in weddings as well, with the Royal Family coming in for attack in 1896 for having spent a large amount of money on such entertainments during a marriage.[43] The favourites of the earlier regime were naturally now in disfavour and this led to a reduction in patronage. Guru Munuswamappa too passed away around this time, leaving Nagarathnam to manage by herself.[44] It was a difficult time for her and she once again migrated to Bangalore, preferring to earn her living through her knowledge of music rather than the trade practised by her family. She began receiving several invitations to sing and soon acquired several admirers. One among these was T Narahari Rao.

Like Nagarathnam, Narahari Rao too had suffered several privations during childhood. His ancestors were from music-rich Tanjavur but squabbles over property had led to his grandparents leaving for Bangalore in order to earn a living. Poverty was a constant feature, till Narahari, by dint of hard work qualified in law and made a name for himself in the profession. He was made a sessions judge of the Mysore Judiciary and was stationed in Shimoga before he was elevated as judge of the Mysore Court in Bangalore. He was held in high esteem by the Maharajah and the *Dewan*s Rangacharlu and Sir K Seshadri Iyer.[45]

Narahari Rao and his wife Sethamma were known for their generosity and their palatial home near the Fort Venkataramana Swami Temple (near the Bangalore Medical College), was open to indigent students, musicians and anyone else desiring assistance. It was said that the kitchen fires were never extinguished, for someone or the other was always being fed at the house.[46] It was therefore Nagarathnam's good fortune that such a noble and highly placed personage extended his support to her. Rather uniquely, this association of the learned judge with a Devadasi was not objected to by his wife[47] and a warm friendship soon sprang up between Sethamma and Nagarathnam, with the latter often calling at the judge's residence for cosy chats with his wife.[48]

The judge himself visited Nagarathnam as often as possible. At the conclusion of the court's business for the day he would hasten in his coach to where Nagarathnam lived. The sight of a judge's carriage bearing the insignia of the court with a uniformed and turbaned mace bearer in attendance, standing outside Nagarathnam's residence in crowded Nagarathpet caused considerable comment, which soon reached the ears of the *Dewan* Sir K Seshadri Iyer. Given that the palace was taking steps to reduce patronage of Devadasis, the *Dewan* felt that the open support given by Narahari Rao to Nagarathnam would undermine the authority of the law courts. Calling on Justice Rao one day, the *Dewan* gently remonstrated with the former and stated that while he had no objection to Justice Rao's patronage of Nagarathnam, it would be wiser for him to keep the symbols of his official position out of it.[49]

Justice Rao concurred with this. In any case he had been on the lookout for a suitable place far from the hustle and bustle of Bangalore where he could listen to Nagarathnam in peace. He selected a hillock amidst a thick forest just outside the then limits of the city. Here he built a house for Nagarathnam and took several of his friends to attend her performances, including brother judges of the court and the *Dewan* Sir K Seshadri Iyer himself. Sometimes his granddaughters went with him.[50] The place and its stellar occupant obviously gave him great happiness for he soon christened the hillock as Mount Joy, a name that still survives. So closely associated was he with the place that the locals gave the hillock a name as well – *Narahari Raya Gudda* (the hillock of Narahari Rao).

Looking out from her bird like perch high above Bangalore city, Nagarathnam would have commanded a fine view. Even as the sun set and the moon rose, the breeze would have carried the scent of several flowers. In the distance, lamps lit in various houses of the town would have been visible. From far away, becoming louder each moment would have been the clip-clop of Justice Narahari Rao's horses even as he hastened in his Victoria coach to keep his tryst with her. From the narrow and congested streets of Nagarathpet, she had been elevated to a hill, almost reflecting her sudden elevation in society. On a more mundane level, the distancing from the city helped her survive the plague, which appeared with alarming regularity, with the worst occurrence being in 1898-99 when thousands died.[51]

The association with Justice Rao was a happy one, on his part all protection, advice and admiration and on her part a respectful awe and gratitude, but with both being strong personalities, occasional differences of opinion did arise. Once it was a little more acrimonious than usual and Narahari Rao stayed away from Mount Joy. They next happened to meet at a public concert of Nagarathnam's and she lost no time in winning his affection once again. The easiest way to his heart was music and Nagarathnam sang the *javali* "Matada Baaradeno". It is ostensibly the song of a woman who is pining for union with Narahari (Narasimha, an incarnation of Vishnu), deity of a temple at Namakkal, near Salem. The piece was set in the raga Kamas, a very popular one for *javalis* and mostly associated with romance.

*Shouldn't you say something, my love?*
*Holder of my very life, having accepted my love,*
*Shouldn't you say at least one word, just now?*
*The moonlight falling on my eyes seems*
*Like the burning sunlight*
*And the buzzing of the bees puts fear in me*
*Shouldn't you say something, my love?*
*The mild breeze is driving me mad*
*My beautiful body is losing its lustre*

*Shouldn't you say something my love*
*Cupid's arrow has pierced my body*
*Is this fair, O Narahari of Namagiri?*[52]

The judge got the hint. There was a warm reconciliation soon after. The origins of this song are obscure and the composer has left no signature. Today, it is common to attribute the song to Nagarathnam and credit her with composing the song on the spot when she saw the judge walking into the concert hall.[53]

Life must have been idyllic for Nagarathnam at this stage. Playing hostess to judges, *Dewans* and other erudite personalities must have given her the confidence and self-possession that were to be her greatest strengths in the years to come. Her association with Justice Rao would have refined her taste in everything, a hallmark of all her future endeavours. She could hold her own in conversation, debate and discussion, aspects that would stand her in good stead right through life. Musicians too, treated her with respect and her music was greatly relished by the Mysore palace artistes such as 'Veena' Subbanna and Seshanna. Once at the conclusion of her concert at Subbanna's residence she was given valuable gifts, but as she left the room she could not help noticing several bottles of perfume which had been purchased at an exorbitant price by the luxury loving Subbanna that very day. Always a woman who believed in asking for anything she desired,[54] she requested Subbanna to give her a bottle. He simply opened his cupboard and gave her the entire stock which had cost him Rs. 800 just a few hours earlier.[55]

As though commemorating the happy years spent with each other, Justice Rao renovated and extended a Shiva temple that stood at the summit of Mount Joy and over the lintel carved the words "Mr T Narahari Rau, MC, 1901". Though he may not have known it, the beautiful relationship was coming to an end. His health began to fail.[56] Sir K Seshadri Iyer retired from the post of *Dewan* in March and passed away soon after. The charmed coterie that had supported Nagarathnam had begun to collapse. Worrying about her future, Justice Rao arranged for Nagarathnam to be taken care of by CS Rajarathna Mudaliar, a businessman of Madras. He would become Nagarathnam's protector in the future.[57] The judge had acted with foresight, for hardly had the handover been completed when he passed away in 1902. Realising that Bangalore would not be the safe haven it had been while she was under Justice Rao's protection, Nagarathnam began spending increasing amounts of time in Madras. By 1903 she had decided to settle permanently in that city.[58]

## References

[1] Ramanujachari, C; p 565.

[2] Nagarathnam, Bangalore; Last Will and Testament; Madras; 3rd January 1949; p 2.

[3] Lewis Rice, B; Mysore, A Gazetteer Compiled for Government; Revised Edition 1897; Reprinted by Government of Karnataka; 2004; p 249.

[4] Bai, C Banni; "Srimati Vidya Sundari Bangalore Nagarathnam Ammayarin Suyacharitai"; Sami Printers; Madras; 1953; hereinafter referred to as Bai, C Banni. p 1.

[5] Ibid.

[6] Grihalakshmi; "Tyagasevasaktha, Vidyasundari, Ganakalavisharada, Life History of Srimathi Bangalore Nagarathnamma", article in Grihalakshmi, March 1949, Madras, p 10, hereinafter referred to as Grihalakshmi.

[7] Of the five published accounts of Bangalore Nagarathnamma's life, three, namely those of T Sankaran, the 1949 account in the Grihalakshmi magazine and C Banni Bai agree on the fact that there was a split which caused the shift to Mysore. The fourth account, that of DV Gundappa, states that the shift was made keeping Nagarathnam's education in mind. The fifth, by Mysore Vasudevachar does not speak of a rift at all and states emphatically that "Subba Rao, who discerned

the range of Nagarathnamma's talent even when she was a young girl, brought her to Mysore".

8 Grihalakshmi, p 11.

9 Vedavalli, Dr MB; Mysore as a Seat of Music; CBH Publications; Trivandrum; 1992; p 19

10 Ibid; p 26.

11 The most famous one being Seshanna's *tillana* in raga Janjhooti which contains the ruler's name. Latter-day musicians changed the wording to accommodate the name of his successor, which is how the song is sung today. Ref -Vedavalli, Dr MB; Mysore as a Seat of Music; CBH Publications; Trivandrum; 1992; p 25.

12 Vasudevacharya, Mysore; With Masters of Melody; Translated from the original in Kannada by S Krishnamurthy; Ananya GML Cultural Academy; Bangalore; 1999; hereinafter referred to as Vasudevacharya, Mysore; p 69.

13 Grihalakshmi; p 11.

14 Ibid.

15 Bai, C Banni.

16 Vasudevacharya, Mysore; p 57.

17 Grihalakshmi; p 11-12.

18 Ibid.

19 Ibid.

20 Ibid.

21 Sankaran T; "Kanchipuram Dhanakoti Ammal"; article in Sruti; Issue 11; September 1984; p 31.

22 Nair, Janaki; The Promise of the Metropolis, Bangalore's Twentieth Century; Oxford University Press; New Delhi; 2005; hereinafter referred to as Nair, Janaki; p 42-45.

23 Gundappa, DV; Jnapaka Chitrashale, Vol 2, Kalaposhakaru; Kavyalaya Publishers; Mysore; 1990; hereinafter referred to as DVG.

24 Ibid; p 46.

25 Chandrashekar Gayatri; "Kadur Venkatalakshamma: Lifetime of Dedication to Dance"; article in Sruti; Issue 37/38; October/November 1987; Madras; p 23.

[27] Sankaran T; "Bangalore Nagaratnammal; A Devadasi True"; article in Sruti; Issue 4; January/February 1984; hereinafter referred to as Sruti; BNR; p 14.

[28] Sankaran, T; Isai Medaikal; Tamil Isai Publications; Madras; 1962; hereinafter referred to as Isai Medaikal.

[29] Ibid.

[30] Bai, Banni C; p 4.

[31] Nair, Janaki; p 32.

[32] Grihalakshmi; p 13-14.

[33] Ibid.

[34] Ibid.

[35] Bhagavatar, Soolamangalam Vaidyanatha; Karnataka Sangeetha Vidwangal; Kalakshetra Press; Madras; 1994; p 60.

[37] Ibid; p 69.

[38] Grihalakshmi; p 13-14.

[39] DVG.

[40] Grihalakshmi; p 13-14.

[41] Nagarathnamma, Bangalore; Article in the souvenir of the Sri Thyagabrahma Mahotsava Sabha; Tiruvayyaru; 1951.

[42] Kamath, Dr. Suryanath U; A Concise History of Karnataka; Jupiter Books; 2002; hereinafter referred to as Kamath, Dr Suryakanth U; p 257.

[43] Vijaishri, Priyadarshini; Recasting the Devadasi, Patterns of Sacred Prostitution in Colonial South India; Kanishka Publishers; Delhi; 2004; p 156; hereinafter referred to as Vijaishri, Priyadarshini.

[44] Grihalakshmi; p 13-14.

[45] Rao, KKA; "Justice T Narahari Rao"; handwritten manuscript dated 13th April 2001 with Mrs Saradamba, great granddaughter of Justice Narahari Rao and her son Mr P Vijayasimha Rao; hereinafter referred to as Rao, KKA.

[46] DVG.

[47] Ibid.

48 Author's interview of Mrs Saradamba, great granddaughter of Justice T Narahari Rao at Bangalore on 1st February 2007.

49 DVG.

50 Rao, KKA.

51 Kamath, Dr Suryakanth U; p 257.

52 Translated by VR Anilkumar.

53 Anecdote of music historian BVK Sastry and related to author by VAK Ranga Rao, dance critic and collector of 78 rpm records.

54 Vasudevacharya, Mysore; p 11.

55 Rao, KKA.

56 DVG.

57 Grihalakshmi; p 15-16.

# Chapter 2

*"To my heart's content you have made my glory shine in far off countries"* (Tyagaraja in "Daasharathi", raga Todi, tala Adi)[1]

~

Making a name as a singer in Madras city was then as now no easy task. When Nagarathnam arrived there in her 25th year,[2] it was a veritable beehive of not only singing but active music making and writing treatises on music. George Town which more or less comprised metropolitan Madras then, was full of musicians, scholars and patrons. There had been a steady increase in the number of *Sabha*s extending support to music and *Harikatha* performances.[3] The Komati and Beri Chetty communities of the city, as well as the Mudaliars, all of them in trade, built plenty of temples and employed musicians and dancers. There were a number of *nagaswaram* artistes attached to these establishments. The Peyazhwar festival at the Chenna Kesava Perumal Temple, Devaraja Mudali Street was well known for its *nagaswaram* performances. Edapalayam, near the Central Station was where many percussionists and pipers lived.[4] There were orchestras which played Carnatic Music, such as the Nathamuni Band and the Corporation Band which performed at public parks and on special occasions. Hindustani music too, was patronised by many. In addition, there was the theatre with plenty of musical plays being staged.

It was however the Devadasi community that really lent colour to the city and there was a large contingent of these professional singers

and dancers in residence. Coimbatore Palanikunjaram or Thayi as she
was better known, was a leading light. Her home in Nattu Pillaiyar
Koil Street was a haven for musicians.[5] There were besides several
others such as Salem Papa and Radha, the daughters of another well-
known singer Salem Meenakshi. The sisters lived in Krishnappa Naicken
Tank Square. Another famous name was Salem Godavari who lived in
Thambu Chetty Street.[6] A formidable duo was that of the Enadi Sisters,
Lakshminarayani and Rangaiah. They were renowned for their repertoire
of *padams* and *javalis* and for their reluctance in parting with any of
them to aspirants.[7] The well-known *Dubash* and philanthropist, Raja
Sir Savalai Ramaswami Mudaliar was one of their patrons.[8] Though
not a part of the George Town group, but highly respected among
them, was Mylapore Doraikannu, the dancer of the Kapaleeswarar
Temple, known for her ravishing beauty and dancing prowess.[9] Her
daughter Mylapore Gowri was also making a name for herself in dance.[10]
Among those who did not live in Madras but visited it frequently to
perform were the Dhanakoti Sisters of Kanchipuram.

The queen bee among all these women was 'Veena' Dhanammal.
Residing in Ramakrishna Chetty Street and rarely stirring out of it,
Dhanam commanded clout and respect that is unimaginable today.
Descendant of a proud line of Devadasis who could trace their ancestry
to Papammal, a dancer in the Tanjavur court[11], the family had moved
to Madras at the time of Dhanam's grandmother, Tanjavur Kamakshi,
at the request of a rich businessman of George Town, Rangoon
Krishnaswami Mudaliar.[12] The transition from dance to music also
happened simultaneously and without difficulty, for Kamakshi was a
talented singer, having learnt from Syama Sastri's descendants.[13]
Kamakshi's adopted daughter[14] was Sundaram and the two teamed up
to sing as a pair. The family home in Nattu Pillayar Koil Street, George
Town[15] was a veritable storehouse of music and it was into this musical
environment that Dhanam and her eight siblings[16] were born. In course

of time Dhanam and her sister Rupavathi paired off as singers.[17] However, the veena enchanted Dhanam and soon she broke off from Rupavathi and became a solo artiste, making the veena her voice and occasionally singing along with it.[18] Having a long and fruitful association with Dharmapuri Subbarayar[19], the composer of *javalis*, Dhanam had the singular honour of being the subject of three of his songs.[20]

Convinced that the veena was complete in all respects and needed neither amplification nor accompanying instruments, Dhanam restricted her performances to her own home and to only once a week. Her Friday evening sessions were looked forward to by the cognoscenti who flocked to her house and abided by the strict rule of silence in her household which even frowned on people sneezing during her performances.[21] To be able to appreciate Dhanam's music demanded extreme refinement and to be appreciated by Dhanam was an impossibility. Such exclusivity naturally curtailed Dhanam's potential to earn money and yet she never gave up on luxuries, such as the finest perfumes from Lucknow and the best quality betel leaves and nuts.[22] Extravagances soon led to insolvency and by the time Nagarathnam came down to Madras, Dhanam and her four formidable daughters Rajalakshmi, Lakshmiratnam, Jayammal and Kamakshi were living in a grace and favour residence on Ramakrishna Chetty Street, arranged for them by their ardent admirer 'Jalatarangam' Ramaniah Chetty, a chit fund owner of George Town.[23]

Ramaniah was not the only patron. Most of the Komati Chettys of George Town were ardent lovers of music and the wealthier ones such as the members of the V Perumal Chetty clan, owners of the famed Hoe and Company were avid patrons.[24] In addition there were other *dubash* clans further away in the city such as the Dare House Naidus of Luz, the descendants of Sami Naidu in Chintadripet[25] and the Savalai Ramaswami Mudaliar family of Poonamallee.[26] Madras was also home to several Telugu-speaking princely families such as Bobbili,

Vizianagaram, Pithapuram, Wanaparthi, Challapalli and Venkatagiri and all of them had music lovers among their members.

It was into this melting pot that Nagarathnam fell headlong and worked hard to come up to the top. She must have called on the seniors in the field and this must have definitely included Coimbatore Thayi and 'Veena' Dhanammal. The first meeting between Nagarathnam and Dhanam has sadly gone unrecorded. It is interesting to speculate what must have passed through Dhanam's mind even as she shaded her rapidly failing eyes to assess the newcomer, ten years her junior. Outwardly, they were totally unlike each other. Nagarathnam was talkative and made friends easily. She was humorous in speech and like a professional comedian could keep audiences in splits of laughter.[27] Dhanam was reserved and sardonic and most people hesitated approaching her.[28] Nagarathnam was fair in complexion and quite plump[29], while Dhanam was dark and small made.[30] Jewels and high-quality silks were Nagarathnam's great loves[31], while Dhanam hardly had any jewels and wore ordinary cotton cloth. Nagarathnam's voice was powerful[32], while Dhanam's was soft.[33] Nagarathnam was financially sound, while, for Dhanam money had no importance.

Despite all this, a warm friendship sprang up between the two women, a friendship that was to strengthen and last till Dhanam's passing in 1938. Nagarathnam became a family member of sorts and was a confidante to Dhanam's daughters. And yet, while they all liked and respected her, they did not entirely approve of her music![34] But that was the way of the Dhanam clan. Through Dhanam, Nagarathnam was introduced to Dharmapuri Subbarayar. He taught her several of his *javalis*.[35]

Nagarathnam continued giving performances of music and dance after moving to Madras. While no records are available of her dance performances, Mysore Vasudevachar has given his impressions about her music and these are worth quoting:

"Nagaratnamma's style of singing was religiously classical. She had an accurate sense of *laya*. A unique characteristic of her voice was that it combined in itself the melodic sweetness of the female voice and the dignity of the male voice. As she had a sound knowledge of *Bharatanatya* also, her singing was endowed with emotion. In her concerts, Nagaratnamma devoted more time to *ragalapana* than to *swarakalpana*.

There was hardly a concert in which she did not sing the raga Yadukulakambodhi. To listen to her singing the *kirtana* "Sri Rama Jayarama" in that raga was an unforgettable pleasure. It was Nagaratnamma who popularised the *ragamalika* "Nityakalyani". She used to sing *devaranama*s and *Mukundamala sloka*s such as "Bhaktapaya bhujanga" and "Satruchhedaikamantram" in a characteristic style of her own. As she had a sure knowledge of her art, Nagaratnamma was never afraid of any challenge from other musicians."[36]

In order to enhance her musical prowess, Nagarathnam apprenticed herself under Ramanathapuram 'Poochi' Srinivasa Iyengar.[37] Like her guru Munuswamappa, Iyengar too traced his lineage to Tyagaraja, through his own guru 'Patnam' Subramania Iyer, who had learnt music from Tyagaraja's cousin Manambucchavadi Venkatasubbier.[38] There are varying theories as to how he acquired the prefix 'Poochi', with the most musical reason being that the ring in his voice was like the humming of a bee.[39] Iyengar was a talented composer and a very popular musician who was patronised by the Ramanathapuram Estate and therefore chose to live there.[40] His concert opportunities however made him visit Madras often and whenever he did, he taught Nagarathnam. Yet another artiste who frequently called on her and taught her, was the violinist Tirukodikkaval Krishna Iyer.

Nagarathnam performed during a time when the popular press of the day rarely published reviews. However, a rather unusual source has left behind his impressions of one of her performances and this was the Hindustani maestro, Vishnu Narayan Bhatkhande. In 1904 he travelled to South India on a religious pilgrimage during which he also sought to study the Carnatic system. During his stay in Madras, Bhatkhande was scheduled to meet C Tirumalayya Naidu, a well-known patron of music, at the Cosmopolitan Club on 18th November 1904. A long wait for the tram delayed him and the appointment was cancelled. Recollecting his having seen an announcement in that day's issue of *The Mail* of a concert being held under the auspices of the Gana-manohari Association in Ramaswami Street, George Town, Bhatkhande made his way there. The concert was on the first floor of a building and he joined the gathering which was listening to a woman singer.

The Hindustani maestro was rather self-conscious about having gatecrashed into a *Sabha* without buying a ticket and sitting unobtrusively in a corner listened to the performance.

"The singer's name was Nagarathna and the music was good. I was able to see shades of several ragas of our system of music. Not knowing their names and not wanting to expose my ignorance by asking others I was unable to identify them accurately... Her speciality was in the elaboration of the raga around particular notes. The *Bai* had a deep voice. At many places she modulated her voice which did not make much of an impression on me, but it was precisely at these places that the audience came out with exclamations of praise. Towards the end of the performance there were requests for raga *alapanas* alone. The violinist played very sweetly and so did the percussionist who provided able support. I found that unlike the courtesans of Bombay this *Bai* was dignified. Probably all her songs were religious in content. I came to know that she was in the service of the Mysore palace and that after the demise of the ruler she had come to Madras".[41]

By 1905, Nagarathnam had made a powerful impression on the music-loving public of Madras and was being spoken of in the same terms as Coimbatore Thayi and 'Veena' Dhanam.[42] In order to distinguish her from Kolar Nagarathnam, also a student of Bidaram Krishnappa and 'Poochi' Iyengar who though her junior had lived more years in Madras, fans began prefixing 'Bangalore' to her name.[43] She thus became Bangalore Nagarathnamma.

Concert opportunities were pouring in and performances in the homes of the high and mighty brought rich rewards and by 1905 she had begun to pay income tax,[44] one of the earliest artistes and among the first professional women to do so. She religiously maintained a diary in order to keep track of her professional engagements and the income accruing from them.[45] Unlike most women of her time, Nagarathnamma was financially savvy and invested her money wisely and well. Jewels were her greatest passion, perhaps in order to make up for a poverty-stricken childhood. Photographs taken of her at this time show her bedecked in a variety of jewels. Apart from the standard diamond earrings, she has rings on both sides of the nose, a variety of chains around her neck, a heavy waistband, armlets, bracelets and bangles, anklets and toe rings.[46] In addition to purchasing jewellery, always a liquid security, she invested in bank deposits and government promissory notes.[47] In all this, she may have been advised by CS Rajarathna Mudaliar, her patron-in-chief. She also acquired her own house in Madras at No 7, Srinivasa Iyer Street, George Town.[48] Nagarathnamma retained her house in Bangalore for a few years as well,[49] before disposing it off, when the prospect of returning to that city became remote.

The house-warming ceremony in George Town was a lavish affair, with many noteworthy residents of the city attending, including Kasturi Ranga Iyengar[50], who in 1905[51] had become the new proprietor of what was to become the city's leading daily – *The Hindu*. For the evening's entertainment, Nagarathnamma invited her guru, Bidaram Krishnappa to give a concert. It was her way of introducing a leading musician of Mysore to the citizens of Madras.[52] It had been a quick climb to the top within three years. From a relative nonentity she had become a personality whose backing was needed even for a reputed musician like Bidaram Krishnappa. The concert, at Nagarathnamma's request, comprised only *Devaranamas*, the songs of the *Dasa Koota*, all of them in the Kannada language. It was her homage to her mother tongue and also a demonstration that Purandara Dasa's songs could be presented in the same elaborate and scholarly manner as those of Tyagaraja.[53]

Her popularity though, was not universal. Having come up the hard way, Nagarathnamma not only fought for her rights but also demanded and obtained whatever she felt should be hers. In the initial years at least, it manifested itself in aggression which sometimes riled her acquaintances. An incident in Tiruvarur illustrates this. Nagarathnamma's patrons included landlords from the fertile Kaveri delta. One among these was a scion of the wealthy Vadapadimangalam family whose tutelary deity was Lord Shiva as Tyagaraja in Tiruvarur, the town where the Carnatic Trinity took birth. Dance was an integral part of worship offered to Lord Tyagaraja here and He Himself was said to be ever in the midst of a mystic dance called the *Ajapa Natanam*. Whenever the deity was brought out in procession it was customary for the bearers to dance and this was said to be symbolic of the Lord's cosmic dance. Among the various musical pieces dedicated to this deity was the "Tyagesa Kuravanji", an opera comprising 65 songs, the creation of an unknown composer dated tentatively to the 18th century.[54] The opera was performed during the float festival for three nights in the Devashraya, a great hall in the temple.[55] Performing the opera was the right of the Kondi family, a line of illustrious Devadasis belonging to the temple, who traced their lineage to Kondiammai or Kathyayani the consort of Shiva-Tyagesa and who could count as their ancestor, Kamalam – a famed disciple of Muttuswami Dikshitar.[56]

During one of her sojourns in the Tanjavur belt Nagarathnamma saw the "Tyagesa Kuravanji" being performed and became enamoured of it. She expressed a desire to perform the same along with her troupe at the temple, but was refused permission by the authorities who did not want to tamper with tradition. Undaunted, Nagarathnamma used her influence with her local patron who forced the temple manager to allow her to stage the dance drama in the forecourt of the temple. Fearing protests by the members of the Kondi line, security personnel were posted at all entrances to the temple with instructions to bar anyone in dance costume from entering the temple.

However none of them had contended with the steadfastness of Kutti Ammal, the then head of the Kondi clan. Her only asset was the house where she lived and she pledged this in order to finance a civil suit demanding restitution of her hereditary right. Then having dressed herself up as a Brahmin woman, Kutti Ammal gained entry to the shrine along with a lawyer armed with a stay order barring Nagarathnamma's performance. Nagarathnamma had to obey the law and accepted defeat. However, on coming to know of the sacrifice that Kutti Ammal had made, she magnanimously gave up any idea of performing the *Kuravanji* and returned to Madras.[57]

Her survival instincts also made her shrewdly grasp new opportunities as and when they arose. Beginning with 1905, Nagarathnamma began featuring in a new form of entertainment, namely recorded music. By the end of the 19th century, music companies in India were importing a variety of equipment such as phonographs, recording cylinders, gramophone and discs from the USA and Europe.[58] By 1900, The Gramophone and Typewriter Limited (GTTL), the forerunner of the Gramophone Company Limited, had a presence in India through agents and in 1901 had sent its own representative to assess the local markets.[59] Encouraged by his report, the GTTL sent its first recording expert, Frederick William Gaisberg, along with a business manager and an assistant on a recording tour of the Far East, including India.[60] The Indian leg of the visit was restricted to Calcutta and whilst there, the team recorded among others, the 'Cuckoo of Calcutta', Gauhar Jan[61], a woman whose rags-to-riches story largely paralleled that of Nagarathnamma. By April 1903, gramophone discs with the Indian recordings began arriving in Calcutta and were soon distributed all over the country.[62]

Encouraged by the response, the GTTL sent William Sinkler Darby and Max Hempe, two recording engineers at its Berlin office, on a second recording tour of India in 1904.[63] Arriving in December that year, the duo travelled across India, finishing in Madras in 1905.[64] This was the first time that South Indian artistes were recorded and, unlike the earlier one, this tour was to focus on artistes whose style appealed locally and also those who were renowned classical and theatrical vocalists and instrumentalists of the time, including musicians who were retained in the court or 'durbar' service of Maharajahs, Princes and nobility of India.[65] Featuring among them was "Miss Nagaratnam of Bangalore".[66] It speaks volumes about her popularity that another artiste who recorded at the same time as she, was Kanchipuram Dhanakoti, the doyenne whom she and her mother had approached for music lessons less than 20 years previously. Nagarathnamma herself later confessed that she had been diffident about accepting the invitation to record.[67] She may have been influenced by the then prevailing notion that recording of the voice reduced the vocal power of the singer. Ultimately an elderly female relative had convinced her to do it.[68] Some like Nagarathnamma's younger contemporary Tiruvarur Rajayee and Kanchipuram Dhanakoti's nephew Naina Pillai never recorded, fearing that their songs would be played at "hair dressers and tea shops".[69] 'Veena' Dhanam herself was to remain aloof from the recording industry for many years, succumbing to the pressures of her friends only in the last year of her life.[70]

The recordings must have happened at the place where the engineers stayed and in keeping with the then practice, Nagarathnamma would have arrived decked in jewels and silks. By today's standards the recording equipment would have appeared rudimentary. Singers and accompanists were ushered into a recording booth set up in a room. The process was mechanical, wherein the artistes would be required to sing or perform into a huge horn at the end of which was a diaphragm which vibrated purely by means of the force of the sound produced and which was connected to a needle. The vibrations caused the needle to cut the grooves on the wax-coated surface of a disc mounted on a turntable rotating at 78 rpm. This disc became the 'shell' or master for the recording. These shells were then shipped back to Hanover where they were pressed into discs for sale and arrived back in India.[71] The 'South Indian' Catalogue of the GTTL, "with songs in Tamil, Telugu, Malayalam, Canarese and Sanskrit" was released in 1905[72] and must have met with good response.

Nagarathnamma remained an active recording artiste and when the GTTL organised its third recording tour in 1906/07, she was to record many more discs for them.[73] Recording remuneration was usually a flat fee for the troupe apart from reimbursement for the travel to and from the place of recording. It is not certain as to what was paid to Nagarathnamma, but a contemporary singer Janki Bai of Allahabad was able to command Rs 3000 per session and this is probably an indication of what was paid to her.[74] Over the years, like Gauhar Jan, Nagarathnamma too, achieved fame as a recording artiste, though the most popular voice was that of her friend Coimbatore Thayi.[75] However, Nagarathnamma was never comfortable with the recording process and was to recall years later about the travails it involved. Firstly, there was just about enough space for the main artistes and the accompanists to sit. Secondly, the singer had to be very loud so that the force of the voice would cause the diaphragm to vibrate. Lastly, what irritated her most was the dominance of the recording engineer, owing to the limitation stipulated by the three-minute duration of the disc. The engineer dictated when she was to start and when to stop and this was something that according to her even her guru had not done.[76] It was common practice for artistes, made nervous by the time limit, to finish the song before the disc had been recorded in full, whereupon the recording engineer would brusquely signal to the singer to continue. As a result, some of them resorted to a small snatch of raga *alapana* after the song was over, contrary to convention.[77] Nagarathnamma's discs were reissued time and again and the lyrics of several of them were published in gramophone songbooks[78], which were very popular publications and helped those interested in music to learn songs from the gramophone discs.

There was sound logic in becoming a recording artiste. The Anti – Nautch Movement, a continuous attempt at outlawing the Devadasis was gathering momentum. The dance of the Devadasi, rather than her music, was being scrutinised with increasing concern by the British Raj and the Princely states. More and more social reform organisations, government officials and western-educated members of the public began demanding legislation against the Devadasi system which they perceived to be a social evil. Dance, being the more visible element of the Devadasi trade was targeted. Within the Government however, there were conflicting opinions, but it was clear that sooner or later legislation of some sort was bound to happen against the system of dedicating girls to temples and training them in dance.[79] As a consequence, more and more Devadasis began giving up dance and switching to music. By 1907-8, Nagarathnamma too, began refusing invitations to give dance performances.

Nagarathnamma's native state, Mysore, continued to lead the way when it came to legislation against the Devadasi system.[80] In 1909, a rule was passed that the state controlled temples would not avail themselves of the services of Devadasis. This was received with great jubilation all over the country and Mysore was portrayed to be a 'bastion of reformed Hinduism'.[81]

If the future of dance looked bleak, a new opportunity was opening up for women. *Harikatha* had been an exclusive male bastion till a year before when the path was cleared by C Saraswathi Bai, a Brahmin girl of seventeen and her guru, Pt. Krishnachar. Saraswathi's debut as a discourser in the true *Harikatha* style had taken place in Mylapore in the teeth of great opposition to an upper caste woman taking to a performing artiste's career.[82] The most virulent opponents had been the male *Harikatha* artistes who felt threatened by the advent of a woman. A vicious campaign of slander was launched against her, causing her great personal suffering. But a strong-willed mother and an equally ardent love for the art ensured her triumph and in times to come she was to be hailed as the "First Lady *Bhagavatar*".[83] The Devadasi community, one of whose members, Elayanarvelur Saradambal had also attempted the same act earlier with less success[84], was silently supportive of Saraswathi's endeavour.[85]

Nagarathnamma was one of the earliest to follow Saraswathi's lead. While others switched over to music, she decided to put her extensive knowledge of Sanskrit, acquired thanks to her tutelage under Giribhatta Thimmayya Sastri, to good use and took to religious discoursing as well.[86] She however did not become a *Harikatha* artiste and preferred to perform *Upanyasams*, or religious discourses. Here, the main artiste remained seated and the performance was generally high-brow, involving copious quotations from Sanskrit texts, plenty of music and generally extolling high moral values. Nagarathnamma however did not focus on a career in discoursing and performed selectively. She enjoyed a clientele for this in the homes of the rich business families of the city and all her *Upanyasam* performances were privately held. The Maharajah of Cochin became an ardent admirer of her oratorical skills and at the end of a performance in Trichur, presented her with gold bracelets and an expensive brocade shawl.[87] Taking a cue from her, other women such as Padamasini Bai took to the field of *Harikatha*.

Giving up dance made life more sedentary and Nagarathnamma gradually began putting on weight. She made up for lack of height by an impressive increase in girth. The Bengal Nagpur Railway was one of many private railway companies that operated lines in India and wags, noticing that she shared her initials with those of the company soon began comparing her in size to the steam locomotives of the company.[88] To the admiring public she became BNR Ammal. Needless to add, Kolar Nagarathnam became KNR, probably beginning a long-lasting trend in Carnatic Music where musicians were usually referred to by initials, which mostly numbered three.

## References

[1] Ramanujachari, C; p 518.

[2] Grihalakshmi; p 13-14.

[3] Madras Tercentenary Volume; p 435.

[4] Sankaran, T; "Bala's Musicians"; article in Sruti; Issue 5; March 1984; p 46.

[5] Sundaram, BM; Marabu Tanda Manikkangal; Dr V Raghavan Centre for Performing Arts; Chennai; 2003; hereinafter referred to as Sundaram, BM; p 50.

[6] Subrahmanyan, Sanjay; Ramnath, Bombay Jayashree and Krishna, TM; Professor Sambamoorthy, The Visionary Musicologist; The Music Academy; Madras; 2001; p 36.

[7] Sankaran, T; Pattabhiraman N & Rajagopalan KR; "Veena Dhanammal, A Mere Musician but a Great Artist"; article in Sruti; Issue 23/23 S; June/July 1986; hereinafter referred to as Sruti, Veena Dhanammal; p 31.

[8] Menon, Indira; p 53.

[9] Sundaram, BM; p 265.

[10] Ibid; p 267.

[12] Menon, Indira; p 56.

[13] Sruti; Veena Dhanammal; p 26.

[14] The information on adoption was given by T Muktha to the author during an interview in 2001.

[15] Menon, Indira; p 56.

[16] Subba Rao, TV; Studies in Indian Music; Asia Publishing House; Delhi; 1962; p 195.

[17] Sruti; Veena Dhanammal; p 26.

[18] Menon, Indira; p 58.

[19] Sruti; Veena Dhanammal; p 27.

[20] The three songs being "Smara Sundaranguniki" in Paras, "Narimani" in Khamas and "Sakhi Prana" in Jhanjooti.

[21] Sruti; Veena Dhanammal; p 29.

[22] Ibid; p 33.

[23] Ibid; p 31.

[24] Sriram, V; "Musical Movements in Madras"; article in Madras Musings; Vol XIV No 15; November 15-30; 2004; Chennai.

[25] Ibid

[26] Menon, Indira; p 53.

[27] Bai, C Banni; p 7.

[28] Sruti; Veena Dhanammal; p 29.

[29] Observation made to author by several people who have met Bangalore Nagarathnamma.

[30] Observation of S Rajam, eminent painter, musician and musicologist.

[31] Observation made to author by several people who have met Bangalore Nagarathnamma.

[32] Bai, C Banni; p 7; Banni Bai states that Nagarathnamma's voice did not need a loudspeaker to reach large audiences.

[33] Menon, Indira; p 57.

[34] Comment made by T Muktha to the author during an interview in 2001. She said that her entire clan admired Nagarathnamma but her musical prowess was not above the ordinary.

35 Sankaran, T; "Dharmapuri Subbarayar"; article in The Hindu; 20th September 1970.

36 Vasudevacharya, Mysore; p 69-70.

37 Sruti; BNR ; p 14.

38 Sambamoorthy P; Great Musicians; Indian Music Publishing House; Madras; 3rd Edition, 1996, p 43.

39 Ibid; p 47.

40 Ibid; p 44.

41 Bhatkhande, Vishnu Narayan; Meri Dakshin Bharat Ki Sangeet Yatra; Chaube, Amaresh Chandra - Trns.Indira Kala Sangita Vishwavidyalaya, Khairagarh 1986; Hindi (Trns. from Marathi).

42 Grihalakshmi; p 13-14.

43 Isai Medaikal.

44 Grihalakshmi; p 13-14.

45 Ibid.

47 Nagarathnamma, Bangalore; "Last Will and Testament"; Madras; 3rd January 1949; p 8.

48 Ibid; p 7.

49 Grihalakshmi; p 13-14.

50 DVG.

51 Parthasarathy, Rangaswami; A Hundred Years of The Hindu, The Epic Story of Indian Nationalism; Kasturi and Sons Limited; Madras; 1979; p 163.

52 Vasudevacharya, Mysore; p 71.

53 Ibid; p 71.

54 Seetha, S; p 84.

55 Sriram, V; "The Tyagesa Kuravanji", article in Sruti Issue No 255, Chennai; December 2005; p 32.

56 Ibid; p 28.

57 Anecdote of Tiruvarur PR Thilagam, interviewed by the author in November 2005.

58 Kinnear, Michael S; The Gramophone Company's First Indian Recordings, 1899-1908; Popular Prakashan Pvt. Ltd; Bombay; 1994; p 9; hereinafter referred to as Kinnear, Michael S.

59 Ibid.

60 Ibid; p 11.

61 Ibid; p 12.

62 Ibid; p 21.

63 Ibid.

65 Ibid.

66 Ibid; p 25.

67 As conveyed by Nagarathnamma to VAK Ranga Rao.

68 Ibid.

69 Menon, Indira; p 78.

70 Sriram, V; "The Star of a Star Rich George Town"; article in Madras Musings; Vol. XI, No. 19; Chennai; p 6.

71 Kinnear, Michael S; p 12.

73 Ibid; p 121.

74 Ibid; p 28.

75 Gohil, Jay; "Growth of Music in Tamil South India – Historical Outlook"; sourced from the Internet.

76 As conveyed by Nagarathnamma to VAK Ranga Rao.

77 Ibid.

78 Mudaliar, A Madurai; Gramophone Sangita Kirtanamrtam, Parts 2 & 4; Shanmukhananda Puttagasalai; Madras; 1930; p 169-173 & p 111-119 respectively.

79 For a detailed account on litigation and early attempts at legislation against Devadasis see Jordan, Kay K.

80 Vijaisri, Priyadarshini; p 156.

81 Ibid; p 157.

82 Sriram, V; "C Saraswathi Bai (1892-1974), Lady Bhagavatar", article in Sruti Issue No 262, Chennai; July 2006; hereinafter referred to as Sruti; CSB; p 27.

83 Ibid.
85 Sruti; CSB; p 30.
86 Bai, C Banni; p 5.
87 Ibid;  p 6
88 Sruti; BNR; p 16.

≈≈

# Chapter 3

*"Catching the brocaded saris of some, pushing the feet of some
away from his own, gazing at the beauty of some, speaking to
some after reading their thoughts,, lying on the laps of some,
painting red the lips of some, sporting with the bodies of some,
Krishna played with the Gopis"* (Tyagaraja in "Tanayande
Premayanuchu" raga Bhairavi, tala Chapu)[1]

~

"I have been doing some study of literature from childhood onwards
in the language of my land, Kannada and later had read many works in
Telugu. Since settling in Madras I have taken up the study of Tamil
works and yet nothing can match my passion for Telugu literature in
which I have studied many works from the *Bharatham* onwards". There
was pride in the above lines that Nagarathnamma penned and it was
the pride of a woman who, unusually for those times was exceedingly
well read. She considered the learned and erudite courtesans of yore
to be her ideals. She was held in high esteem by Telugu scholars and
poets and preferred to spend time in their company. Symposia of Telugu
poets were common in those times and she was often an honoured
invitee. Once, arriving at a Ganda Penderam festival (an event in which
a scholar is honoured by gift of an anklet) in Rajamundry town, she
was welcomed at the station by the assembled poets with a garland of
camphor and a poem in her praise. She later addressed the festival.[2]
By 1910 such honours and recognitions were commonplace to her.

In all this, she clearly had an ideal and role model and that was Muddu Palani, the court poetess and concubine of Pratapasimha[3], the 18th century Maratha ruler of Tanjavur. His long reign, which stretched from 1739 to 1763, witnessed peace and prosperity in Tanjavur. The ruler was a munificent patron of the arts and was also a composer. In his court were several scholars and Muddu Palani, the court dancer was also one of them. Highly accomplished in Telugu, she had worked on a Telugu version of the *Tiruppavai*, the creation of the 10th century Tamil poetess, Andal. Not being content with a mere translation, Muddu Palani introduced certain original elements and the resulting work, in verses of seven lines or *Saptapadulu* was hailed as a scholarly work for which she was rewarded in court.[4] Subsequently, Muddu Palani also wrote, the *Radhika Santwanamu* (the Appeasement of Radha) also known as the *Ila Deviyamu* (The Story of Ila). This work, speaks of the love that Radha had for Krishna. Unlike the standard *bhakti* interpretations which preferred to treat Radha as the soul yearning for union with Krishna as the supreme being, Muddu Palani looked at the relationship as one of a woman in her prime, consumed with passion and enjoying a great relationship with her nephew, Krishna.[5] The twist in the story comes with Ila, the niece that Radha brings up, being given away to Krishna on attaining puberty. Radha, hiding her own pangs of jealousy, advises Ila on how to conduct herself and also rather unusually, advises Krishna on how he ought to handle a young and tender girl while making love to her. The marriage of Krishna and Ila is consummated but Radha is unable to bear the separation. Krishna returns to her and appeases her.[6] The work holds the distinction of being one of the few surviving examples of an erotic classic written by a woman.

Muddu Palani, introduces herself as one who is unequalled in her patronage of scholars and as one who is acclaimed in the arts. She proudly traces her own lineage through her grandmother and aunt and in this she follows the practice of male composers who always traced their paternal line when introducing themselves. Rather uniquely, Muddu Palani also records that she has had epic works dedicated to her, surely a first, for almost all scholars and poets dedicated their works to male patrons.[7] *Radhika Santwanamu* was thus in every way the creation of a woman who considered herself to be an equal to any male scholar of her times. What is even more interesting is that this assertion of status is not laboured but emerges very naturally, a clear indication of perfect self-assurance and confidence.

The work had probably been first noticed in modern times by Charles Philip Brown, the renowned Oriental scholar and lexicographer, who had while leaving India in 1855 left behind a collection of manuscripts ready for printing at the Madras Oriental Manuscripts Library.[8] *Radhika Santwanamu* was one among this collection. The work was published in 1887 and later in 1907 by Venkatanarasu, an associate of Brown.[9] It had also received attention of sorts from Kandukuri Veeresalingam Pantulu, the Andhra reformer who in 1887 published his compilation of the lives of Telugu poets in which he included a brief write-up on Muddu Palani and the *Radhika Santwanamu*.[10] Veeresalingam was a staunch supporter of the Anti-Nautch movement and held the Devadasi system responsible for most of society's ills.[11] He therefore used derogatory forms of address such as *idi* and *dani* in his account of Muddu Palani. On the work itself, while commending the style and the ideal admixture of Sanskrit and Telugu in it, Veeresalingam claimed to be shocked by its contents. Having denounced Muddu Palani as an adulteress, he declared that the shamelessness of the work was not surprising as it was written by a prostitute.[12]

At the Ganda Penderam symposium held in Rajamundry, Nagarathnamma was surprised to find that 'Kaviraja Sarvabhauma' Sripada Krishnamurthy Sastri talked about the translations of Andal's

*Tiruppavai* into Telugu by an 18th century male poet named Muthu Palani. She laughed aloud and chided the speaker for not knowing that the poet was a woman and a Devadasi like herself.[13] Nagarathnamma had first come to know of Muddu Palani and the *Radhika Santwanamu* through the work *Panigruhita* written by her friends and admirers the two Tirupati Venkata Kavis. Curious to know more about it she managed to lay her hands on the Venkatanarasu edition of the poem and read it with great interest. She read it again and again and found the work to be immensely beautiful, almost as beautiful as the subject of the work – Lord Krishna. She also noted that several errors had crept into the text. With great difficulty she managed to obtain through a friend an annotated manuscript of *Radhika Santwanamu* and compared the same with the printed work. She found that the latter did not have the prologue in which Muddu Palani had proudly traced her ancestry through her aunt and grandmother and also written about her own greatness.[14] Upset over the fact that several verses of the work were not even published, Nagarathnamma decided to publish a new edition of the *Radhika Santwanamu*. Little did she realise that in doing so she was going to stir up a controversy that would convulse the entire community of Telugu and Sanskrit scholars, the Government of Madras and the printing house of Vavilla Ramaswami Sastrulu and Sons.

When the manuscript was ready, Nagarathnamma added a prologue in which she spelt out the reasons for which she had worked on it. Firstly, the fact that the author was a woman and that too from Nagarathnamma's own community of Devadasis was a matter of pride. Secondly, though she did not state this, she clearly felt that a strongly worded rejoinder was needed to counter Veeresalingam's remarks on the author and her work. The prologue was a rebuttal in every way to what he had stated about Muddu Palani in his book on Telugu poets.

Nagarathnamma began by quoting, out of sheer necessity she said, from Veeresalingam's writings where he had stated that "Muddu Palani was one of the women who wrote *padya kavya*s (works of poetry). She was a *veshya* (prostitute) and wrote the *Radhika Santwanamu*, a *shringara prabandham* (erotic work) in four chapters. Her mother's name was Muthyalu. That she was the kept woman of Pratapasimha; the Lord of the Tanjavur *Samasthanam* (court) can be gathered from her work which is also called *Ila Deviyamu*".

Pointing out the errors he had made in tracing Muddu Palani's ancestry, Nagarathnamma opined that, had Veeresalingam only taken the trouble to read the preface to the poem he would have known that Muthyalu was the father and not mother of Muddu Palani.

Veeresalingam had gone on to write that "this woman was proficient in music, literature and dance as per her own claims. This woman's poetry is undoubtedly sweet and simple and she evidently knows of Sanskrit and Telugu. There are occasional mistakes but these are found in the works of men also". Reacting strongly in particular to the last sentence, Nagarathnamma wrote that when there were errors in works from the *Bharatam* onwards it was not necessary to look for mistakes in the work of a woman.

In his comment, Veeresalingam had condemned the work as "having been written by a woman whose profession was prostitution. It is bereft of the modesty that one expects of a woman and she has filled the book with graphic descriptions of lovemaking in a very crude manner. Parts of the work are such that they should not be heard or read by women."

Nagarathnamma came down sharply on the assumptions that Muddu Palani was a prostitute and unchaste. She challenged Veeresalingam's contention that Muddu Palani was an adulteress just because she was a Devadasi. According to Nagarathnamma, an adulteress was a woman, who having married a man with fire as witness, eloped with another, while a Devadasi, the divine handmaiden, could not be termed so. Such terms as chastity, according to her, did not apply to her community as was clear to anyone who had read Vatsyayana's *Kamasutra*. Her community was ordained to perform this task as a duty, as per divine command. She noted that Veeresalingam, while denouncing Muddu Palani's writing on sex, had edited works written by men with far more graphic descriptions, some of which he had recommended to the Madras University as text books. Nagarathnamma questioned if a sense of shame was a virtue only for women.[15]

Appealing to those who respected women to receive this book favourably on the grounds that it was written by a woman and edited by another, Nagarathnamma completed the foreword and the manuscript was duly sent off to the Tiruvottiyur High Road offices of Vavilla Ramaswami Sastrulu and Sons, the pioneering Telugu publishers of Madras city since 1863[16], on 9th March 1910. It was Maha Sivaratri, the holy day dedicated to Lord Shiva when women in particular, fasted all day and worshipped the deity during the night. The edition comprising 750 copies was printed at SN Tirumala-charya's India Printing Works of 15, Broadway, Madras and released at a price of 6 annas on 30th March 1910.[17] Copies were available at the Vavilla book depot at 192, Esplanade Road, Madras and also at various other locations. For almost a year after this, nothing much happened except that scholars read the work and commended its publication.

In January 1911, the new edition came to the attention of *Sasilekha*, a highly moralistic Telugu publication from Madras. The magazine's editorial strongly condemned the work stating that it was "to be regretted that wretched books full of rude, depraving and obscene descriptions are now brought out in good and attractive editions in Telugu literature". It went on to point out that a "prostitute composed a book under the name of "*Radhika Santwanam*" (Radha Reconciled) and that another prostitute corrected errors therein and edited it!" Having summarily dismissed the author and editor it went on to marvel at how "the firm of Messrs Vavilla Ramaswami Sastri and Sons have printed this book on good paper without fear of law and openly published it for sale." The reviewer denounced the book "as full of obscene descriptions calculated to deprave pliable minds." Lord Krishna was not spared either. The writer confidently stated that "no well behaved literate gentleman can realise God by reading descriptions depicting God that He without heeding the prohibited degrees of relationships enjoyed sexual embrace in forty different ways with an adulterous woman." The article wondered at the editor (Nagarathanamma) defending "the obscenities in this book on the ground that they relate to divine topics." In a flight of imagery the reviewer stated that the publishers may plan an illustrated edition, encouraged by the success of the book and the Government turning a blind eye to its sale. The article concluded that it was "not possible to gauge the evil effects of this book, seeing that it is written in fine composition within the grasp of even ordinary minds".[18]

Advance copies of the article were forwarded to the Telugu Translator of the Government, as was required by law. The man occupying the post was Goteti Kanakaraju Pantulu, a staunch follower of Veeresalingam. On 4th February, he sent a letter to the Chief Secretary, Government of Madras, enclosing free translations of some of the obscene verses along with a copy of the Sasilekha review. In his letter he stated that the poem was "grossly obscene" and that the "author was a prostitute as also the editor". He was of the view that the "descriptions in the verses" would "deprave and corrupt the young minds of both sexes, by suggesting to their minds thoughts of the most impure and libidinous character". He also added that in his view "the conduct of the editor and the publisher comes under the provisions of section 292 of the Indian Penal Code".[19]

The Chief Secretary, on 7th February forwarded the letter to the Criminal Investigation Department, where an officer wrote the following cryptic memo:

"The Printers and Publishers – Messrs V Ramaswami Sastrulu and Sons.

Shops at :  (1) 323 Tiruvattur High Road, Tandiarpeta

(2) 192, China Bazaar Road, Esplanade

(3) Rajahmundry

The Editor – Bangalore Nagaratnam, a well-known prostitute of Madras.

The name of the book is *Radhika Santwanam* or *Ila Deviyam* (Radha Reconciled or the Story of Ila Devi)"[20]

On 6th March 1911, PB Thomas, DIG of Police, CID sent a memo to the Chief Secretary assuring him that a "prosecution would be initiated". The matter was deferred for some time as complaints on eight more titles had come in and the Telugu Translator's opinion of them was awaited.[21] It was however soon clear as to where his sympathies lay for he stated unambiguously that all eight were as "injurious to public morals as *Radhika Santwanamu*".[22] The Government swung into action on 22nd May 1911 and a posse of policemen led by Deputy Commissioner Cunningham, raided the offices and depots of several publishers and in a classic case of misplaced zeal seized 18 titles in all, including some Tamil books and also most ironically Veeresalingam's *Rasikajana Manoranjanam*[23], which in Nagarathnamma's opinion had as much description of sex as *Radhika Santwanamu*.[24] When the list of books was made public, however, care was taken to remove all mention of his name and the title of the book was simply given, with no other details.[25] On the other hand, complete details of all the remaining titles were published, with *Radhika Santwanamu* being second on the list. The author of the work was cited as a man – Maddu Pillai[26], something that must have enraged

Bangalore Nagarathnamma no end. Three hundred and eighty eight copies of *Radhika Santwanamu* were seized.[27] It was however quite clear that not much logic had been applied in deciding which books were to be seized. Among them was *Nandanar Natagam*[28], a dramatised version of the *Nandan Charittiram* of Gopalakrishna Bharati, which was the story of a devotee of Lord Siva and had no eroticism in it.

A second scanning of the list was evidently conducted, for the case of obscenity was eventually filed against only nine titles, all of them in Telugu and all published by Vavilla Ramaswami Sastrulu and Sons.[29] Veeresalingam's book was among those excluded, but *Vaijayanti Vilasamu*, a work edited by him was retained.[30] A case was registered against the publisher in the Chief Presidency Magistrate's Court, early in June under section 293 of the Indian Penal Code.[31] Nagarathnamma was not proceeded against probably on the grounds that she was not the author and had only edited an existing manuscript. In the meanwhile, she and the publisher did not remain idle. They decided to take their case to the wider public, on the grounds that the books being acted against were not recent creations but were classics which could not be subject to latter-day laws.

Consequently on 22nd June, G Venkataranga Rao, Secretary to the Madras Landholders Association and a great patron of the arts, had an interview in Ootacamund with Sir Arthur Lawley, the Governor of Madras Presidency. Rao strongly defended the books and said that these "works were classics and were written by poets who lived one or two centuries ago or are translations of old Sanskrit works and that other editions of them are now extinct". The Governor was also alerted to the possibility of a diplomatic incident as one of the books seized, *Sringara Padya Ratnavali*, had been published with the support of the Rajah of Venkatagiri, a powerful landholder of the Madras Presidency. The minutes also recorded that there was a "good deal of feeling in Madras about these cases". The Governor requested Venkataranga Rao to send a note to him regarding the books. [32] A feeler was also immediately sent to Sir Harold Stuart, Acting Chief Secretary to the Government in Madras asking if prosecution could not be stayed. [33] In his response Stuart admitted that this was the first time that the Government was informed that the books pertained to ancient literature. [34]

In the meanwhile the prosecution was appealed against in the High Court by Peri Narayana Murthy, the lawyer [35] representing Venkateswara Sastri, the proprietor of Vavilla Ramaswami Sastrulu and Sons. A stay was obtained on 26th June which lasted till 17th July when the High Court opened after the summer vacation. [36]

The note from Venkataranga Rao was received on 7th July, wherein he commented that the controversy had arisen because "a small coterie of radical social reformers seem(sic) to have carried the matter from the press to the police with the object of justifying their position by a magisterial decision". He differed from the Telugu Translator in his analysis of the *Radhika Santwanamu* and noted that it was an "amatory poem of high literary merit in four cantos. The subject of the poem is the love of Krishna for the beautiful cowherdess Radha, the estrangement of the lovers and their final reconciliation. It is an adaptation of a Sanskrit poem called *Radha Madhava Samvadamu*. The story is puranic in origin and has been immortalised in the well-known Sanskrit lyric *Gita Govinda* by Jayadeva, a native of Bengal and contemporary of a Bengal king named Lakshmana Sena. *Gita Govinda* has been translated into German by Ruckert and into English poetry by Sir Edwin Arnold under the name of Indian Song of Songs. *Radhika Santwanamu*, like its Sanskrit original and prototype contains passages which describe the transports of sensual love with all the exuberance of an impassioned imagination. As in the case of Solomon's *Song of Songs* in the Bible, there is in this poem and other works relating to the love between Radha and Krishna a widely recognised undercurrent of spiritual allegory and divine devotion".

The note went on to defend the remaining eight titles in a similar vein and then in eight structured passages, put forward a strong case for the Government to refrain from interfering with literature, stating that the books were "the products of an age and surroundings in which delicacy of sentiment and refinement of thought in the depiction of the sensuous were not what they are now required to be according to the ideas of a class of puristic critics... After all there can be no absolute and inviolable standard of decency in the artistic treatment of human love". He compared the works with those of several European writers and asked if Shakespeare in works such as *Venus and Adonis* and *The Rape of Lucrece* did not overstep the bounds of decency. "If stray obscene passages in poems be a legitimate ground of prosecution, there is hardly a Telugu or Sanskrit work that will escape and the publications of Telugu *prabandhams* must cease. If, however, it is a question of degree in respect of such obscenity, it will be utterly impossible to draw the line and of all places the Police Court is the one least fitted to be entrusted with this delicate function of drawing the line", he went on. He then quoted CP Brown as having said that "some who have not studied Hindu books speak of them as licentious. But there is more license in Ovid's Metamorphoses, in Congreve's plays and in Lesage's Romances than will be easily found in all Hindu literature".

Venkataranga Rao concluded his defence of the works, stating that the prosecutions for the publication of "accepted literary works of classical merit on the ground of their alleged indelicacy are certainly ill advised. A magisterial decision in the present condition of Telugu literature will tend to establish a standard of decency which will either sweep away all the old and much of contemporary Telugu literature or legalise the literary morals of an earlier age in a period of transition, both of which are results far from wholesome or helpful".[37] The Governor went through the papers but decided that it would not be necessary to interfere with the prosecution.[38]

In the meanwhile, the Governor's Council began interesting itself in the matter. The eminent *vakil* V Krishnaswami Iyer, then a member of the Council, asked to see the papers.[39] His contention was that the Telugu Translator was not of a neutral disposition and was a follower of Veeresalingam.[40] Sir Murray Hammick, also a member of the Council opined that "there could be no doubt that the person who possesses this book *Radhika Santwanamu* for sale has made himself liable under 293, Indian Penal Code. It is proper that the circulation of books containing these passages should be stopped". He however added that it was very likely that the publisher may not have brought the book out with an intention to deprave and if he consented to destroy the books and not sell unexpurgated editions in future, the prosecution may be dropped.[41] The CID was asked to get such a commitment from the publisher and a note was also sent to the Chief Presidency Magistrate asking to adjourn the case.[42] The CID was also asked to investigate and ascertain the moral character of the publisher[43] and it set its Acting Assistant Commissioner of Police, Rao Sahib Saravana Bavanandam Pillai[44], a man who was known for his support of the arts, on the job. Pillai, on 31st July furnished a fairly factual assessment of the nine works and concluded his note with the observation that the publisher was of a respectable character and good reputation. However, he also recorded that during the investigation several aristocratic and therefore western-educated Indians opined that they could not allow the books to be read in their houses and this carried weight with the powers that be.[45]

In the meanwhile, on 20th July, a meeting of "Telugu and Sanskrit scholars and others interested in Telugu literature" under the auspices of the South Indian Association of which V Krishnaswami Iyer was a founder, was held at the Ranade Hall in Mylapore. Attending it was a veritable galaxy of Telugu pundits such as Veduri Prabhakara Sastri of the Oriental Library, Madras and noted teachers of the language such as V Subba Rao of the Presidency College. The legal aspects of the matter also attracted several lawyers such as Sriman Srinivasa Iyengar and P Nagabhushanam. Editors and publishers of Telugu works were also present as was most surprisingly G Seshacharyulu, the editor of the *Sasilekha*, whose writings had triggered the controversy. He appears to have had some pangs at what he had stirred up, for he warmly seconded the first of three resolutions passed that evening which stated that "in view of the fact that the nine Telugu publications in respect of which a prosecution is now pending in the Court of the Chief Presidency Magistrate, Madras, are amongst ancient classical Telugu literary works and in view of the general character of Telugu literature which is largely modelled on Sanskrit literature, the Government be humbly requested to drop the said prosecution".

The second resolution however contained the seeds of an idea that was acceptable to the Government. The resolution stated "that efforts should be made to induce publishers to bring out expurgated editions of Telugu classical works, where they contain objectionable passages and that a conference of Telugu people be held for the purpose at such time and place as may be notified". The third resolution concerned the forming of a committee for organising the conference and for forwarding the first and second resolutions to the Government. These resolutions were forwarded to the Chief Secretary of the Government on 22nd July 1911, by GV Appa Rao Pantulu who had chaired the meeting at the Ranade Hall.[46]

On 1st August, V Krishnaswami Iyer concurred with Sir Murray Hammick that the prosecution should be "withdrawn on an undertaking from the man not to publish in future, unexpurgated editions. They are old books many times published though very obscene in parts. They don't stand on the same footing as new works".[47]

Taking every aspect of the case into account, the Government ordered the Chief Commissioner of Police on 24th August to obtain an undertaking in writing from the publisher that he would not publish thereafter unexpurgated editions of the nine works. The choice of the passages to be expurgated was left to the publisher. Subject to such an undertaking the Government ordered that the prosecution may be withdrawn. The publisher was also asked to destroy all printed copies of the nine works then available with him.[48]

On 5th September 1911, Vavilla Venkateswara Sastri sent a reply on behalf of his firm to F Armitage, the Commissioner of Police, in which he stated that unless he was told as to which passages were considered objectionable, he would not be in a position to take up the expurgation of passages in any of the books. He also stated that he did not, while publishing the books "even for a moment feel that I was doing anything wrong, particularly because they were widely current and well-known works, freely published by others engaged like me in the book publishing trade. That it was possible to look upon these publications as objectionable, in fact, came to my knowledge for the first time when the printed copies of the said books in my possession were seized by the Police". Sastri went on to request that instead of the stocks being destroyed he be allowed to block out objectionable passages, once they were decided upon. He could then be permitted to sell the books so that the loss to be sustained by him would be minimised. In order to impress upon the Government that he was a reputed publisher he attached testimonials from rulers, lawyers, professors of history and several prominent citizens of the Madras Presidency. A copy of a Government Order sanctioning purchase of certain books from the publisher was also enclosed. In a moving passage, Sastri narrated the losses he had already suffered in seeking legal advice and in frequently appearing in court and other places, all of which had been too heavy for a man of his circumstances. There is mention of his being ill which had resulted in delays in the progress of the case.[49]

The Veeresalingam faction was however not idle. Their main interest lay in getting the *Radhika Santwanamu* proscribed, principally because of Nagarathnamma's spirited attack on their idol. It was probably not to their liking that the book, with only parts of the main text expurgated and the preface written by Nagarathnamma be circulated intact. A new tack was therefore tried out, which worked successfully. On the very same day when Venkateswara Sastri made his representation to the Government, G Venkataranga Rao, Chairman of the Board of Studies for Telugu, met Sir HA Stuart, the Chief Secretary. During the conversation it emerged that Veeresalingam himself had been the prime mover in the matter of the prosecution. Venkataranga Rao represented that the *Radhika Santwanamu* could not be expurgated with "objectionable passages being found on nearly every page". It was decided that all copies of the work would be destroyed. As for the remaining works, among which was *Vaijayanti Vilasamu*, edited by Veeresalingam, it was decided that a committee of three, comprising Venkataranga Rao, Goteti Kanakaraju, the Telugu Translator to Government and Professor Rao Bahadur M Rangacharya, the Registrar of Books would assess them and decide which sections of each were to be expurgated.[50]

The disclosure that Veeresalingam was an interested party in the prosecution was noted with some glee by V Krishnaswami Iyer, who wrote on the margin of the file, which had by then become huge in size, that he had "never thought that the Telugu Translator was disinterested. He is the follower of Viresalingam".[51] On the basis of this, Krishnaswami Iyer demanded that the Telugu Translator be removed from the committee and be replaced either with P Rama Rayaningar (later the Rajah of Panagal) or P Srinivasa Charlu, a scholar.[52] But this was not agreed upon and the committee went ahead.

On 27th September 1911, the Government formally issued a memorandum to the Commissioner of Police stating that it had been decided "that all copies of the book *Radhika Santwanamu* should be destroyed as objectionable passages are found on nearly every page of that work." Regarding the remaining titles, the Commissioner was asked to obtain one copy of each and submit to the Government, which would pass them on to the examining committee. Venkateswara Sastri was asked to submit an undertaking that he would not publish or sell any unexpurgated copies of the remaining eight titles in future.[53]

In December 1911, the committee of three made its recommendations for expurgation of passages in the other books.[54] It was found that the Telugu Translator had dissented and filed a separate list of passages; an act which the other two members felt was a breach of etiquette.[55] The Telugu Translator's list which dealt harshly with seven of the eight titles left the *Vaijayanti Vilasamu*, edited by Veeresalingam practically untouched.[56] On 4th March 1912, the Government directed that three more titles among the eight, namely *Hamsa Vimsati*, *Tara Shashanka Vijayamu* and *Vithi Natakamu* ought to be proscribed and the remaining five could be printed after deleting the offensive passages as detailed by the Telugu Translator. The Government Order pressed Vavilla Ramaswami Sastrulu and Sons to give their undertaking as demanded in August 1911.[57]

G Venkataranga Rao, who had rather tamely accepted the decision to proscribe the *Radhika Santwanamu* put up a strong defence in favour of lifting the ban on the other three titles. He met the Chief Secretary in June 1912 and demanded that the three titles be treated on par with the other five that had been returned to the publisher.[58] Vavilla Venkateswara Sastri in the meantime dawdled over giving his undertaking and it appears that a powerful lobby within the Government was now working in his favour. Translations in Government files of the period show that works such as *Tara Sashanka Vijayamu* and *Hamsa Vimsati* were much more graphic in their description of sex than the *Radhika Santwanamu* and yet these were not measured by the same yardstick. The general attitude appeared to be that with the *Radhika Santwanamu* out of the way, there was very little left to worry about. P Hannyngton, the Commissioner of Police was asked not to revive prosecution of the publisher until further orders.[59] On 4th July 1912, it was decided that the three remaining titles would be returned to the publisher and that he ought to be given an opportunity to publish expurgated copies.[60] Thus the only book to be really proscribed in the end was the *Radhika Santwanamu*. Venkateswara Sastri used his own judgement regarding expurgation and continued bringing out the remaining titles until 1927. The drama of seizure and prosecution was once again repeated[61] then, but that does not concern the story of Nagarathnamma.

*Radhika Santwanamu* practically went out of existence. The book had been singled out largely because it was an erotic classic written by a woman and while editing it, another woman, namely Naga-rathnamma, had been bold enough to attack a pillar of the establishment namely, Kandukuri Veeresalingam. Talking about the episode as late as in 1949, Dr KN Kesari, the well-known physician and philanthropist stated that "it required enormous courage to oppose Veeresalingam and only Nagarathnamma could have done it".[62]

The publishing of the book however raised Nagarathnamma's stature enormously in the public eye and she was now acclaimed as not only a leading musician but also as a scholar and a bold personality who stood up to be counted. Her wide circle of friends and admirers now included several scholars and poets and some such as Sripada Krishnamurthy Sastri and 'Shatavadhani' Chellapilla Venkateswara Sastri sang her praises in their works.[63] She was given a seat of honour in poetry symposia and in scholarly discussions and was asked to be seated in the presence of the rulers of Mysore, Bobbili and Venkatagiri.[64] In time, she turned author as well, penning a work in Telugu titled *Madya Paanam*, which dealt with the evils of alcohol, in the form of a conversation[65] Interestingly, for someone whose mother tongue was not Tamil, she also wrote a philosophical work *Panchikarana Bhautika Viveka Vilakkam* in that language.[66] This had a preface in her praise by Tyagaraja Siva Yogigal, probably a scholar and her guru in Tamil. She had truly acquired the same stature as the courtesans of the Maratha court.

## References

[1] Parthasarathy, TS; Sri Tyagarajaswami Kirtanaigal; Sri Sadguru Sangeetha Samajam; Madras; 1967; p 640; translated from the original in Tamil by the author.

[2] Isai Medaikal.

[3] Seetha, S; p 98.

[4] Ibid.

[5] Tharu, Susie & Lalita,K; Women Writing in India, Vol.1, 600 BC to the Early Twentieth Century; Oxford University Press; New Delhi; 2000; p 117; hereinafter referred to as Women Writing in India.

[6] Rao, Dr Pappu Venugopala; email to author with a précis of the book.

[7] Ibid.

[8] Ari, Sitaramayya & Paruchuri Sreenivas; Charles Philip Brown; website of the Telugu Literary and Cultural Association.

[9] Women's Writing in India; p 118.

[10] Ibid; p 2.

[11] Vijaishri Priyadarshini; p 269.

[12] Women's Writing in India; p 3.

[13] Jackson, William J; Tyagaraja and the Renewal of Tradition, Translations and Reflections; Motilal Banarsidas; Delhi; 1994; hereinafter referred to as Jackson, William J; p 149.

[14] Nagarathnamma, Bangalore; "Prasthavana"; *Radhika Santwanamu;* Vavilla Ramaswami Sastrulu and Sons; Madras; 1910; p 80.

[15] Ibid; p ii.

[16] Grihalakshmi; p 19.

[17] Tamilnadu Archives; notes to GO No 348; Judicial; 4th March 1912; p 14.

[18] Annexure to letter from Telugu Translator to Government to Chief Secretary; 4th February 1911.

[19] Ibid.

[20] Tamilnadu Archives; GO 348, Judicial; 4th March 1912; Page 7 of Notes.

[21] Tamilnadu Archives; notes to GO 348, Judicial; 4th March 1912; letter from PB Thomas, DIG of Police, CID to the Chief Secy, Govt. of Madras; 6th March 1911.

[22] Tamilnadu Archives; GO 348, Judicial; 4th March 1912; Minutes of Dissent to the Report of the Registrar of Books and the Chairman of the Telugu Board of Studies; 15th December 1911; p 17.

[23] Tamilnadu Archives; notes to GO No 348; Judicial; 4th March 1912; p 14.

[25] Tamilnadu Archives; notes to GO No 348; Judicial; 4th March 1912; p 14.

[26] Ibid.

[27] Ibid.

[28] Ibid.

[29] Tamilnadu Archives; GO 348, Judicial; 4th March 1912; letter from F Armitage, Commissioner of Police to the Chief Secy., Govt. of Madras; 7th August 1911; p 4.

[30] Tamilnadu Archives; GO 348, Judicial; 4th March 1912; note from Sir HA Stuart, Acting Chief Secy.; p 21.

[31] Ibid.

[32] Tamilnadu Archives; notes to GO No 348; Judicial; 4th March 1912; p 23.

[33] Tamilnadu Archives; notes to GO No 348; Judicial; 4th March 1912; Demi Official from AYG Campbell, PS to Governor, addressed to Sir HA Stuart, Chief Secy., Govt. of Madras; 27th June 1911; p 23.

[34] Tamilnadu Archives; notes to GO No 348; Judicial; 4th March 1912; Reply from Sir HA Stuart to AYG Campbell; 28th June 1911, p 23.

[35] Women's Writing in India; p 4.

[36] Tamilnadu Archives; notes to GO No 348; Judicial; 4th March 1912; note from SH Slater, Under Secy., Govt. of Madras to the Chief Secy., 1st July 1911; p 24.

[37] Tamilnadu Archives; notes to GO No 348;Judicial; 4th March 1912; Letter from G Venkataranga Rao; 7th July 1911, p 24-29.

[38] Ibid; p 29.

[39] Tamilnadu Archives; notes to GO No 348; Judicial; 4th March 1912; Note from Sir HA Stuart, Chief Secy., Govt. of Madras to SH Slater, Under Secy., 20th July 1911; p 30.

[40] Tamilnadu Archives; notes to GO No 348; Judicial; 4th March 1912; Memo by V Krishnaswami Iyer on the margin of letter to him from Sir HA Stuart; 13th September 1911.

[41] Tamilnadu Archives; notes to GO No 348; Judicial; 4th March 1912; note from Sir Murray Hammick to Chief Secy., Govt. of Madras; 12th July 1911.

[42] Ibid.

[43] Ibid.

[44] Tamilnadu Archives; GO 348; Judicial; 4th March 1912; letter from F Armitage, Commissioner of Police to Chief Secy., Govt. of Madras; 7th August 1911; p 4.

[45] Ibid.

[46] Tamilnadu Archives; GO 348; Judicial; 4th March 1912; letter from MR Ry Appa Rao Pantulu to the Chief Secy., Govt. of Madras; 22nd July 1911; p 2-4.

[47] Tamilnadu Archives; notes to GO No 348; Judicial; 4th March 1912; Note from V Krishnaswami Iyer to Chief Secy., Govt. of Madras; 1st August 1911; p 31.

[48] Tamilnadu Archives; GO 348; Judicial; 4th March 1912; Official Memorandum No 3505-3; Judicial; 24th August 1911; p 5.

[49] Tamilnadu Archives; GO 348; Judicial; 4th March 1912; Enclosure to letter from F Armitage, Commissioner of Police to Chief Secy., Govt. of Madras; 5th September 1911; p 6.

[50] Tamilnadu Archives; note to GO No 348; Judicial; 4th March 1912; letter no 547 I-D from Sir HA Stuart to V Krishnaswami Iyer and the Governor; 5th September 1911; p 32.

[51] Ibid.

[52] Tamilnadu Archives; notes to GO No 348; Judicial; 4th March 1912; note from V Krishnaswami Iyer; 16th September 1911; p 33.

[53] Tamilnadu Archives; GO 348; Judicial; 4th March 1912; Official Memorandum No 4370-1; Judicial; 27th September 1911; p 9.

[54] Tamilnadu Archives; GO 348; Judicial; 4th March 1912; letter from Registrar of Books, Madras and the Chairman, Telugu Board of Examiners, University of Madras to the Chief Secy., Govt. of Madras; 4th December 1911; p 10.

[55] Ibid.

[56] Tamilnadu Archives; GO 348; Judicial; 4th March 1912; letter from Telugu Translator to Government to the Chief Secy., Govt. of Madras; 15th December 1911; p 16.

[57] Tamilnadu Archives; GO 348; Judicial, 4th March 1912; Order no 348; 4th March 1912; p 21.

[58] Tamilnadu Archives; notes to GO No 1077; Judicial; 4th July 1912; Letter from Chief Secy., Govt. of Madras to HE The Governor; 12th June 1912; p 1.

[59] Ibid; p 2.

[60] Tamilnadu Archives; GO 1077; Judicial; 4th July 1912.

[61] Tamilnadu Archives; GO 355; Public Confidential; 22nd April 1927.

[62] Grihalakshmi; p 52-53.

[63] Isai Medaikal.

[64] Grihalakshmi; p 17-18.

[65] Ibid; p 19.

[66] Ibid.

*Nagarathnamma dressed as an Iyer lady*
*at the instance of her friends. Circa 1902*
Picture courtesy Amarajeevi Potti Sriramulu Library, Chennai

*After a command performance at Mysore, circa 1905.*

Picture courtesy Amarajeevi Potti Sriramulu Library, Chennai

*Nagarathnamma circa 1910.*
Picture taken from the 1950 edition of *Radhika Santwanamu.*
Published by Vavilla Ramaswami Sastrulu & Sons

*Nagarathnamma circa 1935.*
Picture courtesy Amarajeevi Potti Sriramulu Library, Chennai

*At the height of her performing career.*
Picture taken from *A Dictionary of South Indian Music and Musicians* by Prof. P Sambamurthy.

*Offering prayers at Tyagaraja's Samadhi, 1940.*
Picture courtesy Tyagaraja Aradhana Souvenir 1941.

*At the fund raising concert series in RR Sabha, 22nd September 1941.*
*Along with her are C Saraswathi Bai & Mrs. S Sathyamurthy*
Picture courtesy S Thyagarajan, The Musiri Subramania Iyer Collection.

*A cartoon of Nagarathnamma which appeared in Ananda Vikatan, Jan. 1943.*
Picture courtesy Tamilnadu Archives, Chennai

*Aradhana of 1950,*
*Janaki Subramaniam, Shakuntala Sethuraman & Nagarathnamma.*
Picture courtesy Tyagaraja Aradhana Souvenir 1951.

*Nagarathnamma with friends and admirers in Tiruvayyaru, 1949.*
Picture courtesy Amarajeevi Potti Sriramulu Library, Chennai

*Receiving the Swarna Kankanam award from Dr K N Kesari, 16th March 1949.*
Picture courtesy Amarajeevi Potti Sriramulu Library, Chennai

*Last photo taken of Nagarathnamma, early 1950.*

# Chapter 4

*"What if they perform yagas…adopt other's sons? What if they build palatial houses and fit them up with rows of lights?"*
(Tyagaraja in "Emi Jesitenemi", raga Todi, tala Chapu)[1]

~

"In these 26 years, Nagarathnamma has performed in 146 cities," wrote a source in 1931. "On the whole, 1235 concerts were performed in the Tamil speaking country. In Madras alone she has performed 849 concerts."[2]

It was a considerable number for an era when transport and communication were still in the nascent stage. She was much in demand in places such as Tiruchirapalli, Venkatagiri, Nellore and Tanjavur. Audiences would not let her go and performances often extended up to 10:30 or 11:00 pm at night, an advanced hour in those conservative days. Nagarathnamma also crossed the seas, in what must have been a daring move at a time when such travel was considered taboo. She performed in Jaffna in Ceylon (present day Sri Lanka).[3]

She had to frequently travel by train. Using a *tambura* for the drone was de rigueur and carrying it over long distances became a major problem. Nagarathnamma solved this by designing a portable instrument,[4] perhaps the first of its kind. Mysore Vasudevachar who called on her had his attention drawn to a *tambura* that stood in the corner of her, music room. Nagarathnamma placed the instrument before him and demonstrated how the stalk and the keys could be dismantled from the gourd, thereby making for easy transportation. The *tambura* did not suffer any loss of tone, which Vasudevachar described as rich and pure.[5] In her concerts, Nagarathnamma strummed the *tambura* herself, by placing it horizontally on her lap or on the floor in front of her.[6]

While it is not clear as to who her accompanists were in the first half of her career, it was Sivasubramania Iyer, a violinist of Madras who became her stock accompanist in the later years.[7] He was in many ways an ideal accompanist for her, for he was an equally strong-willed personality who did not hesitate to publicly state his views about musicians whom he did not approve of.[8] The *mridangam* artiste was Ramamritham Iyer.

Weddings in the families of well-heeled landlords of the Tanjavur district were rarely complete without music performances. Such events involved entire villages becoming absorbed in their arrangement and celebration. Usually celebrated in the post-harvest seasons, the ceremonies would last for eight days and more, with lavish feasts three times a day. Concerts in the evening would comprise western bands, dance performances, *nagaswaram* performances, *Harikatha* sessions and mimicry. Among the prominent Devadasis who were frequently invited to sing was Bangalore Nagarathnamma. Mudicondan Venkatarama Iyer, the latter-day musician remembers attending performances of Nagarathnamma's during such weddings. He later wrote that Nagarathnamma's voice was majestic yet sweet and that she had a forceful manner of singing. Her performances would last between three and four hours. She also invariably sang *ragam tanam pallavi* suites and often selected complicated *pallavi*s set to intricate *tala*s.[9] This again was a deviation from the tradition that women were generally not supposed to sing *pallavi*s. Areas such as Mudicondan and Mayavaram were noted for audiences who were experts in the mathematics of *pallavis*[10] and to have taken up singing this form of music in their presence must have required plenty of self-confidence. Nagarathnamma was not alone in this. Kanchipuram Dhanakoti had begun the trend and had been closely followed by Coimbatore Thayi.[11] Nagarathnamma had followed their lead and was knocking down a male bastion. She also included a *javali* or two in her performances.[12] She evidently had a large repertoire of these songs. She also appears to have possessed an extensive repertoire of the works of Mysore Sadasiva Rao.[13]

Her gurus traced their lineage to the composer Tyagaraja and she therefore knew many of his songs. Given her deep knowledge of the Telugu language, it was not long before she came to appreciate the depth and meaning of Tyagaraja's songs. In time her concerts came to largely comprise his compositions.[14] Once a fan had asked her as to why she did not sing songs of Tyagaraja's great contemporary Muttuswami Dikshitar. She replied that to sing Dikshitar kritis one needed extensive knowledge of Sanskrit, which she did not possess and to comprehend the composer's works was a tough task.[15] This was stretching the truth somewhat as she had enough knowledge of Sanskrit to conduct conversations in it.[16] Perhaps her repertoire of Dikshitar's works was scanty, for the composer's songs were not yet well known. But clearly Tyagaraja was her favourite composer. Writing about him was perhaps the only task that made her diffident. "Is it not a task akin to counting the grains of sand by the sea or estimating the number of rays that come from the sun?" she asked.[17]

Concerts apparently also involved plenty of repartee and banter with the audiences. Nagarathnamma, like a stand-up comedian had the talent to make people laugh uproariously. She could also be quite sardonic, though her speech was never sarcastic unlike that of 'Veena' Dhanam. Like Kanchipuram Dhanakoti, Nagarathanamma was also largely intolerant of people asking her to sing particular songs of their choice during her performances. Dhanakoti had once faced an insolent young man in the audience, who, addressing her in the disrespectful singular had asked her to sing a song from Arunachala Kavi's *Rama Natakam*. Stung to the quick but not showing it, Dhanakoti immediately launched into Ravana's song from the play which being addressed to Hanuman began with the lines "*Yaarada Kurange?*" (Who are you, monkey).[18] A contemporary account of Nagarathnamma states that once when asked to sing a song in raga Kapi, she had punned on its name and the way the word coffee is pronounced in South India and had asked the person who made the request to come to her house the next day where she would treat him to good Kapi.[19]

On the days when she was not performing, Nagarathnamma was at home to visitors and of these there were plenty. Many times, her fans would call on her the day after her performance and ask her to sing their favourite songs once again.[20] Patrons such as Rajarathna Mudaliar and Kasturi Ranga Iyengar were frequent visitors. Besides, musicians would call at all times of the day. The residence itself was similar to a town house and comprised two floors.[21] The front room was where Nagarathnamma received most of her guests. There was in addition, a music room where she practised.[22] This had besides several *tamburas*, a harmonium as well.[23] Several pictures of the gods done in the Mysore style, lined the central passage of the house. It was said that the decorative work on these were of real gold leaf and precious stones and that the pictures had been gifted to Nagarathnamma by the Mysore royalty.[24] Somewhere in this house also stood a large iron safe which "overflowed with cash"[25] and contained her extensive collection of jewellery.[26] She had a great liking for diamonds in particular and preferred them to be of the uncut variety.[27] It was no exaggeration according to Banni Bai, to say that Nagarathnamma was covered with diamonds from head to foot. For these, Nagarathnamma did business with the famed house of Tawkers, traders in gems and jewels. After that firm went into a decline she patronised the Surajmal Lallubhai Mehta family whose outlet was in Broadway.[28] In course of time Surajmal, the proprietor himself, became an ardent admirer and patron.[29]

Nagarathnamma detested the summer heat of Madras and devised an ingenious method of reducing the temperature in the house. Several cotton saris would be drenched in water and hung all around the room. In the middle would be a huge block of ice. Seated in this room she would have iced juices and relax in the company of her friends such as 'Veena' Dhanam and Coimbatore Thayi.[30]

Correspondence regarding concert invitations was extensive, for the *zamindars* of Andhra considered auspicious events in their households incomplete if Nagarathnamma did not perform on the occasion. She made routine visits to Bobbili, Venkatagiri, Nuzvid, Telaprole and Vizianagaram and at all these places she would always be referred to as *"Amma"* and never by name.[31] The women in the *zenana* loved her company, for she was sparkling in her conversation. Her quaint use of Urdu terms in her Telugu, as characteristic of one who came from Kannada-speaking regions caused much amusement and laughter in which she too joined.[32]

Within the city of Madras, Nagarathnamma moved around in considerable state, always in a horse carriage and surrounded by a retinue of servants. There were evidently maids with individual responsibilities. Many years later Dr KN Kesari remembered, as a child, seeing Nagarathnamma visiting the Park Fair and Carnival of Sport organised by the South Indian Athletic Association. This was a landmark event in the social calendar of Madras especially during the inter-war years. Dr Kesari described the arrival and his impression of Nagarathnamma thus:

"At the main entrance, I saw people hurriedly running to see something. Curious, I asked them what the commotion was all about. "Bangalore Nagarathnamma is coming", was the reply. Enthusiastically,

I ran to catch a glimpse of that person. I still recollect the picture of Nagarathnamma with her entourage. One maid walked in front with a silver pot of coffee. Another carried hot water and yet another a box of betel leaves. Swaying a fan made of palm leaf followed another maidservant. They were all richly ornamented. Then like a ray of light enhanced by diamonds and dressed in a sari came this goddess walking elegantly. That was the image I formed of Nagarathnamma then. I kept looking at her, but she did not notice me. After all when she was the cynosure of so many eyes, how could she have made note of any one person? When questioned as to who she was several said that she was a scholar, a very learned person. Since then, I became a regular at all her *kutcheris*."[33]

As befitting her status as a leading Devadasi, she did not ever enter her kitchen, preferring to employ a cook. In culinary matters, her tastes were extremely spartan and despite her size she was a very poor eater, with the quantity she ate often being compared to that of a small child.[34] She was however extremely fond of milk and of this she could evidently never have enough. Her nightcap was elaborate and involved adding several spices and condiments to milk which was placed over the embers of coal in a mud stove, a good two hours before bed time. The milk would boil over repeatedly and thicken until only a condensed quantity was left, which Nagarathnamma would consume with relish. She would repeatedly test the consistency of the milk during this process, not wishing to have it till it was perfect. This would at times take so long that she would even doze off and wake up sometime at night and drink the milk.[35]

Rituals prescribed for her station in life held great importance for Nagarathnamma and she religiously followed them all. Her mother and her guru were objects of veneration for her and she observed the days of their passing, each year with great devotion. She observed without fail the annual *puja* in memory of her guru.[36] In remembrance of her mother, Nagarathnamma conducted for many years the annual festival or *Brahmotsavam* at the Fort Sriramaswami Temple in Bangalore.[37] Later, having had a vision of Hanuman in her dream she resumed the practice in Madras, conducting the event at the Prasanna Seetharama Anjaneya Swami temple on Thatha Muthiappan Street, George Town. This was observed on the thirteenth day of the waxing phase of the moon in the month of *Margazhi* (Dec/Jan).[38] The deities were ceremonially bathed and offered flowers, to the chanting of 108 names of the Lord and then taken out in procession. Gifts for them would be placed on trays and decorated as though they were being offered at a wedding. The heavily bejewelled and perfumed Nagarathnamma would follow the procession and with her collared blouse, her cascading gold chains, her rich sari and her heavy silver-encased walking stick, would make for a most dignified and majestic personality.[39]

*Bhajan* or congregational singing took place regularly at several aristocratic homes of Madras. Some of the Devadasis also conducted them at their own residences. Coimbatore Thayi had them each month at her home when the asterism *Rohini* was in the ascendant.[40] Nagarathnamma preferred *amavasya* and on that day several *sadhus* and singers would assemble at her house and she would lead the congregation in singing *bhajans*.[41] Feeding of the poor was done each month when the asterism *Krittika* was in the ascendant.[42] On the birthday of Rama, she would distribute buttermilk, jaggery mixed with water (*panakam*), palm leaf fans and betel leaves to those who passed by her home.[43] Each year Nagarathnamma donated extensively to the annual *Vairamudi* festival at Melkote.[44] In 1911, she purchased land near the French Rocks at Harpanahalli, so that each year a temporary shelter could be constructed for pilgrims on their way to the same festival.[45] In Madras, she bought an entire market in the ancient district of Tiruvottiyur and donated it to the Nandikeswara temple there, with the proviso that the income from the rent be used for lighting lamps.[46]

Similarly, the Nataraja temple on Govindappa Naicken Street was a beneficiary and on *Ardra Darshanam* day, which falls each year in December, special worship was offered there at her expense.[47] Besides all this, there were several poor students who were helped with money for school and college fees, as were several girls who had their marriages conducted at her expense. The godman Sorakkai Paradesi, who lived in Perambur and whose mere glance was said to bring good fortune[48] was greatly venerated by Nagarathnamma who donated lavishly to his establishment.[49]

Her daily *puja* was also elaborate. The family owed allegiance to Lord Venkateswara of Tirupati and an idol of this deity was worshipped by Nagarathnamma.[50] A crystal Shiva *linga* and a silver frieze of Rama with consort Sita, brother Lakshmana and attendant Hanuman occupied positions of importance. All these idols were housed in a wooden pavilion in her *puja* room. To this was added a statue of Goddess Kameswari which was acquired by Nagarathnamma from a visiting Brahmin.[51] This idol gradually became central to Nagarathnamma's *puja*. Every Friday, a Brahmin came and offered special worship to the deity.[52] Nagarathnamma herself recited the *Lalitha Sahasranama*, the hymn containing the 1000 names of the Goddess and at the conclusion of it, distributed *kumkum* and turmeric to women of the neighbourhood. A lamp was kept burning in front of the idol night and day.[53]

Given her piety and her erudition, it was not long before the public began attributing special powers to her. Her crystal *linga* was said to bless the public with copious rains if Nagarathnamma prayed to it.[54] Her *kumkum* was looked upon by women as a blessing for a long and happy married life.[55] The *Zamindarini* of Chikkavaram, Saraswathi Devi sought her blessings when she became pregnant for the third time and hoped that unlike the earlier deliveries, this would result in a son. Nagarathnamma gave her a lime fruit and asked her to keep it in her *puja*. Saraswathi Devi did so and when the baby was indeed a son she attributed it to the blessings of Nagarathnamma. The dried up and shrivelled fruit still remains in the possession of the son in question, VAK Ranga Rao.[56]

Awards and titles came to her in plenty. The first was *Vidyasundari* which was conferred on her by Puranam Suryanarayana Teertha, a well known Andhra poet.[57] This was to be her favourite title and she used it as a prefix to her own name. She was given medals and bracelets by the ruling princes of South India and *zamindars*.[58] All this was in an era when women were rarely bestowed with titles and honours.

Nagarathnamma had everything that life could offer and yet she lacked children. There are some accounts that aver that she had given birth to a daughter who died young.[59] As the years went on, the hopes of bearing a child must have receded. All around her she must have seen her friends bringing forth their offspring and raising families. Adoption was a common feature among childless Devadasis and it was only very rarely that there were instances like the Enadi Sisters, who died without passing on either their knowledge or their wealth to anyone. It was common for indigent families of all castes to give away their daughters in adoption to Devadasis, for the girls stood to gain property, education and a good grounding in the arts. In the years of famine, such adoptions reached an all time high. Dhanam's mother Sundarammal had been adopted by grandmother Kamakshi from a Brahmin family, many years earlier.[60] Nagarathnamma's friend Perumalkoil Narayanamma had more recently adopted a girl child Lalithangi from a Brahmin household[61] and the girl was already showing promise of becoming a good singer. Encouraged by this Nagarathnamma too adopted a girl child and lavished affection on her. She tried teaching her all that she knew.[62] But over the years the relationship soured. The girl was found to be more interested in Nagarathnamma's wealth,[63] which by 1920 had reached Rs two lakhs in value.[64] The girl's parents were also proving to be a baneful influence and one night they tried poisoning Nagarathnamma's cup of milk. But she saw through the plot.[65] She settled thousands of rupees on the girl and returned her to her parents, rescinding the adoption.[66] In later life she would never speak of the circumstances in which she parted from her adopted daughter.[67] It was left to chroniclers such as Banni Bai to bring the story to light.

Divested of the child, Nagarathnamma once again pined for company, especially in the evenings. Among the many attendees of her evening *puja* to Kameswari, was Dorasani Ammal, a practitioner of the arts, who lived in Krishnappa Naicken Tank Square of George Town.[68] The two women became close to each other and Naga- rathnamma would often visit Dorasani. She was particularly fond of Dorasani's third daughter. The child, born in 1912 had been named Alamelumanga Thayar but her unusually fair complexion made a visiting Marwari *seth* in the neighbourhood refer to her as Baniya Bai, a name representative of his own community. This soon became Banni Bai.[69] Nagarathnamma mothered Banni Bai, who became the daughter she never had. The relationship was to be warm and close till Nagarathnamma's death in 1952. In later years, Banni Bai was to state that Nagarathnamma was the mother who nourished her in the arts.

For some time a young lad named Subramania Naidu, who was hopeful of learning music from 'Veena' Dhanam stayed with Nagarathnamma.[70] But soon he was to realise that Dhanam was not going to teach him beyond a few songs, one of which was Tyagaraja's "Merusamana" (raga Mayamalavagaula). He had to repeat the song so many times, that this became a standing joke among Dhanam's burgeoning brood of grandchildren who began calling him Merusamana.[71] He gave up and apprenticed himself under Naina Pillai, the nephew of Kanchipuram Dhanakoti. This necessitated his move to Kanchipuram. Later he would shine as Chittoor Subramania Pillai, in many ways the true inheritor of the Naina Pillai tradition.

Yet another youngster for whom Nagarathnamma had great affection was Kothainayaki, a talented young Brahmin girl of Triplicane. Kothai, born in 1901 was married at the age of five to Vai Mu Parthasarathy, the nine-year-old son of an orthodox Brahmin Iyengar family. By the time Nagarathnamma got to know her she was a teenager. Kothai was very good in music and her husband used to take her to listen to concerts of Nagarathnamma and her contemporaries such as Bangalore Thayi and Tiruvarur Rajayee. The introduction may have happened on one of these occasions. Hearing Kothai sing, Nagarathnamma wanted her to perform in public. But in those days it was unheard of that a Brahmin woman could take to a concert career, even if C Saraswathi Bai had shown the way. Nagarathnamma however did not give up and finally succeeded in persuading Kothai's in-laws. The concert took place at a *Sabha* in Thambu Chetty Street, George Town. By way of giving confidence to the young woman, Nagarathnamma herself strummed the *tambura*. The audience was very impressed with the performance and 'Kirtanacharya' CR Srinivasa Iyengar, a great scholar who was in the audience was full of praise for Kothai's performance.

Not content with this, Nagarathnamma sent Kothai to Mysore with a letter of introduction to her guru, Bidaram Krishnappa. He was in those days involved with a shrine for Rama and arranged for her concert to be held there. The two-hour performance was hailed by musicians such as T Chowdiah and Mysore Vasudevachar. Later Kothai was also presented at court and was honoured by Maharajah Krishnaraja Wodeyar. In later years, Kothai would blossom into a multifaceted personality running her own magazine, *Jaganmohini* and turning into a prolific novelist, writing under the name of Vai Mu Ko. She recorded several 78 rpm records and became a fine speaker. She would also participate in the freedom struggle and become one of the prominent women of Madras city.[72]

Kothai was an exception to the general Devadasi dictum, whereby knowledge was not easily imparted to outsiders and the arts were considered the exclusive preserve of the community. Nagarathnamma herself strongly believed in this. When she called on Saraswathi Devi, the *zamindarni* of Chikkavaram, shortly after she had given birth, the latter wanted her to bless the baby so that he would become a musician. Nagarathnamma, on the other hand, blessed him with the words that he would be greatly appreciative of the arts. When questioned, she said that if everyone got into a palanquin nobody would be around to carry it and similarly the arts needed patrons to sustain them as much as they needed artistes. In her view the Devadasis and their menfolk were meant to be artistes and the *zamindars* the much-needed patrons. The two ought not to trespass on each others' territory.[73] On the other hand she was generous with members of her own community and taught *abhinaya* to some Devadasi girls of Madras.

In the meantime, it was back to loneliness for her. A woman, particularly wealthy and living alone was easy target for burglars. Sivasubramania Iyer, worried about her well-being and safety, stationed his wife's brother, a young man named Meenakshisundaram at Nagarathnamma's house. This lad too was looked upon by her as a son. He was to remain a close acquaintance till the end of her life.[74] Working as he did as a teacher in the Tondaimandalam High School on Mint Street[75], he was able to frequently visit Nagarathnamma and also run errands for her.

In order to alleviate her loneliness, Nagarathnamma acquired a dog of which she became very fond. The animal soon became an icon in the music community, for when it barked it remained faithful to pitch, always barking in the tonic note of "*sa*". It was also said to be highly intolerant of anyone who sang off-key and did not hesitate in biting them.[76] In many ways, it was the forerunner of another dog, the pet of Hindustani singer Abdul Karim Khan, whose fidelity to pitch while barking, elicited admiration even from 'Veena' Dhanam.[77] Nagarathnamma's dog provided her with the necessary security, when a burglar came calling one night. It pinned him down and held on till its mistress obtained help from the neighbourhood.[78] When the animal died a few years later, Nagarathnamma was inconsolable.

Next in line was a parrot. The bird was kept in a bejewelled cage and also had gold anklets for its feet. It learnt most of the songs that Nagarathnamma sang and would often join her during her practice sessions and at times even dance to her music. Nagarathnamma fed the bird the choicest of fruits and nuts and often let it sit on her shoulder.[79] The cage was usually hung at the entrance to the house and whenever a visitor came, the bird would announce that someone was at the door. Nagarathnamma or one of the maids would then let the person in.[80] A few years later this companion also passed away. However Nagarathnamma was always to remain fond of animals. An eagle would always respond to her call and come and eat the food that she gave it everyday.[81] She had her way with poisonous snakes as well. Once on realising that her maid was not responding to her calls Nagarathnamma went to the kitchen to see the woman lying on the floor, speechless in fright for a snake had coiled itself around her leg. Nagarathnamma coolly stared at the snake for a while and the reptile slid away. Later she revealed that she had also been chanting the *Bhaktapaya Bhujanga* that was said to ward off snakes.[82]

The canonisation of Tyagaraja was gaining momentum during this period and one day Nagarathnamma purchased a portrait of the composer for seven rupees from Umayalpuram Panchapakesa Bhagavatar, who sold it to her, claiming that regular worship of the saint would ensure that all her wishes would be fulfilled.[83] She had the picture encased in silver leaf work and placed it in her *puja*. Every day she lit a lamp before it and sang the songs that she knew.[84] In course of time Tyagaraja became central to her existence. She read the lyrics of his songs and marvelled at the meanings in them, she revelled in the music of the composer and was overwhelmed by his greatness. *Harikathas* on Tyagaraja's life had already become popular and perhaps listening to them and reading the various books that had begun to be published about him, she became obsessed with his worship. She began carrying the portrait wherever she went.

One October night in 1921, Nagarathnamma had dozed off in a reclining chair. The monsoon had come to the city and the weather was cool. In the kitchen the milk was simmering in the mud stove. The servants had retired for the day and she was alone. It was then that she had a vision of Tyagaraja raising his hands and blessing her.[85] Awakening with a start and perhaps confused over what had happened she sang a song not of Tyagaraja but of Mysore Sadasiva Rao.[86] She was however quite clear that the dream was a significant one.

Early next morning she was surprised to receive a letter from her guru, Bidaram Krishnappa. He was writing from Tanjavur where he was camping after a visit to Tiruvayyaru. In his letter Krishnappa lamented about the condition of Tyagaraja's Samadhi. He was pained at the dilapidated condition of the structure and the insanitary conditions of its surroundings. According to Krishnappa, if at all there was someone who had the means to restore and renovate the Samadhi, it was Nagarathnamma. He asked her to take immediate action.[87] To Nagarathnamma, Krishnappa's word was law and she never tired of stating that he was her *Adi* (first) guru. She decided to do something about it. Oddly enough, it was the first time she had heard about a Samadhi for Tyagaraja.[88] She wanted to get some details about the Samadhi and its history. C Muniswami Naidu, the secretary of the Bhagavat Katha Prasanga Sabha which operated from the Tondaimandalam School, Mint Street[89], was an active participant in the collection of funds for the annual *Aradhana* held in commemoration of the composer's passing at Tiruvayyaru.[90] She therefore called on him and asked for information.

By coincidence, Tanjavur Nagaraja Bhagavatar, a musician who was actively involved in the *Aradhana* was also present and between them, Naidu and Bhagavatar gave Nagarathnamma a concise history of the Samadhi and the annual *Aradhana* celebrations.[91]

## References

[1] Ramanujachari, C; p 121.

[2] Grihalakshmi; p 15.

[3] Grihalakshmi; p 15-16.

[4] Sruti; BNR; p 14.

[5] Vasudevacharya, Mysore; p 72.

[6] Iyer, Mudicondan Venkatarama; "Mun talaimuraiyil irunda sila sangita vidushigal"; Forty Second Conference Souvenir; Music Academy; Madras; 1968; hereinafter referred to as Mudicondan.

[7] Sruti; BNR; p 14.

[8] Comment made by S Rajam during an interview with the author in 2003.

[9] Mudicondan.

[10] Sriram,V; Carnatic Summer; East West Books (Madras) Pvt. Ltd; Chennai; 2003; hereinafter referred to as Carnatic Summer; p 166.

[11] Mudicondan.

[12] Ibid.

[13] DVG.

[14] Vasudevacharya, Mysore; p 70.

[15] Vasudevacharya, Mysore; p 70.

[16] Interview with Smt Rukmini Ammal who was an eyewitness to a conversation in that language between Sengalipuram Anantharama Dikshitar and Nagarathnamma in Tiruvayyaru.

[17] Nagarathnam, Bangalore; article in souvenir of the Sri Thyagabrahma Mahotsava Sabha; Tiruvayyaru; 1951; p 11.

[18] Sankaran T; "Kanchipuram Dhanakoti Ammal"; article in Sruti; Issue 11; September 1984; Madras; p 31.

[19] Grihalakshmi; p 52-53.

[20] Bai, C Banni; p 8.

[21] Sriram V; The House of Nagarathnam; www.sangeetham.com

[22] Vasudevacharya, Mysore; p 72.

[23] Nagarathnamma, Bangalore; Last Will and Testament; 5th January 1949.

[24] Interview with Chellam Iyer; 2005.

[25] Bai, C Banni; p 9.

[26] Nagarathnamma, Bangalore; Last Will and Testament; 5th January 1949.

[27] Interviews with VAK Ranga Rao; 2004-7.

[28] Interview with Seethapathi, assistant to Bangalore Nagarathnamma at Tiruvayyaru, May 2006.

[29] Ibid.

[31] Interviews with VAK Ranga Rao; 2004-7.

[32] Ibid.

[33] Grihalakshmi; p 52-53.

[34] Interview with Nagarathnamma's coachman Krishnan at Tiruvayyaru, May 2006.

[35] Interview with Seethapathi, assistant to Bangalore Nagarathnamma at Tiruvayyaru, May 2006.

[36] Isai Medaikal.

[37] Grihalakshmi; p 15-16.

[38] Bai, C Banni; p 9.

[39] Isai Medaikal.

[40] Sundaram, BM; p 51.

[41] Sriram V; The House of Nagarathnam; www.sangeetham.com

[42] Bai, C Banni; p 8.

[43] Ibid.

[44] Grihalakshmi; p 15-16.

[45] Nagarathnam, Bangalore; Last Will and Testament; 5th January 1949.

[46] Grihalakshmi; p 15-16.

[47] Nagarathnam, Bangalore; Last Will and Testament; 5th January 1949.

[48] Ashokamitran, T; "Lurdhu Mary, Ramalingar and Suraikkai Siddhar", article in www.chennaionline.com; September 2001.

[49] Grihalakshmi; p 15-16.

[50] Ibid.

[51] Nagarathnam, Bangalore; Last Will and Testament; 5th January 1949.

[52] Ibid.

[53] Bai, C Banni; p 8.

[54] Sruti; BNR; p 16.

[55] Bai, C Banni; p 8.

[56] Interviews with VAK Ranga Rao, 2004-7.

[57] Sruti; BNR; p 15.

[58] Ibid.

[59] Ibid; p 16.

[60] Interview with T Muktha in 2002.

[61] Ibid.

[62] Grihalakshmi; p 52.

[63] Ibid.

[64] Grihalakshmi; p 15-16.

[65] Bai, C Banni; p 10.

[66] Grihalakshmi; p 15-16.

[67] None of her writings, be it her will, the article in the Tyagaraja Aradhana souvenir or the profile on her in Grihalakshmi in 1949 mention this episode.

[68] Bai, C Banni; p 10.

[69] Rajagopalan, N; A Garland, A Biographical Dictionary of Carnatic Musicians and Composers; Bharatiya Vidya Bhavan; Bombay; 1990; p 26.

[70] Sruti; BNR; p 16.

[71] Orr, P; "T Sankaran Recalls"; article in Sruti; Issue 168; September 1998; Chennai; p 28.

[73] Interviews with VAK Ranga Rao, 2004-7.

[74] Interview with Seethapathi, assistant to Bangalore Nagarathnamma at Tiruvayyaru, May 2006.

[75] Nagarathnam, Bangalore; Last Will and Testament; 5th January 1949.

[76] Grihalakshmi; p 52-53.

[77] Sruti; Veena Dhanammal; p 39.

[78] Grihalakshmi; p 52-53.

[79] Ibid.

[80] Giri, Sandhya Vinjamuri; "Vinjamuri Varadaraja Iyengar"; article in www.sangeetham.com

[81] Mudicondan.

[82] Grihalakshmi; p 22.

[83] Ibid; p 16.

[84] Ibid.

[85] Ibid.

[86] Ibid.

[87] Ibid; p 15-16.

[88] Nagarathnam, Bangalore; article dated 29th November 1950 in Saint Thyagaraja Aradhana Festival Souvenir; 1951; Tiruvaiyyaru; p 11-14.

[89] Iyer, Soolamangalam V Radhakrishna; "Tiruvayyaru Sri Tyagabrahma Aradhanai Utsava Varalaru"; article in Bharata Devi; 1949; reprinted as a book by M Rammohan; Chennai; 2003; hereinafter referred to as Soolamangalam; p 2.

[90] Appeal dated 9th December 1909 issued by the organisers of the Aradhana; Caxton Press; Madras; The Chellam Iyer Collection.

[91] Grihalakshmi; p 16.

# Chapter 5

*"Worldly men will assert that theirs is the only path. Don't follow it and get deceived"* (Tyagaraja in "Sri Raama Raamaasritulamu Gaama", raga Saveri, tala Chapu)[1]

~

Hailed as the greatest composer of all time in Carnatic music, Tyagaraja passed away on 6th January 1847[2] in Tiruvayyaru. He had attained fame even in his own lifetime[3] and his death was an event witnessed by many of his disciples and admirers. Three principal branches had emerged among Tyagaraja's disciples, namely the Wallajahpet, Tillaisthanam and the Umayalpuram schools.

The last moments of Tyagaraja are mentioned in brief by Wallajahpet Krishnaswami Bhagavatar, one of his disciples and an eyewitness, as follows:

"On the fifth day before the dark moon in the month of *pusya*, a Sunday, and in the year *Prabhava*, after bathing in the Kaveri and performing other sacrificial rituals, Tyagaraja entered the order of *sanyasins* at the end of his life, having respectfully called on Paramahamsa Parivrajaka Sri Brahmanandasvami for initiation.

And after giving offerings to *brahmanas* and the poor, while *bhajans* were being sung, with the appearance of a great sound (or in the presence of a great sound) he merged with Brahman."[4]

Later accounts became increasingly exaggerated and soon more and more stories gained ground about the last moments, as they also

did about the composer's life in general. Whatever be the exact
sequence of events building up to Tyagaraja's passing, the obsequies
that followed would have been according to time-honoured customs.
The honour of presiding over Tyagaraja's funeral must have gone to
Panchapakesiah, his grandson, through his only daughter Sitamaha-
lakshmi. There are specific rules and observances for the last rites of
a *sanyasi* and Tyagaraja's must have followed these. A *sanyasi's* body
would usually be washed and draped in two cloths, dyed ochre. Sacred
ash or *vibhuti* would then be rubbed all over and a chain of *rudraksha*
beads would be fastened around the neck. The body would then be
seated with legs crossed in a bamboo basket hung from a pole and
borne by four Brahmins. In the meanwhile, a circular pit would have
been dug near a river or tank and a thick layer of salt would have been
spread in it. The body would be lowered into the pit and the hole
would be filled with salt till only the head of the *sanyasi* was visible.
The salt would be pressed down firmly so that the head would not loll
to any side. Then several coconuts would be smashed on the exposed
head of the *sanyasi* till the skull was completely fractured. Then the
remains would be covered with further layers of salt till the body was
obscured. A brick or stone structure would be placed on the spot by
way of a memorial. This structure was usually cylindrical in shape,
with the top open to the skies and filled with soil in which a *tulasi*
would be planted. This was called a *brindavanam*. Those assembled
would light lamps and offer cooked food to the structure. Cooked rice
and some fruit would be distributed to all assembled. All this would
take place to the accompaniment of chanting of hymns and the singing
of *bhajans*. Obsequies would be performed for a further ten days at
the structure.[5]

In the case of Tyagaraja, the burial took place at what was called
the Mangudiar Samadhi near the Bhavaswami Agraharam on the banks
of the river Kaveri. This was a spot earmarked for the burial of *sanyasis*,

who died in the Tanjavur kingdom and the land was controlled by a trust administered by members of the Maratha royal family. Several *brindavanams* dotted the landscape and one among these was the memorial to Tyagaraja's guru, Sonti Venkataramanayya. It is said that Tyagaraja identified the spot for his burial himself and even specified to his disciples the exact dimensions of the pit and the quantity of salt to be poured in. [6]A superstructure made of baked clay was erected over the spot and this became the Samadhi of the great composer.[7] The top of this cylindrical structure was filled with soil and a *tulasi* was planted in it.

The anniversary of the composer's passing was observed each year at Tiruvayyaru by his grandson. The ceremony involved a *shraddha* in which food cooked in a ritually pure fashion was offered to Brahmins, after the chanting of several hymns. The observances took place at the ancestral home on Tirumanjana Veedhi. Grandson Panchapakesiah and fellow disciples may have also paid their respects at the *brindavanam* of the composer on that day. Those disciples who could not make it to Tiruvayyaru conducted similar *shraddha* ceremonies at their own residences. The annual rite was observed at Tiruvayyaru till 1855 when Panchapakesiah passed away at a relatively young age, leaving behind his childless wife, Guruvamma. The *shraddha* ceased to be observed at Tyagaraja's ancestral home in Tiruvayyaru. For a while, the annual ceremony was observed in the house of Subbarama Bhagavatar, one of the disciples of Tyagaraja.[8] The *brindavanam* became one of the many on the banks of the river Kaveri and was soon covered with weeds. Soon, the spot which was once described as a "quiet place near a coconut grove, on the river bank, south of the road leading to Kumbhakonam and south east of Tiruvayyaru" became an "inaccessible spot full of foul odour".[9]

In 1903, the last surviving disciples of Tyagaraja, Krishna and Sundara Bhagavatars, known as the Umayalpuram Brothers came over to Tiruvayyaru with a view to worshipping at the Samadhi. They were appalled by what they saw. The *brindavanam* itself was identified with great difficulty. The brothers, despite their own advanced ages, got the *brindavanam* renovated with the help of musicians belonging to the Tillaisthanam lineage of Tyagaraja's disciple Rama Iyengar. They used slabs of good quality granite.[10] A slab was put up on the rear side of the monument commemorating the repair works which read that the renovations had been done by the brothers Krishnan and Sundaram, on the 28th of the *Chitra* month of the Tamil year *Sobhakritu,* which corresponded to 10th May 1903.[11] The brothers appointed a gardener to ensure that the area surrounding the monument was kept clean and also got a priest to go there twice a day, light an oil lamp and place offerings.[12] They also roped in their disciple Umayalpuram Panchapakesa Bhagavatar to help in the annual ceremony. It was he who had sold a portrait of Tyagaraja to Nagarathnamma.

Shortly after the renovation, two brothers belonging to the Tillaisthanam lineage, Narasimha Bhagavatar and Panju Bhagavatar, interested themselves in the observance of the annual rite. Narasimha Bhagavatar was a well-known *Harikatha* exponent and under his leadership in 1904 the observance of the *Aradhana* shifted to Tiruvayyaru itself. The venue for the *Aradhana* was a *Choultry* (guest house) belonging to the Pacchaiyappa Mudaliar Trust, a charitable body instituted by a wealthy *dubash* of the East India Company.

The brothers Narasimha and Panju Bhagavatars created a format for the *Aradhana* which was followed for the next six years or so. Enlarging on the traditional *shraddha,* they brought in music and the ritual of *unchavritti* or alms-seeking into the *Aradhana.* *Unchavritti Bhagavatars* were a regular sight in Tiruvayyaru. "Strumming his *tambura,* keeping time with the clappers and tinkling anklets, the alms dependent singer had a pot tied to a sash dangling from his turban, in which villagers would place rice".[13] Tyagaraja himself had practised this and had according to tradition maintained his family and retinue of disciples by the food received during the *unchavritti*. Over the years his reputation for such *unchavritti bhajans* became so well known that he was often invited to perform them in suburbs of Tanjavur such as Manambucchavadi, Karuntattangudi and Kalyanapuram.[14] Indeed in later years it became customary to associate the *unchavritti* with Tyagaraja and so, an *Aradhana* without the enactment of the musical alms-seeking was incomplete.

On the day of the *Aradhana*, the traditional *shraddha* would be observed in Tyagaraja's residence. Musicians, singers and instrumentalists included, would go as a group to the Samadhi accompanied by priests chanting hymns. The structure would be ceremonially washed and decorated with flowers, and food offerings would be made to it. After the traditional waving of camphor lamps, the musicians would leave for *unchavritti*. They would return to the Pachaiyappa Mudaliar *Choultry* and the feeding of Brahmins would take place with the food being made from the ingredients gathered during the *unchavritti*.

After the Brahmins had had their fill, the assembled musicians would eat and then the poor would be fed. That night there would be music and *Harikatha* performances and the *Aradhana* would conclude.[15]

Narasimha Bhagavatar was however not a person to rest content with such a celebration, which according to him was not befitting the stature of Tyagaraja. He had many performance opportunities in Madras and whilst there he began discussing the matter with musicians and music lovers. He held the view that musicians who owed a large part of their livelihood to Tyagaraja's *kritis* ought to consider it their duty to participate in the *Aradhana* and make it a grand success. He was greatly assisted in his efforts by Muniswami Naidu, Secretary of the Bhaktimarga Prasanga Sabha, an organisation established in Madras in 1895 for the conducting of *Harikatha* performances. The eminent violinist, Malaikottai Govindasami Pillai, also began interesting himself in the proceedings.

The ageing Umayalpuram Brothers issued an appeal titled *"Tiruvayyaru Sangeeta Shikhamani"* to the public on 24th November 1907 asking them to donate liberally for the conduct of the *Aradhana*, to be held on 23rd January 1908. Donations in cash or kind were to be sent to the brothers themselves, their disciple Umayalpuram Panchapakesayyar or to Malaikottai Govindasami Pillai.

In 1908, efforts were taken to make the 1909 *Aradhana* a grand affair. On 20th December 1908, Narasimha Bhagavatar performed a *Harikatha* on "The Life of the *Swamigal*" at the Tondaimandalam High School, Mint Street and "after briefly explaining the noble features in the life of the *Swamigal*, he exhorted the audience to subscribe liberally for the celebration of his anniversary with greater pomp and enthusiasm and also for the performance of daily puja and other ceremonies at the grave of the *swamigal* with due solemnity".[16] Narasimha Bhagavatar's performance touched the audience's heart and his appeal resulted in a good collection for the *Aradhana*. Several musicians came forward to participate in the celebrations.

Handbills were circulated detailing the programme for the *Aradhana*, which fell on 28th January 1909. For the first time in its history, the single day event expanded to a five-day celebration beginning on 24th January. The first four days witnessed music concerts and *Harikatha* performances from 3:00 to 6:00 pm and 8:00 pm to midnight. On *Aradhana* day the programme was as follows:

7:00 to 9:00 am – Worship at the Samadhi

9:00 am to 12:00 noon – *Aradhana*

(performance of *shraddha* rites)

12:00 noon – Feeding of Brahmins

5:00 pm – Procession with Tyagaraja's portrait

8:00 pm – *Kathakalakshepam* on the life of Tyagaraja

The appeal states very significantly that the *Aradhana* of Tyagaraja was proposed to be held on a grand scale from that year onwards. Presumably the Umayalpuram Brothers had passed away by then, for the appeal was issued in the names of the Tillaisthanam Brothers, Narasimha and Panju Bhagavatars and it is clear that by 1909 they had emerged as the main forces behind the conduct of the *Aradhana*.[17]

The handbill roused great interest in Tiruvayyaru and the surrounding towns and huge crowds began to descend on the village in anticipation of some wonderful music and more importantly, non-stop feasting for five days. In order to cater to the needs of such a vast gathering, the brothers divided the responsibility. Narasimha Bhagavatar being a resident of Kumbhakonam busied himself in collecting cash for the festivities, while Panju Bhagavatar called on the landlords and other well-heeled patrons of the Tanjavur delta and its environs and collected rice, vegetables and condiments.[18]

The concerts and *Harikatha* performances were great successes as was the catering. However, at the instance of certain diehard conservatives it was decided that *nagaswaram* artistes would not be allowed to perform from the dais during the *Aradhana*.[19] This was not out of the ordinary, for *nagaswaram* artistes were considered to belong to a very low stratum of society. They were expected to stand when playing their instruments and generally were to make their appearance without an upper garment. It was also an accepted tradition that they would perform only when deities were taken out in procession. Since *nagaswara* artistes had contributed to the conduct of the *Aradhana* it was necessary to keep them happy. It was therefore decided that the portrait of Tyagaraja would be taken out in procession in a floral palanquin late at night to the accompaniment of their music. This was to remain an unwritten rule at the *Aradhana* for many years to come.[20]

Yet another unspoken and unwritten rule that was tacitly understood and accepted by all, was that women would never be allowed to offer musical homage to Tyagaraja by participating in the *Aradhana*. This did not necessitate a via media solution like the floral palanquin procession for the *nagaswara* artistes. For no woman attended the *Aradhana*. The only women who could offer music were the Devadasis and as for *Harikatha*, the first woman performer, C Saraswathi Bai, a Brahmin, was just then making a name for herself in distant Madras.[21] The popular view was that Devadasis were prostitutes and were therefore immoral. After all, had Tyagaraja himself not warned his followers about the evil ways of women in songs such as "Menu Joochi"(raga Sarasangi)?[22] Moreover women were subject to menstrual cycles, which meant they were ritually impure necessitating their being kept away from the Samadhi. No matter that all the *vidwans* assembled had mothers, sisters, wives and daughters and several of them had relationships with Devadasis themselves.

Be that as it may, the *Aradhana* of 1909 was a huge success and encouraged by it, the Tillaisthanam Brothers decided that this would be the pattern to follow in future years to come. With increasing support from the public and from musicians like Malaikottai Govindasami Pillai, the 1910 celebrations in Tiruvayyaru were sumptuous.[23] There was however no dearth of jealous onlookers who did not like the idea of the two brothers working together. Thanks to their insinuations, doubts arose in the mind of each brother about the integrity of the other. A bitter quarrel over financial matters ensued and by the end of 1910, they were no longer on speaking terms with each other. When it came to the *Aradhana* celebrations of 1911, Narasimha Bhagavatar made it clear that he would not be coming to Tiruvayyaru and also distributed letters of invitation to musicians and well-wishers for an *Aradhana* that he planned to conduct in Kumbha-konam. On hearing of this, several well-wishers along with Panju Bhagavatar called on Narasimha Bhagavatar to effect reconciliation. In their view, it was not correct to observe the *Aradhana* of the composer in a place other than his own Samadhi.[24] This was a new argument, given that the practice of observing the annual ceremony at the villages of Tyagaraja's disciples had been going on for almost 60 years.

However the expected rapprochement did not happen and Narasimha Bhagavatar remained firm in his resolve. The Tiruvayyaru group returned disappointed but with the resolve that they would not abandon the celebrations in their village. Prominent residents of the area involved themselves and so did several musicians. Invitations and handbills were prepared and distributed and collections in cash and kind poured in. The festivities began as in the previous years, five days prior to the *Aradhana* and concluded on *Aradhana* day with Panju Bhagavatar performing the rituals at the Samadhi.[25] As always, the last ritual was the worship of Anjaneya or Hanuman, the God who cleared obstacles.

Festivities were no less spectacular in Kumbhakonam with Narasimha Bhagavatar leading a rival team comprising many musicians including Malaikottai Govindasami Pillai. However, within a few days of the festivities Narasimha Bhagavatar passed away, thereby putting his group in a quandary as to what ought to be done in future years. Some of the musicians felt that the early demise of Narasimha Bhagavatar was due to the shifting of the *Aradhana* from Tiruvayyaru to Kumbhakonam and a decision was taken that from 1912, the Kumbhakonam group would also observe the annual rites in Tiruvayyaru.[26]

With two groups thus descending on the village, the local people identified the Kumbhakonam faction as belonging to the elder brother Narasimha Bhagavatar and referred to it as the Periya Katchi (elder faction). Panju Bhagavatar's group therefore became the Chinna Katchi (the younger faction).[27] A competitive spirit prevailed between the two groups and each made preparations to strengthen their respective factions with the addition of prominent musicians. Govindasami Pillai being a resident of Trichy concentrated on collecting funds there for the Periya Katchi while Munisami Naidu did the same for them in Madras. The Chinna Katchi, left without support in the city roped in TS Sabhesa Iyer, a renowned musician of Madras belonging to the lineage of Tyagaraja whose ancestors belonged to the *Padinaindu Mandapam* or Street of 15 pavilions of Tiruvayyaru in which Tyagaraja's father had distributed land on behalf of the ruler.[28]

Beginning with 1912, the residents of Tiruvayyaru witnessed the strange spectacle of two simultaneous *Aradhana*s being conducted for Tyagaraja. The Periya Katchi held its events in the Kalyana Mahal, a large rest house built by the erstwhile rulers of Tanjavur, while the Chinna Katchi conducted its programmes at the Pacchaiyappa Mudaliar *Choultry*. On *Aradhana* day, the Chinna Katchi would first conduct its worship at the Samadhi, followed by the Periya Katchi. The processions of both groups were spectacular. The Chinna Katchi would begin early in the morning and having bathed in the river would, to the accompaniment of the *nagaswaram* and *tavil*, proceed to the Samadhi where Panju Bhagavatar would perform the rituals, followed by the rendering of select songs of the composer by some of the assembled musicians. Leaving the Samadhi by 8:30 am, they would be met by the Periya Katchi at the Kumbhakonam Road. A large crowd would gather here to witness the meeting of the two groups. The Periya Katchi would then proceed to perform its worship.[29]

Rituals for this group were conducted by Ramudu Bhagavatar, a descendant of Tyagaraja's brother Japyesa. The choice of Ramudu Bhagavatar is something of a mystery, for he was certainly not a musician or *Harikatha* performer of renown. The sole factor in his favour appears to have been that he could claim some sort of kinship with Tyagaraja. This too was subject to ridicule by many, as Tyagaraja was tormented in life by his brother as some of his songs such as "Anyayamu Seyakura" (raga Kapi) attest.[30] That such a man's descendant ought to be allowed to lead the worship at the Samadhi could not be accepted by some of the ardent devotees of the composer.

The simultaneous conduct of the *Aradhana* by two groups presented some interesting situations. Poor feeding was done on a lavish scale by both groups and this and the music offered by them, meant most residents of Tiruvayyaru and its environs had a good holiday with food and entertainment thrown in for five days. However, there were several causes for concern as well. The Chinna Katchi would feed the masses after the Periya Katchi and gluttons made merry by eating in the first batch served in the Periya Katchi and then once again eating well in the last batch of the Chinna Katchi. Concerts presented a bigger problem. If a prominent musician was performing for one of the groups, it meant an exodus from the audience of the other group. If musicians of equal stature were performing in both, it meant a continuously floating population, thereby disturbing the artistes and serious listeners. Often mischief-makers intervened during very crowded performances by letting loose harmless water snakes among the audience.[31] This caused great panic, often leading to concerts being abandoned midway, as it happened in 1911 during the performance of Mangudi Chidambara Bhagavatar.

Chidambara Bhagavatar or Brahmasri Chidambara Bhagavatar of Agara Mangudi to give his full name was a giant in both physical and musical stature. Giving up the study of law he had taken to *Harikatha*[32] and was an authority on Tyagaraja's songs.[33] In 1911, Bhagavatar who had preferred to remain neutral was invited to perform by the Periya Katchi. Halfway through his performance, the water snakes made their appearance leading to pandemonium. Bhagavatar was convinced that fellow practitioners of *Harikatha* in the Periya Katchi had engineered the sabotage. He immediately declared allegiance to the Chinna Katchi and became a pillar of support to it.[34] Yet another star *Harikatha* performer who became associated with the Chinna Katchi at this time was Soolamangalam Vaidyanatha Bhagavatar. He was a forceful personality with wide contacts and soon he established himself as a power centre in the Chinna Katchi.[35] However, none disputed the supremacy of Panju Bhagavatar, who retained with himself the right to perform worship at the Samadhi.

With the Chinna Katchi too, becoming a group with influential backing, it became apparent to Govindasami Pillai that having two *Aradhana*s at the same time was not beneficial to anyone. In 1912, he therefore shifted the Periya Katchi's celebrations by five days, preferring to commence them on the day of Tyagaraja's passing.[36] Thus the Chinna Katchi ended its five-day celebrations on the day of the *Aradhana* while the Periya Katchi began its festivities on that day and carried on for four more days. The residents of Tiruvayyaru too benefited, for now there was music and feasting for nine days at a stretch and without the stresses and strains of having to make a choice between simultaneous concerts and free lunches. By then the need for a larger venue was felt by the Chinna Katchi and that year they began observing the *Aradhana* at a larger public building called the Palayi Chattram.[37]

In 1914, the Periya Katchi, through Malaikottai Govindasami Pillai succeeded in getting the eminent musician, composer and *Harikatha* exponent Harikesanallur Muthiah Bhagavatar to come to Tiruvayyaru to perform a *Harikatha* during its five-day festival. Muthiah Bhagavatar was quite unaware of the schisms that existed in the *Aradhana* celebrations and it was only on arrival in Tiruvayyaru and seeing the Chinna Katchi festivities in progress that he came to know of the rival groups. He immediately set about arranging a meeting between the leaders of the two groups on 17th January, in order to effect reconciliation. However, the kingpin of the Periya Katchi, Malaikottai Govindasami Pillai abstained from attending the meeting and in his absence all talks of unification were inconclusive. The groups decided to remain independent in their observance of the *Aradhana*. A disappointed man, Muthiah Bhagavatar did not give up and decided to continue with his efforts at unification in the years to follow.[38]

The Chinna Katchi, prompted largely by Soolamangalam Vaidyanatha Bhagavatar decided to go ahead with the registration of a formal body to observe the *Aradhana*. A meeting was held in Madras on Ist February at the residence of Pt. Lakshmanachar, a noted *Harikatha* exponent and a new registered organisation, the Tyagaraja Parabrahma Vaibhava Prakasa Sabha came into being with an executive committee comprising sixteen prominent musicians. Pt. Lakshmanachar was the President, Ramanathapuram 'Poochi' Srinivasa Iyengar (Nagarathnamma's guru) was Vice President, Soolamangalam Vaidyanatha Bhagavatar became Secretary, Mangudi Chidambara Bhagavatar the Assistant Secretary and Tanjavur Panchapakesa Bhagavatar, the Treasurer. Though he figured way below, in the Sabha hierarchy as a Director[39], it was understood that Panju Bhagavatar was the leading light of this group and Rs 25 was taken from him as seed money for the organisation. It was also understood that as long as he was alive, he would lead the musicians of the Chinna Katchi in the worship at the Samadhi.[40]

Accountability was considered a matter of prestige in the Chinna Katchi and it took its new avatar as a registered body very seriously. It began publishing statements of accounts at the end of each year's celebrations, which were distributed to donors and musicians who contributed to the event. The statement of accounts also gave the names of musicians who performed concerts during the *Aradhana* celebrations.[41] This was probably insisted upon by Panju Bhagavatar who even in the previous year had under his own name published a statement of income and expenditure.[42] In 1917, with increasing participation, the Chinna Katchi found the Palayi Chatram to be insufficient for its programmes and moved to the Pushya Mandapam, a beautiful pavilion on the banks of the river for its celebrations.[43]

The Periya Katchi which continued to operate from the Kalyana Mahal also went from strength to strength. However, it largely depended on Malaikottai Govindasami Pillai for its funds and he, given his stature in the world of music could rustle up large amounts very easily.[44] He was ably supported by the *mridangam* exponent Kumbhakonam Azhagianambia Pillai. Harikesanallur Muthiah Bhagavatar continued with his policy of strict neutrality till 1915 and participated in programmes of both the groups. He also kept up his efforts to effect a unification of the celebrations. That year, frustrated at the lack of response to these initiatives he decided to stay away from the *Aradhana* in future years.[45]

By 1919 however, the Chinna Katchi was found to be weakening. Many of its stalwarts passed away and that year its President, Pt. Lakshmanachar passed on. Mayavaram Vaidyanatha Iyer, a noted exponent of the veena succeeded him, only to pass away within a few weeks. Tanjavur Govinda Bhagavatar became President and died shortly thereafter. Soon, a story began to circulate that the position of President in the Chinna Katchi was cursed.[46] When the offer was made to Soolamangalam Vaidyanatha Bhagavatar to take over as President he refused and preferred to remain as Secretary. The position of President was never filled after this and Vaidyanatha Bhagavatar as Secretary became the kingpin of the Chinna Katchi.[47] He stemmed the erosion of confidence in the Chinna Katchi's ranks and personally led the way in collecting funds and ensuring the proper conduct of the *Aradhana*. The flautist Palladam Sanjeeva Rao supported him greatly in his efforts. By this time, Tillaisthanam Panju Bhagavatar, the founder of the Chinna Katchi had passed away and the right to perform the worship at the Samadhi was assigned to his chief disciple Rajagopala Bhagavatar.[48]

Both groups campaigned for their cause among the young and upcoming musicians of the period. By 1918 or so, the Periya Katchi managed to rope in Kanchipuram Naina Pillai, the nephew of

Kanchipuram Dhanakoti.[49] His 'full bench' concerts, comprising nine accompanists were enormous successes at the *Aradhana*.[50] In 1920, the Periya Katchi appeared to have pulled off yet another coup when Ariyakkudi Ramanuja Iyengar, a rapidly rising star, agreed to sing for it.[51] However Malaikottai Govindasami Pillai made a maladroit move when he planned the concert schedules for the *Aradhana*. He slotted Ariyakkudi directly after Naina Pillai.[52] If this was bad enough, matters got worse when Naina, given that his full bench of accompanists had to display their virtuosity, overshot his time slot. "Telegraph" Mani, the man in charge of time slots simply snatched the *tambura* from the hands of Naina's assistant and brought the concert to an abrupt halt.[53] Naina Pillai was upset but he had the last laugh. A conventional concert by Ariyakkudi after the thunderous impact of Naina's full bench made the audience restive and irritated the musician no end. Feeling that this was a calculated insult by Govindasami Pillai, Ariyakkudi left the Periya Katchi's ranks and joined the Chinna Katchi. He was warmly welcomed and at the end of his performance that year, Soolamangalam Vaidyanatha Bhagavatar, realising that a cash cow had landed in his hands, made a speech lasting an hour, in which he profusely praised Ariyakkudi. A greatly pleased Ariyakkudi became Assistant Secretary in the Chinna Katchi. His admission into the group greatly strengthened it, for with his rising popularity he ensured that money was available in large quantities for the celebrations.[54] Not to be outdone, the Periya Katchi managed to rope in yet another star, Maharajapuram Viswanatha Iyer. However, that maverick musician did not have it in him to indulge in any factionalism and began giving concerts for both the groups.[55]

The ding-dong battle for supremacy continued in the area of catering as well. Plantain leaves, bags of rice, vegetables and spices would arrive by the cartloads and be stocked in the various guest houses of Tiruvayyaru. Kalyanapuram Viswanatha Sastrigal was in charge of the board for the Chinna Katchi and a cook from the Madhva community which was well known for its culinary skills, brought in by Palladam Sanjeeva Rao would take care of the preparations. The food would be served at the Seethabai Chattram and hundreds would flock to partake of the breakfast, comprising hot steaming *idlis* soaking in *sambar*. The Periya Katchi had Vikravandi 'Mottai', a master chef in charge of its kitchen. The food was conventional, with enormous quantities of rice, pickles, curds and *sambar* made with eggplant, pumpkin or French beans. But the taste was extraordinary, with vegetables coming from the fertile Kaveri delta and rice being plentiful in the area.[56]

Despite all this rivalry, the musicians belonging to the two groups remained friendly with each other. Throughout the year they attended weddings in each other's families, performed concerts together and often went on pilgrimages together as well.[57] But come October, when preparations for the *Aradhana* would begin, attitudes would harden and each musician would campaign for his own group. Expenditure mounted with larger and larger crowds participating and given the rivalry that existed, each group spent lavishly in order to score points off the other.[58]

Neither group could manage any surplus funds for the proposed construction of a permanent structure over Tyagaraja's Samadhi. Each group claimed to have plans in this regard but financial constraints prevented them from doing anything about it. Throughout the year the Samadhi presented a picture of neglect and it was only during the *Aradhana* celebrations that a temporary structure was erected over it. During the remaining part of the year, casual visitors to the Samadhi had to walk over thorny bushes, all the while praying that no snake would be trodden on and come to a structure that was covered with bird droppings. This was what Bidaram Krishnappa had lamented about in his letter to Nagarathnamma.

## References

1 Parthasarathy, TS; p 456; translated from the original in Tamil by the author.

2 Raghavan, Dr.V; "Introductory Thesis"; The Spiritual Heritage of Tyagaraja; The Sri Ramakrishna Math, Madras, 1958; p 6.

3 As evident in his song "Dasarathi" (raga Todi), wherein Tyagaraja states that by the grace of Rama he had attained fame in distant lands.

4 Jackson, William J; p 65.

5 Dubois, Abbe JA; Hindu Manners, Customs and Ceremonies; Oxford; Third Edition Reprinted 1943; p 539-540.

6 Sambamurthy, Prof. P; Great Composers Book II, Tyagaraja; Third Edition; The Indian Music Publishing House; Chennai; August 2002; p 293.

7 Nagarathnam, Bangalore; article dated 29th November 1950 in Saint Thyagaraja *Aradhana* Festival Souvenir; 1951; Tiruvaiyyaru; p 11-14.

8 Rajagopalachary, TV; "Memorial to Sree Thiagaraja"; undated manuscript of letter addressed to The Hindu.

9 Soolamangalam; p 2.

10 Appeal dated 24th November 1907 issued by Umayalpuram Krishna and Sundara Bhagavatars and Panchapakesayyar; The Chellam Iyer Collection.

11 Devnath, Lakshmi; "Place of Umayalpuram in Carnatic Music"; article in Sruti; Issue 217;October 2002; p 21.

12 Bhagavatar, Duraiyappa; "Tiruvayyaru Tiruvizha", Chapter 1 "Ankurarpanam"; Serial article in Kalki; Madras; hereinafter referred to as Bhagavatar, Duraiyappa.

13 Jackson, William J; Tyagaraja, Life and Lyrics; Oxford University Press; New Delhi; 1999;p 48.

14 Sambamurthy, Prof P; Great Composers Book II, Tyagaraja; 3rd Edition, Indian Music Publishing House, Chennai; 2002; p 245.

15 Bhagavatar, Duraiyappa; "Tiruvayyaru Tiruvizha", Chapter 1 "Ankurarpanam";

16 Rajagopalachary, TV; "Memorial to Sree Thiagaraja"; undated manuscript of letter addressed to The Hindu.

[17] *Aradhana* Utsava Patrikai – handbill/ invitation issued by Narasimha Bhagavatar and Panju Iyer; printed at The Commercial Press, Triplicane; Madras; 1908; The Chellam Iyer Collection.

[18] Bhagavatar, Duraiyappa; "Tiruvayyaru Tiruvizha", Chapter 1 "Ankurarpanam".

[19] Soolamangalam; p 13.

[20] Ibid.

[21] Bai, C Saraswathi; "En *Harikatha* Anubhavam"; Ananda Vikatan Deepavali Malar; Madras; 1935; reprinted in the "Srimati C Saraswati Bai's Commemoration Volume"; 16th December 1939; edited by MS Ramaswami Iyer.

[22] Ramanujachari, C; p 9.

[23] Bhagavatar, Duraiyappa; "Tiruvayyaru Tiruvizha", Chapter 2 "Ghoshti Pirivinai"; p 21.

[24] Ibid; p 22.

[25] Ibid.

[26] Ibid.

[27] Ibid; p 23.

[28] Sriram V; "Musicians from Padinaindumandapam"; article in Sruti Issue 242; Chennai; November 2004; p 33.

[29] Soolamangalam; p 17.

[30] Ramanujachari, C; p 441.

[31] Bhagavatar, Duraiyappa; "Tiruvayyaru Tiruvizha", Chapter 2 "Goshti Pirivinai"; p 23.

[32] Rajagopalan, N; A Garland; Bharatiya Vidya Bhavan; Bombay; 1990; p 36.

[33] Gurumurthy, Dr Premeela; Kathakalakshepa, A Study; International Society for the Investigation of Ancient Civilizations; Madras; 1994; p 133.

[34] Bhagavatar, Duraiyappa; "Tiruvayyaru Tiruvizha", Chapter 2 "Ghoshti Pirivinai"; p 23.

[35] Sriram V; "Tyagaraja *Aradhana* in Tiruvaiyaru, The Chinna Katchi and Soolamangalam Bhagavatar"; Article in Sruti Issue 234; Chennai; March 2004; p 11-19.

[36] Soolamangalam; p 16.

[37] Ibid; p 19.

[38] Bhagavatar, Duraiyappa; "Tiruvayyaru Tiruvizha", Chapter 3 "Muthiah Bhagavatarin Muyarchi"; p 38.

[39] Proceedings of the Meeting of the Sri Thiagaraja Parabrahma Vaibhava Prakasa Sabha; 17th February 1914; The Chellam Iyer Collection.

[40] Handwritten minutes of meeting held on 1st February 1914; The Chellam Iyer Collection.

[41] Annual Reports of the Sri Thiagaraja Parabrahma Vaibhava Prakasa Sabha 1914, 17, 20, 23; The Chellam Iyer Collection.

[42] Statements of accounts published by TP Panjuvayyar; D'Silva & Co Printers; Trichy; 1913; The Chellam Iyer Collection.

[43] Bhagavatar, Duraiyappa; "Tiruvayyaru Tiruvizha", Chapter 4 "Potti Utsavam"; p 58.

[44] Ibid; p 59.

[45] Ibid.

[46] Ibid.

[47] Bhagavatar, Duraiyappa; "Tiruvayyaru Tiruvizha", Chapter 5 "Moonravadu Utsavam"; p 62.

[48] Ibid.

[49] Bhagavatar, Duraiyappa; "Tiruvayyaru Tiruvizha", Chapter 6 "Adhishtana Kumbhabhishekam"; p 24.

[50] Ibid.

[51] Soolamangalam; p 29.

[52] Ibid; p 30.

[53] Ayyangar, R Rangaramanuja; Musings of a Musician; Wilco Publishing House; Bombay; 1977; p 27.

[54] Soolamangalam; p 30.

[55] Ibid; p 31.

[56] Iyer, Chellam; "Chinna Katchi X Periya Katchi"; article in Music Supplement of Dinamani Kadir; Chennai; 9th December 2001; p 34.

[57] Bhagavatar, Mahakathaka Kanteerava Brahma Sree Chidambara; "The Late Mr Govindaswami Pillai"; article in The Hindu; Madras; 18th March 1931.

[58] Bhagavatar, Duraiyappa; "Tiruvayyaru Tiruvizha", Chapter 6 "Adhishtana Kumbhabhishekam"; p 24.

❧ ❧

# Chapter 6

*"Are you not happy that you have secured a charming and excellent place known as Panchanada Kshetra in the Chola country, beautiful in all this world, worthy of being coveted by Shiva, on the banks of the Kaveri over which blows the incomparable zephyr?"* (Tyagaraja – "Muripemu galige", raga Mukhari, tala Adi)[1]

~

Nagarathnamma's mind was made up even as the narrative of Muniswami Naidu and Nagaraja Bhagavatar wound to a close. She decided to proceed to Tiruvayyaru at the earliest and gauge the situation for herself. Insisting that Nagaraja Bhagavatar accompany her, she made arrangements for the trip and a few days later she and Bhagavatar proceeded to the village, which Tyagaraja had made famous.

The place was a short distance from Tanjavur. Its name meant the land of five rivers as it was separated from Tanjavur by the Kaveri and three of its distributaries Vennar, Vettar and Kudamurutti, with the Vadavar flowing on the other side. Tiruvayyaru stood on the banks of the Kaveri with large and artistic pleasure pavilions and charitable hostelries dotting its banks. These had been built in prosperous times by the royal family of Tanjavur for the use of nobles and common men when they visited this holy town. Green fields surrounded the village on all sides and as Tyagaraja himself put it "the incomparable zephyr from the Kaveri" wafted through the streets. The Panchanadeeswara temple dominated the settlement with its tall *gopurams* and its famed sanctum for the Goddess Dharmasamvardhini, where each member of the Carnatic Trinity, Tyagaraja, Dikshitar and Syama Sastri had worshipped and composed songs.[2] Subbaraya Sastri, the son of Syama Sastri and a disciple of the Trinity had composed a song at the sanctum in the presence of Tyagaraja and had been blessed by him.[3] The temple was well known for its *Sapta Sthanam* festival, when deities from six villages surrounding Tiruvayyaru, joined Panchanadeeswara and Dharmasamvardhini in a journey on palanquins, around the neighbouring area. The route was through the dry river bed, just before the onset of summer and was always an occasion for some great music. Tyagaraja and his contemporaries, the Anai Ayya brothers had led *bhajan* sessions during the festival and walked the entire stretch of the journey.[4]

Musicians such as Maha Vaidyanatha Sivan and Patnam Subramania Iyer had been residents of Tiruvayyaru and Nagarathnamma's guru, Ramanathapuram Srinivasa Iyengar and her friend Mysore Vasudevachar had during their tutelage under Patnam, stayed at the village for many years.[5] The Bhavaswami Agraharam, a locality close to the temple was well known for its *Harikatha* performers. Padinaindu Mandapam or the street of 15 pavilions ran parallel to the riverbank at the entrance to the village. It was well known for its own musical lineage, beginning with the composer Doraiswami Iyer whose descendant was the renowned musician TS Sabhesa Iyer.[6] Tiruvayyaru in short was a place known for its erudition and learning. To Malaikottai Govindasami Pillai, it was such a hallowed spot that he would dismount from his conveyance on entering the village and walk the rest of the stretch. It was unthinkable for him that he should be in a vehicle and taken through the streets where Tyagaraja once walked.[7]

The arrival by horse carriage of a much bejewelled and impressive woman created a stir in sleepy Tiruvayyaru. Nagaraja Bhagavatar, by now completely under her spell, gave out her identity in hushed whispers to the assembled onlookers. The horses were unyoked and the carriage was gradually tilted backwards so that the enormously stout Nagarathnamma could slide off on to a stone platform.[8] Seated there, she asked for Ramudu Bhagavatar. While someone was sent to fetch him, she was conducted to the Tuesday Ghat of the River Kaveri, by which stood a *choultry* built in the artistic style of the Marathas. This was to be Nagarathnamma's camp, whenever she visited Tiruvayyaru.[9]

Ramudu Bhagavatar was ushered into her presence a short while later and she requested him to take her to the Samadhi of Tyagaraja.[10] The descendant of Tyagaraja's brother was an emaciated personality, who was physically as far removed from the woman whom he now faced, as much as he was musically removed from the composer with whom he claimed kinship. However, from the first meeting with her he became a trusted lieutenant of sorts to Nagarathnamma. Living as he was in penury it was perhaps clear to him that a woman as prosperous and generous as she, would be a powerful benefactress. Together, the two journeyed to the Samadhi.

Nagarathnamma was to later describe her first visit to the Samadhi thus: "The premises of this great Samadhi had been neglected and subjected to all kinds of misuse and abuse. It sorely pained my heart to look at the state of things... There was then only the *Brindavan* with a stone slab on one side feebly announcing to the world that the remains of the great soul lay interred within the said slab."[11] Later she was to recall that the Samadhi was surrounded by thorny shrubs, bamboos and ferocious serpents and that it was impossible to move around even during daytime.[12]

The "pained feeling" which she experienced when she saw the condition of the Samadhi served, in her own words, as a "source of inspiration" to her "to begin a life of dedication to his cause".[13] In the Devadasi tradition, it was necessary that each girl be dedicated to a deity and then seek out an earthly patron. There is a good deal of uncertainty as to whether Nagarathnamma was ever dedicated to a temple, given the travails of her early years. She had of course had any number of patrons. But now in her 43rd year, she had found her Lord and Master, a deity and a patron rolled into one. She was to refer to herself as a Tyagaraja Dasi from then on.

Despite all her idealism, she was in essence a practical woman and it was clear to her that before she began any construction on the site, it was necessary to be in possession of the clear title to the land. Nagarathnamma had a number of contacts among the rich land-owning families of Tanjavur, and the scion of one of these, TA Ramachandra Rao, came forward to help.[14] Enquiries by him revealed that the property was still under the control of the aristocratic Soorvey family, whose descendant Mannappa Sahib Soorvey was the trustee of the lands.[15] The Soorveys, their financial situation much altered like most of the aristocrats after the abolition of Maratha rule in 1855, were keen on selling the land. However, meant as it was for a public charitable purpose, it could not be alienated and the local *tahsildar* refused to register a sale.[16] Nagarathnamma found a way out. The land could be exchanged with one of equal value. Without any hesitation she gave away a property in her possession to the Soorveys and took over the Samadhi land. She had given away fertile, revenue-bearing lands and had obtained in exchange a site that was "dead, low-lying and overgrown with prickly pears and wild shrubs" necessitating large sums of money being spent in improvements.[17] Given the pace of life then, Naga-rathnamma must have moved at a blistering tempo, for the transactions had all been completed within a week of her coming to Tiruvayyaru. On 27th October 1921 construction of a temple over the Samadhi began.[18]

The two Katchis must have come to know of Nagarathnamma's activities, but neither evinced much interest in what was going on.

However, Nagaraja Bhagavatar was of the view that Nagarathnamma ought to establish contact with Malaikottai Govindasami Pillai at the earliest and so from Tiruvayyaru they proceeded to Trichy to meet up with the violin maestro who not only gave his blessings but also hosted Nagarathnamma for a few days.[19] Both were great admirers of 'Veena' Dhanam and this forged a bond. As for the Chinna Katchi, its prime mover Soolamangalam Vaidyanatha Bhagavatar, while not approving of Nagarathnamma's involvement in Samadhi matters, was quite happy that Tyagaraja's sepulchre was getting a roof over its head and chose not to interfere.[20]

The courtesy visit to Trichy completed, Nagarathnamma returned to Madras from where she kept up a regular correspondence with Ramudu Bhagavatar and monitored the construction activity. Money was required in increasing amounts as the construction progressed and in order to fund it, Nagarathnamma plunged into her music career afresh, accepting concert opportunities with alacrity.[21] Every rupee earned from these performances was poured into the construction of the shrine and within a short while the temple for Tyagaraja had made remarkable progress. Nagarathnamma worked in close co-ordination with Govindasami Pillai and Ramudu Bhagavatar and by 1924 the building of a hall surrounding the Samadhi and a *gopuram* surmounting it was completed. Whenever she had any free time she thought nothing of travelling down to Tiruvayyaru and overseeing the construction. Each time she departed from the place it was with fresh energy and renewed determination to make the Samadhi a proper temple. In between all these activities she also found time to watch over her protégé Banni Bai's progress and attend her maiden *Harikatha* performance in 1924.[22] Yet another talented woman artiste had been launched.

During this period the Chinna Katchi was facing several problems internally. Owing to what they perceived to be Soolamangalam

Vaidyanatha Bhagavatar's high-handedness in administrative matters, a few musicians decided to observe an independent *Aradhana* in 1923. The third front called itself the Sri Tyagaraja Parabrahma Bhakta Gana Sabha and conducted its celebrations at the Pachaiyappa Mudaliar Choultry from where the Chinna Katchi had originally begun. However, this group did not find great favour with the public, largely due to poor organising capabilities. Sensing this and wanting them to fail completely, Soolamangalam Vaidyanatha Bhagavatar sent letters to the press stating that his group had nothing to do with the third front and saddened as he was at these differences, he had decided that his own group, the Chinna Katchi would not be observing the *Aradhana* in 1924. The notification resulted in most patrons stopping their donations to the third front and though it did observe the *Aradhana* in 1924, the celebrations resulted in a loss to the committee, of Rs.350, which had to be borne by its founders. They consequently lost all interest in the *Aradhana* and by December 1924 it was clear that they would not be interested in celebrating it in 1925. This was the moment that Soolamangalam Vaidyanatha Bhagavatar was waiting for. He triumphantly returned and began making arrangements for the 1925 celebrations. The scene was therefore set for a grand *Aradhana*.[23]

Coming to Tiruvayyaru early in 1925, any visitor would have been taken aback at the transformation of the Samadhi property. Walking through the tall coconut trees that lined the banks of the Kaveri the visitor would have seen that the crude hedge that enclosed the Samadhi had been done away with and in its place had come up a proper compound wall.[24] The low-lying land had been reclaimed by filling it with sand.[25] The shrine was now a proper temple with a square structure topped by a low circular *gopuram*.[26] The entrance was protected by grille gates, which were locked each night by security provided by Nagarathnamma.[27] Stepping inside the shrine the visitor would have been greeted by two sub-shrines flanking the entrance to the Samadhi proper. These were for Bhoga Ganapati, the remover of obstacles and Hanuman (referred to at the Samadhi as Yoga Anjaneya), the one who ensured that all projects were completed without delay. Nagarathnamma had installed them when the work had begun.[28] The construction of a superstructure meant that *brindavanams* dedicated to the memory of other *sanyasis* buried in the area close to Tyagaraja's memorial were in the way. But Nagarathnamma would not agree to their removal and so they remained inside the corridors of the shrine. When the sanctum was built, one of these memorials came to be right inside and there it was allowed to be.

The sanctum to Tyagaraja too had changed. Gleaming silver vessels, the gift of another woman, Padmasini Bai, by then a noted *Harikatha* exponent, were used for worship.[29] While this was all to the good, some of the other changes inside the sanctum came in for sharp criticism. The *brindavanam* had been clad afresh with new stone. The *tulasi* growing on the top had been removed and the opening had been sealed. The orthodox element in Tiruvayyaru had objected to what they termed as a profaning of the Samadhi and quoted the scriptures as stating that any Samadhi must be open at the top and the sealing of it was one of the five deadly sins.[30] The slab commemorating the original renovation by the Umayalpuram Brothers was now hidden from view.[31] The Samadhi itself was screened off by a black marble statue of Tyagaraja depicted as a *sanyasi*. This had been a last-minute decision of Nagarathnamma's. For months she had agonised over the choice of the deity to be installed inside the sanctum. For some reason her mind did not accept the thought of simply leaving the *brindavanam* as it was. Then finally it dawned on her that an idol of Tyagaraja would be the best choice.[32] She had consulted Malaikottai Govindasami Pillai and he had introduced her to a sculptor in Trichy. She had described the composer as she had seen him in her dream and from this image the statue had emerged.[33] Not everyone was pleased with the statue and Soolamangalam Vaidyanatha Bhagavatar in particular referred to it in derisive terms as Karuppannaswami, which could either be an allusion to its black colour or a negative comparison to a tribal God.[34] But the property being Nagarathnamma's, not much could be said and she had her way. The statue was duly installed and the temple consecrated on 7th January 1925. It was a grand affair with many Brahmins, wealthy patrons and above all and perhaps most importantly, several women attending. Nagarathnamma felt that as befitting a proper temple, worship ought to be conducted twice every day at the Samadhi and appointed Ramudu Bhagavatar to perform the same.[35] She also composed an *ashtottaram*, a set of 108 honorific names for Tyagaraja which she had Ramudu Bhagavatar recite each day during the worship.

The Carnatic music world was overjoyed. Their patron saint had a shrine for himself at last. The veteran scholar 'Kirtanacharya' CR Srinivasa Iyengar wrote a congratulatory letter to Nagarathnamma, where he stated that "In South India, among lakhs of music lovers, you have proved that you are the perfect disciple. Utilising the opportunity, you have built the structure to mark the memory of Sri Tyagaraja Swamy. No king, no landlord, no vocalist, has achieved this fame. We all congratulate you for that."[36] Among those who watched in amazement was CV Rajagopalachariar, a leading *vakil* of Tiruvayyaru, who was an important person in the Chinna Katchi's celebrations. Moved by Nagarathnamma's sacrifice he became a great devotee and admirer of hers.

She was praised in prose and poetry.[37] Lyricist Hari Nagabhushanam, vocalist Parupalli Ramakrishnayya and critic Kona Venkataraya Sharma wrote about her in Telugu publications.[38] TS Ganesa Iyer, Government Pleader at Trichy wrote to *The Hindu* that "thanks to the munificence and devotion of Bangalore Nagarathnam a shrine had been constructed for the composer on the banks of the river". The article however lamented over the fact that there was a "rift in the lute" and stated that this was a "regrettable feature that mars the happy and delightful function". It prayed that the two groups ought to see the light and unite in their observance of the *Aradhana*.[39]

This was also Nagarathnamma's dearest wish. She began approaching the two Katchis a week before the celebrations were slated to begin and requested for a meeting at the earliest, during which all differences could be sorted out. Accordingly, a day before the *Aradhana* a meeting was held at the *choultry* on the Tuesday Ghat where Nagarathnamma stayed.[40] Attending it were Malaikottai Govindasami Pillai and Soolamangalam Vaidyanatha Bhagavatar among others. The initial formalities over, the group got down to brass tacks regarding the rights of worship in case a united *Aradhana* was to be performed. Govindasami Pillai stated that the anointing of the Samadhi and subsequent worship ought to be done by Ramudu Bhagavatar as he was a direct descendant of Tyagaraja's brother. Nagarathnamma was also in favour of this. But Soolamangalam Vaidyanatha Bhagavatar held firm to the view that Tyagaraja would be happier if a disciple or one from the musical lineage performed the worship rather than the descendant of an overbearing tyrant of a brother. He therefore demanded that Rajagopala Bhagavatar ought to perform the worship. Enraged at this stubbornness, Govindasami Pillai walked out of the meeting but not before threatening Vaidyanatha Bhagavatar with the complete disruption of the Chinna Katchi's worship the next day. Vaidyanatha Bhagavatar remained his usual calm self, merely stating that everything would happen as per Tyagaraja's wishes. But inwardly he had begun planning his next move.[41]

That very night, Vaidyanatha Bhagavatar accompanied by other members of the Chinna Katchi called on the Sub Magistrate (SM) of Tiruvayyaru and requested his presence at their worship to ensure that it was not disrupted. The SM immediately summoned Malaikottai

Govindasami Pillai and extracted a commitment from him that he had
no objections to the Chinna Katchi performing its worship and that he
would not stand in the way. This done he also summoned Bangalore
Nagarathnamma and Ramudu Bhagavatar and asked for their views.
Nagarathnamma was categorical in asserting that the property was
hers and hence she had absolute right over deciding who could and
who could not enter the Samadhi. So long as the Chinna Katchi did
not agree to unification she felt that they ought not to enter the
premises.

On hearing this Soolamangalam Vaidyanatha Bhagavatar rose to
speak and the trained orator that he was, argued convincingly by
quoting from the scriptures that Samadhis are always open to everyone
who wished to worship and none could be barred from paying their
respects. The SM concurred and decreed that in order that public
peace be maintained, the *Aradhana* of the groups ought to follow a
strict time schedule. He therefore ordered that the Periya Katchi would
worship at the Samadhi from 6:00 to 9:00 am on *Aradhana* day and
then the Chinna Katchi would worship from 9:00 am till 12:00 noon.
The two Katchis accepted this but Nagarathnamma was inwardly
disappointed.[42]

The next morning, the Periya Katchi completed its worship at 9:00
am and left the Samadhi premises. The Chinna Katchi had not yet
made its way there when Ramudu Bhagavatar, on Nagarathnamma's
instructions locked the Samadhi and went away with the key. Tempers
ran high in the Chinna Katchi when the group arrived at the premises
and found it locked, but Vaidyanatha Bhagavatar did not bat an eyelid
and sent word to the SM about what had happened. The SM arrived
with a posse of policemen and ordered the lock to be broken. Ramudu
Bhagavatar who was observing what was going on from a distance
immediately came running and produced the key. The door was opened
and perhaps for the first and last time in its history, police moved into

the Samadhi premises and watched over the conduct of the Chinna Katchi's worship.[43]

Buoyed by their success in thwarting the Govindasami Pillai – Nagarathnamma combine, the Chinna Katchi put up a brilliant show that year. Awed by the performance of flautist Palladam Sanjeeva Rao, a local landholder presented him with a necklace made of nine precious stones costing over Rs 3000. Mangudi Chidambara Bhagavatar performed *Harikatha* on the subject of Rama's coronation and record crowds witnessed his performances.[44] There was however the odd sour note. Angered over the success of the Chinna Katchi, the erstwhile members of the third front organised a felicitation programme for the Periya Katchi's cook and gave him a gold medal commending his services to Tyagaraja.[45] By then the *Aradhana* had begun attracting large crowds and many young and aspiring musicians felt that it would prove auspicious for their careers if they performed at the composer's memorial. With the pressure on both Katchis to accommodate a large number of singers, a strict time schedule was devised and musicians were asked to adhere to the time slots provided for them. If anyone dared to exceed the time limit, he met with the same fate as Naina Pillai had in 1920, namely being peremptorily ordered off the stage or even worse having the *tambura* snatched from his assistant. The evenings were however still given over to just two performances, the first a music concert and the second a *Harikatha*.[46]

In 1926, Nagarathnamma thought of a different ploy and when the time for the *Aradhana* came around, filed a petition before the Second Class Magistrate of Tiruvayyaru, AV Subbiah requesting that no group other than those who recognise the rights of Ramudu Bhagavatar over the Samadhi ought to be allowed to worship there. Summonses were issued to Soolamangalam Vaidyanatha Bhagavatar, Ariyakkudi and others and all of them duly deposed before the magistrate on 3rd January 1926.[47] Last of all came Ramudu Bhagavatar who in the hope that Nagarathnamma would come to his aid, had been putting off his appearance till the magistrate would wait no longer. But strangely she did not come. Perhaps she realised that her stand was weak and would not be viewed sympathetically by the law. Reluctantly giving in, Ramudu Bhagavatar stated that he had waited for "those who were on his side" to come but as they had not, he had no option but to recognise that the Chinna Katchi's worship led by Rajagopala Bhagavatar was valid and that he had no objections to it. He also stated that he would gladly keep the premises open for their worship at the appointed time.[48] The magistrate in his order reconfirmed the hours of worship as structured by his predecessor in the previous year and instructed the Sub Inspector of Police, Tiruvayyaru to ensure that no disturbances occurred during the *Aradhana*.[49]

The Chinna Katchi was jubilant. It decided that the *Aradhana* that year would be the grandest seen thus far and went in for deficit financing to fund it. The Pushya Mandapam was not considered big enough and the group commandeered the Srinivasa Rao High School premises in Tiruvayyaru for conducting its *Aradhana*. The celebrations were conducted on a lavish scale and in order to cover the deficit a special fund raising concert series was organised at the famed 108-pillared hall in Rock Fort, Trichy. The well-known drama troupe owner Cunniah also came forward and donated liberally to the cause, at the instance of Vaidyanatha Bhagavatar. From that year onwards, it became clear that there would be no further hindrances to the Chinna Katchi from Nagarathnamma.[50] But problems came from the *nagaswaram* artistes affiliated to the group who had long chafed at their not being allowed to perform inside the Samadhi premises. They demanded the right to entry and when Vaidyanatha Bhagavatar refused permission, they broke away and formed a separate group and began conducting their own *Aradhana* at the Pushya Mandapam. Not cowed down by this, Vaidyanatha Bhagavatar organised *nagaswaram* artistes from Tanjavur who were willing to abide by his rules and continued with the Chinna Katchi's worship.[51]

The Periya Katchi – Nagarathnamma combine had till then functioned very smoothly. However within days it was to rupture over the issue of not allowing women to worship during the *Aradhana*. To Nagarathnamma, Tyagaraja was a divine personality open to worship by all. After all, Soolamangalam Vaidyanatha Bhagavatar had in his deposition before the Sub Magistrate in 1925, compared the Samadhi with the *linga* of Shiva as Viswanatha in Benares, which anybody could touch and worship irrespective of caste or sex. It therefore meant that women could also be allowed to worship Tyagaraja. She decided to exercise this right in 1926 when the Periya Katchi's *Aradhana* was in progress. At the end of the regular worship the Periya Katchi's musicians began their homage by singing the composer's songs and all of them were accompanied by Govindasami Pillai on the violin and Azhagianambi Pillai on the *mridangam*. When all the musicians had completed their turn, Nagarathnamma came forward and began to sing. Immediately there was dead silence and both the Pillais put down their instruments and Govindasami Pillai explained to her that his group did not, as a matter of principle allow women artistes (read Devadasis) to perform at the *Aradhana*. Nagarathnamma was greatly incensed at what she took to be a calculated insult. An argument with Govindasami Pillai ensued, in which he made it clear that he would not alter his stance for anyone, not even his idol 'Veena' Dhanam. A few years earlier, with a view to offering worship at the Samadhi, or perhaps to watch the discomfiture of Pillai, the grande dame had arrived in Tiruvayyaru in person, complete with veena on the last day of the Periya Katchi's festival. Pillai was completely taken aback but he remained firm in his resolve about not allowing women to offer worship. He found a via media solution for Dhanam. It was customary for the portrait of Tyagaraja to be taken out in an all night procession on the last day of the *Aradhana* to the accompaniment of *nagaswaram* music. The portrait would return to the Kalyana Mahal premises early the next morning. Pillai arranged for a brief performance by Dhanam after the procession had returned and the great woman had contented herself by performing in a specially erected shelter some distance from the Samadhi. For Nagarathnamma, Pillai was not willing to make any change in his principles.[52]

Nagarathnamma stormed out of the Samadhi premises deciding to begin an *Aradhana* celebration by herself, exclusively conducted by women and perhaps a few men who agreed with her point of view on gender discrimination. Members of the Chinna Katchi on hearing all this chuckled amusedly. They could have told Pillai that nothing good could ever come out of associating with that woman.

Nagarathnamma arrived in Tiruvayyaru one morning in January 1927. The Chinna Katchi's *Aradhana* was already underway and the Periya Katchi members had begun preparations for their own festivities also. The day after she arrived it was found that the banana plantation that stood at the rear of the Tyagaraja Samadhi was being cleared and a sheltered stage was being put up there. She then had handbills prepared and distributed informing the public at large of her intention to conduct an *Aradhana* by women for Tyagaraja and invited one and all to participate in it. Two days prior to the *Aradhana*, Nagarathnamma sent word to the bullock-cart owners of the village that around 40 women were expected to come to Tiruvayyaru the next day and would need transport.

Excitement reached a feverish pitch on the day of the *Aradhana*, when the residents of Tiruvayyaru realised that 40 Devadasis had arrived in their midst. Almost everyone in the village found some work or errand to be near the Tuesday Ghat so that they could get a good view of the women who had arrived. The normally solemn *chattram* at the Tuesday Ghat, a hallowed place where the seven palanquins brought out during the *Sapta Sthanam* festival were kept, echoed to loud conversation and laughter. The women went about Tiruvayyaru, enjoying being the cynosure of all eyes. Some of the more adventurous went to bathe in the Kaveri and around midday all of them went to the Panchanadeeswara Temple to worship. In the afternoon they rested and later played games of dice. Some sang and entertained the others. There was much good-natured banter and teasing and as these filtered to those standing around outside, it was clear to many that the Tyagaraja *Aradhana* as they knew it would never be the same again.

Towards evening the entire group along with the accompanists went to the Tyagaraja Samadhi and offered worship. The Periya Katchi's *Aradhana* had begun that morning but thanks to Nagarathnamma and her team of women, not many people had paid attention to what was happening there. Nagarathnamma's group then proceeded to the rear of the Samadhi where she formally inaugurated her *Aradhana* with a short speech.[53] She introduced each of the performers and spoke a word or two in their praise.[54] It was clear that her initiative had the blessings of 'Veena' Dhanam, the de facto leader of the Devadasis. The old lady had not come herself owing to failing health but all her four daughters were present in formidable array.[55]

Nagarathnamma's *Aradhana*, comprising only women artistes, was a big success. Huge crowds gathered to attend the performances. Rather shrewdly, she did not undertake poor feeding and saved herself the expense. Since her five-day festival coincided with that of the Periya Katchi, she left it to them to bear the burden of feeding people and concentrated only on the music programmes. As a consequence, there were large crowds at mealtimes at the Periya Katchi premises and poor attendance during the performances. Malaikottai Govindasami Pillai and his group could only watch with disappointment. Among those who came was Nagarathnamma's protégé Banni Bai and her *Harikatha* on "Rama Das Charittram" which relates the story of Bhadrachalam Ramadas, a composer whom Tyagaraja admired and referred to in some songs, was much appreciated. TA Ramachandra Rao, who had by then attached himself firmly to the Nagarathnamma bandwagon heard the *Harikatha* and became, impressed enough to take greater interest in Banni Bai.

To the women, what mattered was that they now had an opportunity to offer their tribute to Tyagaraja by means of the music they knew. Nagarathnamma had shown them the way and united under her banner they had emerged winners. On the last night of the *Aradhana*, they had one more opportunity to demonstrate their unity. Tired out, they had all retired to rest, when a burglar, no doubt tempted by the tales that were then circulating about Nagarathnamma's jewels, broke into the Tuesday Ghat Chattram. One of the women woke up and raised the alarm and all the Devadasis set up a loud cry, whereupon the thief took to his heels. The women congratulated themselves and felt that the foiling of a burglary augured well for the *Aradhana* and their community. Overall, the preceding five days had greatly boosted the morale of the Devadasis.

When they returned to their respective home towns the next morning, they would not have realised that their community as they knew it had less than eight months to live.

# References

[1] Ramanujachari, C; p 46.

[2] Syama Sastri has composed four songs on the Goddess here. Tyagaraja has left behind as many as ten songs on the Goddess and five on Siva Panchanadeeswara. Dikshitar has composed one song on the Goddess here.

[3] Sambamurthy, Prof. P; Great Composers, Book I; The Indian Music Publishing House; Madras; 5th edition, 1994; p 110.

[4] Seetha S; p 509.

[5] Vasudevacharya, Mysore; p 26-32 & p 51.

6 Sriram V; "Musicians of Padinaindu Mandapam"; article in Sruti; Issue 242; November 2004; Chennai ; p 34.

7 Sankaran T; "Fiddle Govindaswamy Pillai (1879-1931), A Prince Among Musicians"; article in Sruti issue 55; Madras; April 1989;

8 Anecdote related by Chellam Iyer to the author in an interview in 2005.

9 Information given by Seethapathi Iyer, assistant to Bangalore Nagarathnammal during an interview with author in May 2006.

10 Grihalakshmi; p 15-16.

11 Nagarathnam, Bangalore; Last Will and Testament; 5th January 1949.

12 Grihalakshmi; p 15-16.

13 Nagarathnam, Bangalore; Last Will and Testament; 5th January 1949.

14 Bai, C Banni; p 11.

15 Nagarathnam, Bangalore; Last Will and Testament; 5th January 1949.

16 Bai, C Banni; p 11; Banni Bai says that the landowners objected to the building of the temple on the graveyard. Nagarathnamma in her will clearly states that she exchanged her land with the landowners which means that they were agreeable to the transaction. Chellam Iyer states that it was the tehsildar who objected to the sale. This being the most plausible reason, I have reconstructed what could have really happened.

17 Nagarathnam, Bangalore; Last Will and Testament; 5th January 1949.

18 Grihalakshmi; p 15-16.

19 Sruti; BNR; p 16.

20 Soolamangalam; p 47-48.

21 "A Dedicated Life"; The Hindu; 22nd May 1952.

22 Gurumurthy, Dr Premeela; Kathakalakshepa, A Study; International Society for the Investigation of Ancient Civilsations; Madras; 1994; p 139.

23 Bhagavatar, Duraiyappa; "Tiruvayyaru Tiruvizha", Chapter 5 "Moonravadu Utsavam"; p 62-63.

24 Soolamangalam; p 32.

25 Nagarathnam, Bangalore; Last Will and Testament; 5th January 1949.

26 Thyagaraja Centenary Souvenir; The Mulakanadu Sabha; Madras; 1947; p 28.

[27] Bhagavatar, Duraiyappa; "Tiruvayyaru Tiruvizha", Chapter 6 "Adhishtana Kumbhabhishekam"; p 24.

[28] Grihalakshmi; p 15-16.

[29] Information given by Chellam Iyer to the author in 2004.

[30] Aiyar, Bharatam Narayanaswami; "Sri Tyagabrahma Samadhi, An Appeal"; article in The Hindu; January 1948.

[31] Bhagavatar, Duraiyappa; "Tiruvayyaru Tiruvizha", Chapter 1 "Ankurarpanam"; p 22.

[32] Grihalakshmi; p 15-16.

[33] Ibid.

[34] Information given by Chellam Iyer to the author in 2004. Also refer Aiyar, Bharatam Narayanaswami; "Sri Tyagabrahma Samadhi, An Appeal"; article in The Hindu; January 1948.

[35] Grihalakshmi; p 15-18.

[36] Ibid; p 18.

[37] Soolamangalam; p 47.

[38] Grihalakshmi; p 17.

[39] The Hindu; " Music Festival At Trivadi, In Memory Of Sri Tyagayya"; 21st January, 1925.

[40] Soolamangalam; p 32.

[41] Bhagavatar, Duraiyappa; "Tiruvayyaru Tiruvizha", Chapter 6 "Adhishtana Kumbhabhishekam"; p 25.

[42] Soolamangalam; p 41-42.

[43] Ibid.

[44] Bhagavatar, Duraiyappa; "Tiruvayyaru Tiruvizha", Chapter 6 "Adhishtana Kumbhabhishekam"; p 26.

[45] The Hindu; " Music Festival At Trivadi, In Memory Of Sri Tyagayya"; 21st January, 1925.

[46] Ibid.

[47] Soolamangalam; p 43-44.

[48] Statement of Ramudu Bhagavatar, Thiruwadi; 3rd January 1926; The Chellam Iyer Collection.

[49] Proceedings of the Second Class Magistrate of Thiruwadi; 3rd January 1926; The Chellam Iyer Collection.

[50] Soolamangalam; p 42-43.

[51] Bhagavatar, Duraiyappa; "Tiruvayyaru Tiruvizha", Chapter 6 "Adhishtana Kumbhabhishekam"; p 27.

[52] Bhagavatar, Duraiyappa; "Tiruvayyaru Tiruvizha", Chapter 7 "Sri Govindasami Pillaiyin Erpadugal"; p 70.

[53] The entire account of what happened during Nagarathnamma's first Aradhana is based on the author's interviews with Seethapathy Iyer, assistant to Nagarathnamma and coachman Krishnan whose father was an eyewitness to the celebrations.

[54] Bhagavatar, Duraiyappa; "Tiruvayyaru Tiruvizha", Chapter 6 "Adhishtana Kumbhabhishekam"; p 26.

[55] Information given by Seethapathi Iyer, assistant to Nagarathnammal during an interview in May 2006.

# Chapter 7

*" Is it possible to remain firm and not be attracted at the sight
of wily and beautiful women well dressed and with the charm
of curly hair?"* (Tyagaraja in "Tappibratikipova Tarama", raga
Todi, tala Rupakam)[1]

~

In 1727, when the Royal Charter recognising and reorganising the
Mayor's Court of Madras was received, the ceremonial procession
had included "dancing girls who beat time with their feet to the rhythmic
strains of Nautch music".[2] By then, Nautch which was a corruption of
the Hindustani term for dance had come to be equated with the art of
the Devadasi. It was an era of tolerance and many British Sahibs and
Nabobs maintained dancing girls in their retinue. The law courts
however had much to do with Devadasis, for litigation was very common
among them especially over temple hereditary rights, control over
property, adoption and challenges to their status in temples from
avaricious trustees, who often promoted their own favourites. By the
time the modern system of justice came into existence with the setting
up of the High Courts of Calcutta, Bombay and Madras in 1861, it was
accepted that Devadasis "were a distinct group governed by a unique
customary law".[3]

The Madras High Court, in successive judgements between 1862
and 1889, while making it clear that it disapproved of the system,

recognised that Devadasis were a separate social group. The High Court was of the view that given no legislation outlawing the system itself, the law had to respond when cases came up pertaining to rights of status, inheritance, adoption and survivorship of the Devadasis.[4] The law also distinguished between dedicated Devadasis and generally unchaste women and the latter were not governed by the laws applicable to the former.[5] This aspect also applied to certain elements of the Indian Penal Code, which forbade prostitution of minors and which the High Court ruled as not applicable when it came to adoption of children by Devadasis.[6] Over a period of time however it became very convenient to apply laws pertaining to prostitution when deciding Devadasi disputes. Despite this, the High Court remained ambivalent, applying the customary law in a few cases and the IPC in others.[7] The Courts and the Government however never equated the Devadasis with common prostitutes.

With western education gradually gaining ground, the Government was repeatedly pressurised to bring in reforms in the Devadasi system. Social reformers, Theosophists and followers of reformist organisations, such as the Ramakrishna Mission condemned the practice of dedicating girls to temples and equated it with prostitution.[8] A virulent campaign against Devadasis was launched in 1881 under the leadership of Nagarathnamma's bete noire, Veeresalingam Pantulu.[9] The Anti-Nautch movement as it came to be called received the support of Christian missionaries who were appalled at European officers attending Nautch sessions.[10] In 1893, Veeresalingam submitted a memorandum to the Governor, Lord Wenlock, in which he equated Nautch girls with prostitutes and requested the Governor to abstain from any event in which their dance was presented.[11] The decision of the Mysore Government in 1909 to stop availing the services of Devadasis in the state-controlled temples came as a shot in the arm to the reformists and they stepped up their efforts for legislation against the system in the Madras Presidency.[12] The Governments, both in Delhi and in Madras, were however reluctant to intervene in any custom that had religious implications and despite several debates in both the Central and the Madras legislatures, no concrete action was taken.[13]

In 1927, Katherine Mayo, an American journalist brought out a book titled *Mother India* which attacked several Hindu customs then prevalent and also accused the colonial government of inaction in these matters. The book, considered deeply offensive by progressive-minded Indians, led to a debate on the Devadasi system in the Central Legislative Assembly in Delhi. A member from Madras, V Ramdas Pantulu brought forth a resolution requesting the Governor General in Council to prohibit the practice of unmarried minor girls being dedicated to temples as Devadasis. Rather shrewdly, Pantulu observed that the economics of the system, mainly the practice of lands being given to Devadasis in return for their services to temples, ensured its continuation. He suggested that the lands be purchased by the Government from the temples and made over in perpetuity to the Devadasis, thereby freeing them from the necessity of plying their trade to justify their possession of the land. He also recommended that amendments be made to the Religious Endowment Act to prevent temples from spending money on maintaining Devadasis. As a fall-back measure for those who would be affected by the stopping of income, he recommended the setting up of Hindu rescue homes. The Law Member, SR Das, responding to the resolution stated that the Government would support the move to prevent dedication of minor girls but would not take any action against the Devadasi system per se. The Government, he said, did not consider the Devadasi to be the same as a common prostitute and in this he felt that the learned judges of the Madras High Court could not have been wrong. The eminent publisher, GA Natesan, a non-official representative from Madras, opined that it would be better for local governments to regulate the

Devadasi system rather than have the Government of India enact a Bill prohibiting the dedication of women. It was left therefore to the Government in Madras to take steps.[14]

The Madras Legislative Council had in 1926 acquired the distinction of being the first legislature in India to have a woman member – Dr Muthulakshmi Reddy. This remarkable person was a well-known doctor, social reformer and activist. What was less well known was that she was the daughter of a Devadasi.[15] She was elected Deputy President of the Legislative Council immediately on becoming a member.[16] Devadasis were synonymous with prostitutes as far as she was concerned and with the Government of India preferring to wash its hands of Devadasi legislation, she decided to bring forth a resolution in the Legislative Council asking the Madras Government to put an end to dedication of women to temples.

The Devadasis got wind of Dr Reddy's moves and decided to band together. Nagarathnamma was to play a lead role in the confabulations that took place at 'Veena' Dhanam's house and elsewhere, though the nominal head of the group was T Doraikannu Ammal. A petition was drawn up and despatched to reach the members of the Legislative Council on 3rd November 1927.[17]

The document, couched in the most elegant language possible, argued in nine individual sections as to why any move to abolish the system should not be attempted. The Devadasis protested against their being clubbed with common prostitutes, who they said came from other classes and from a wider circle. If the Government was worried about prostitution, they argued, it ought to be taking steps to improve the morality of the public and not be tampering with an age-old institution like the Devadasi system. The Devadasis admitted that a few members from their community had gone astray and asked the Government to punish these rotten apples rather than condemn the system as a whole. Realising that the Madras Government had all along hesitated on legislation mainly because the system was religious by nature, the women cleverly argued that several temples and *mutts* had assigned them these rights and some of the positions they occupied were hereditary by nature and therefore could not be tampered with by legislation. Turning to economics, the Devadasis questioned the members of the Legislative Council as to what they could do for a living if the proposed legislation took away their income from temples. Admitting that the proposed legislation had taken them by surprise, the Devadasis requested for more time to gather support from authorities – religious and legal and to show the strength of their class. They felt that any move to legislate, ought to consider their point of view and requested that the proposed measure be taken up for debate in the first session of 1928, so that they would have sufficient time to represent their case.

A second appeal on the same date took up the matter from a legal point of view.[18] This document, divided into five paragraphs, reminded the members of the Council that the Law Member of the Government of India, SR Das, had refused to accept the Ramdas Pantulu sponsored resolution and the member had consequently withdrawn the same. It also stated that the Madras High Court had "repeatedly laid down in clear and unmistakeable language that the dedication of one's life to worship and service in a temple had nothing to do with prostitution". Admitting that men in their community were all for the abolition of the system they felt that this was mainly due the "accepted political dictum that a man's interests give a basis to his judgement". The appeal ended with a request that the proposed Bill of "Dr Muthulakshmi Ammal be withdrawn for the present like the sister resolution of the Hon'ble V Ramadoss Pantulu in the Council of State".

Notwithstanding this, on 4th November, Dr Muthulakshmi Reddy proposed a resolution stating that "This Council recommends to the Government to undertake legislation or if that is for any reason impracticable to recommend to the Government of India to undertake legislation at a very early date to put a stop to the practice of dedication of young girls and young women to Hindu temples for immoral purposes under the pretext of caste, custom or religion". The resolution was taken up for debate by the Legislative Council on 5th November.[19]

On the same date as the resolution, some of the Presidency's leading publications carried articles criticising the practice of dedication and hailing the efforts of Dr Reddy in trying to bring the system to an end.[20] These articles claimed that her move had the support of several members of the Devadasi community itself and only a few reactionaries had opposed it.

The Devadasis met that very evening at the Mint Street residence of Jeevaratnammal, the senior most member of their community. Led by Nagarathnamma, the Devadasis Association, Madras, was formed with Jeevaratnammal as President and Doraikannu Ammal as Secretary. A resolution was passed stating "that this Association unanimously and emphatically protests against the introduction of the Bill of Dr Muthulakshimi (sic) Ammal regarding Devadasis as it affects the ancient customs and usages of the community and especially their religion". A letter with the resolution was sent to Sir CP Ramaswami Aiyar, Law Member, Government of Madras, on 5th November.[21] A copy was also sent to the Governor's office.[22] The appeal of 3rd November and the resolution of the 4th received widespread attention in the press.[23] The Law Member responded with a letter dated the 10th asking the Devadasis to prepare a full memorandum on the subject.[24]

Almost simultaneously, a handbill written by Padmavathi Ammal of Tirunelveli and Ranganayaki Ammal of Kornad, both claiming to be Devadasis was released by the section that supported Dr Reddy. The pamphlet questioned the credentials of the Devadasis Association and demanded to know how many members it had and how often it met. The two women claimed that all Devadasis of the Madras

Presidency were eagerly awaiting legislation banning the pernicious practice and hoped and prayed that the members of the Legislative Council would stand united and pass the necessary laws.[25] Organisations of which Dr Muthulakshmi Reddy was a member, such as the Women's Indian Association and The Social Hygiene Council sent in letters to the Government supporting her stance.[26]

In the meanwhile, the debate in the Legislative Council continued with several powerful speakers supporting the resolution. In her winding up speech, Dr Reddy stated that she had moved the resolution in "response to the wishes of all the Women's Associations in the presidency who felt the practice of dedicating young girls or young women to temples for immoral purposes as a slur on Indian womanhood". A few amendments to the original resolution, largely semantic, were agreed to. The Law Member, Sir CP Ramaswami Aiyar then rose to make what must have been the tamest speech of his entire career, given that he had the reputation of being a fine speaker. Rather lamely he replied that "while the Government was wholly in sympathy with the motive underlying the resolution, they could not at once give a definite remedy. They would undoubtedly consider the question and with the cooperation of the best brains in the country who had social reform at heart, they would devise some means to meet the real difficulties and dangers inherent in the system of Devadasis which originally was meant not for immoral purposes or prostitution, but whose later results had undoubtedly been calamitous and melancholy". The resolution was then carried more or less unanimously and it therefore became the responsibility of the Madras Government to take action on the matter.[27]

The Devadasis, in the meanwhile, worked on the memorandum. Believed to be largely drafted by Nagarathnamma, it was titled "*The Humble Memorandum of the Devadasis of the Madras Presidency*" and sent on 11th November to Sir CP Ramaswami Aiyar's residence,

The Grove, Teynampet.[28] The appeal received its share of attention in the vernacular and the English press. Couched in the most elegant English and neatly typed, it today reads as a last-ditch effort by the Devadasis to make out a case for their resurrection. The document began with the Devadasis refusing to accept their being equated with prostitutes. They quoted from judgements of Madras High Court which firmly established that "no true relation exists between the ceremony (of tying the *Pottu* or *Tali*) and prostitution". The document went on to highlight the differences between a Devadasi and a common prostitute and stated that the real purpose of the caste was religious and service to God was the main role. It stated that by considering legislation, the Government was tampering with religion. It conceded that a few from the community had strayed, but the whole lot of Devadasis could not be condemned for this. The Devadasis felt that this kind of a wholesale ban was akin to the "mad frenzy of the French Revolution and the barbarous outbursts of the Modern Russian innovators and not legislators". Demanding that their right to live, which was spelt out in the *Sastras*, ought to be protected, they argued that the proposed legislation would only increase the tendency to prostitution as they would be deprived of their "honourable source of living". They would become destitute if the Bill was passed, the document said, and claimed that all of them would be thrown into the "very jaws of hunger, despair and prostitution".

The appeal asked for "gradual evolution". It stated that several courts had accepted that being a permanent concubine was more or less like a marriage and had in some cases even allowed for children born out of such arrangements to claim assets from the father's estate. The Devadasis asked for recognition of out-of-wedlock arrangements and stated that if such a law was passed there would be no difference between such an arrangement and that of a legally married couple.

The appeal then went on to list the steps that the Devadasis Association would take to garner public support. The women proposed to "submit this memorial to the authorities with the signatures of all the adult members of our community scattered over this Presidency. This is a huge and gigantic undertaking but in the interests of the future of our community and the country at large, we have voluntarily shouldered this labour of love. We propose organising ourselves into several associations in the principal towns and cities of this province under the Head Association in the city of Madras. In this way we will be able to show you what we feel in this matter and we trust you will understand the strength of our cause, the legality of our claims and the justice of our demands to you. Our proposal resembles in a large measure the ascertainment of public opinion by the well-known principle of Referendum known to many of the civilised countries of the West".[29]

Meetings protesting against the proposed Bill were held in almost all temple towns of the Madras Presidency. In meeting after meeting, the Devadasis passed almost identical resolutions and sent them on to the Law Member, Government of Madras.[30] In keeping with the multilingual nature of the Presidency, the copies of the resolutions being sent to the Government were in three sections, with identical translations in English, Tamil and Telugu, so that the Devadasi who was signing below could read and understand what she was committing herself to. In some cases such as the Parthasarathy Temple of Triplicane, Madras, the trustees of the temples too, interested themselves in the issue and sent in letters.[31] Within a few days, the Government had a voluminous file recording the protests.

In the meanwhile the prominent Devadasis of Madras city insisted on a personal meeting with the Law Member. Sir CP Ramaswami Aiyar agreed and the meeting took place on November 23rd.[32] Eight Devadasis, including Nagarathnamma met the Law Member and submitted a six-page document which was essentially identical to the memorandum of 11th November, though it was now called a Memorial. Nagarathnamma's signature, one of two in English, stands out in the document, large and confident.[33] The meeting ended with a terse note on the file by the Law Member that "no action was necessary and that the papers may be "recorded".[34] Identical memorials came in from Devadasi associations in various parts of the Madras Presidency, all of which were acknowledged and filed.[35]

Meanwhile, a lively correspondence unfolded in the columns of *The Hindu*, with V Ramdas Pantulu writing in detail as to what he felt should be the action of the Madras Government.[36] Dr Reddy too, penned several letters stating her point of view.[37] She strongly refuted the Devadasi stance that their practices were as per the scriptures and asked as to why if this was so, temples in "other parts of India as in Travancore, British Malabar, Central Provinces, Bengal and Punjab have not paid attention to these sacred books?" She bemoaned the fact that "in this unfortunate land every kind of evil goes under the cloak of religion and custom, which state of things is the chief and true cause of our ill health, poverty and dependent position in the world". She differed from the opinion of the Devadasis that only a few from their community had strayed and stated that "95% of the cases lead a life of prostitution and the remaining 5% take to a life of concubinage". The nationalist, Kamaladevi Chattopadyaya also wrote on the subject.[38] The lone voice of dissent, supporting the cause of the Devadasis, came from AS Natarajan, a *vakil* of the High Court[39], who, going by the similarity in language between his letters to *The Hindu* and the appeal submitted by the Devadasis to the Government, was their advocate and possibly their draftsman.

Nagarathnamma too, turned to writing and drafted what she referred to as a memorandum in Telugu titled *Devadasi Prabhodhachandro-dayam,*[40] which probably contained a plan for restoring the Devadasi to the premier status she once enjoyed in society. No copy of this appears to have survived. Her choice of title was however significant, for *Prabhodha Chandrodaya* of Krishna Misra (12th Century AD) was one of the earliest works in Sanskrit literature to attack the Devadasis.

Inexplicably, the Devadasi Association lost steam. While protest meetings continued to be held till January 1928, it was clear that the initial fire was absent and there was lack of clarity as to what was to be done next. The men of the community who perceived that with proposed legislation becoming law, they could at last gain the upper hand, forced many of the women into submission. An instance of this came to light when two Devadasi women asked for police protection from the *nagaswaram* maestro TN Rajarathinam Pillai who had threatened them with dire consequences if they continued protesting against the legislation.[41] The clubbing of Devadasis with prostitutes hit the community hard and many of the women were forced by their children to deny that they belonged to it. Gradually the protests ceased and the memorials gathered dust in the Government archives. If there was one person on whom none of this had any effect, it was Nagarathnamma. She continued proudly referring to herself as a Devadasi[42] and indeed the events of 1927 only appear to fan her self-confidence to greater levels. It fell to her lot to keep the Devadasi Association going and by drafting younger members such as 'Veena' Dhanam's daughters, she kept up the fight.[43]

In December 1927, attention shifted to the All India Congress Session, which was to be held in the city. An All India Music Conference was held in conjunction with the Congress session and musicians from all over South India participated. Its inauguration was marked by a speech made by the Conference president Dr U Rama Rau, which had among other things a spirited attack on the Devadasi system. While acknowledging that "if today South Indian music is not dead and its glowing embers kept alive, it is due partly if not wholly to the devadasi community, to whom we must acknowledge our gratitude", he also noted that it was "for their unpardonable sins for which they now stand arraigned before the public forum".[44] Dr Rau was then the President of the Madras Legislative Council and represented the official view.

While the Conference listed the concert schedules of the male artistes, it carefully avoided those of women,[45] but a later document from the Music Academy, released in 1928 states that among the 25 vocalists who sang during the concerts held between 24th and 31st December, there were five women.[46] Nagarathnamma was the sole woman singer from Madras Presidency and also the only Devadasi from Madras Presidency.[47]

Pt. Vishnu Digambar, the eminent Hindustani musician who was chairing the debates on Hindustani music during the conference[48] was moved by Nagarathnamma's music to reward her with a gold medal.[49] She was to later recall with considerable pride that she was the sole woman to have been given the award.[50] The Conference was a success and it was from its proceeds that the Music Academy, Madras was founded.[51] Strangely for all her status as a premier artiste, Nagarathnamma was not invited to perform even once by that august body during the remaining years of her life.

In January 1928, Nagarathnamma returned to Tiruvayyaru in order to hold her *Aradhana* for Tyagaraja. More help was forthcoming as compared to the previous year. Her guru, Bidaram Krishnappa, who had come to Madras to attend the All India Music Conference, stayed on and performed at the *Aradhana* she conducted. He promised to send her artistes from Mysore in future years.[52]

The Government of Madras took its time over legislation against Devadasis and this was despite intense pressure from the Secretary of State for India himself. The British parliament was getting interested in the reforms and had been critical of the Government of India's decision of 1927 not to interfere with the custom when Ramdas

Pantulu's proposal was discussed. [53] The Government of India therefore asked all the provincial governments for their opinion on the matter. The Madras Government still opined that it was advisable not to tamper with the system. [54] Dr Reddy felt that she had waited enough. In September 1928 she therefore proposed an amendment to the Madras Hindu Religious Endowment Act of 1926 in order to strike at the economics of the Devadasi system. As per the new Bill, it was envisaged that the lands held by Devadasis by virtue of their duties in temples would be deeded over to them and they would not be required to perform any service in the temples thereafter. Those who were enjoying a portion of revenue from the land would be given the same amount for the rest of their lives. These rights would not be inherited by anyone and therefore there would not be any incentive to adopt girls any further and dedicate them as Devadasis. After much debate the Bill was passed as Act V of 1929. [55] Almost immediately, the Devadasis witnessed the harsher side of temple authorities and trustees. The transfer of lands to their names took time and in many cases was not done. Income for temple services was not paid, leading to severe financial hardship. A particularly poignant example was that of Mylapore Gowri, a close friend of Nagarathnamma's and for whose dance performances the daughters of 'Veena' Dhanam would vie for the honour of singing. Gowri enjoyed the hereditary rights of performing at the Kapaliswarar temple, Mylapore. The authorities evicted Gowri and her ten children from the temple-owned house within a few days of the Bill being passed. Leading a life of dignified penury, Gowri taught music and dance to a deserving few and losing her eyesight later, lived on till 1971, when her funeral expenses were borne by well-wishers. [56] Why the Devadasis did not challenge Act V of 1929 in a court of law is a mystery. Perhaps they did not think they would get justice from the very court which had time and again lamented the absence of legislation banning the system.

The orthodox elements in the Madras Presidency and elsewhere were not very happy with the passage of the Bill for they viewed it as an assault on age-old Hindu customs. These people, referred to as *Sanatanists* were also outraged by the introduction in 1927 of a Bill in the Central Legislature by Rai Sahab Harbilas Sarda which prohibited marriages of Hindu girls under the age of 14 and boys under the age of 18 and which also invalidated such marriages if they were conducted in defiance of the law.[57] Throughout 1928 and 1929, Sanatana Dharma Conferences were held all over the country protesting against the Bill.[58] Nagarathnamma, who was an uncompromising *Sanatanist* played an active role in the Conference that was held in Madras in 1929. She inaugurated the meeting with a prayer in Sanskrit and was honoured on the occasion by the convenor Babu Narendranath Seth.[59] Notwithstanding such protests, the Bill passed on 1st October 1929 and became the Sarda Act, coming into effect six months later. The immediate result was the exact opposite of what the Act set out to prohibit. A phenomenal number of child marriages were conducted in the interregnum[60], many of them with concerts and Nautches.

Matters did not end for the Devadasis with this. In January 1930, Dr Reddy introduced a Bill in the Legislative Council to prevent the dedication of women to Hindu temples. It was decided by a majority of those present that the Bill ought to be circulated to ascertain public opinion. This was the last nail in the coffin for the Devadasi system, for with its passing, the practice would be outlawed forever. There was a reprieve of a few years however. On May 8th, 1930, Dr Reddy resigned her seat in the Legislative Council as a mark of protest against the 5th May arrest of Mahatma Gandhi for his salt *satyagraha*. As she was no longer a member, the Council dropped her Bill temporarily.[61] Outside the Council, Dr Reddy however continued her campaign against what she felt was an encouragement of immorality by the temples.[62]

All remained quiet on the Nautch front for a good two years, though the Devadasi system was clearly on the wane. Performances were now restricted only to the houses of the rich landlords and as it migrated from the temples to private houses; dance became something that was considered unfit for viewing by chaste women. As Dr Reddy herself remarked, the word *Devadiyal*, a corruption of *Devar Adiyal* or handmaiden of God, was considered a gross insult, even by menials in households.[63] The Central Legislature however made some half-hearted attempts at introducing Bills on the subject of prevention of dedication in 1931, none of which was debated or passed, owing to technicalities.[64]

In 1932, the Rajah of Bobbili was elected leader of the Justice Party in the Madras Legislature. He therefore became the Premier of Madras Presidency. This was a cause for celebration and his friends organised a Nautch party in his honour featuring Gaddibhukta Sitaram, a palace dancer who had, at the instance of the Rajah moved to Madras and stayed with Nagarathnamma to learn the Tanjavur style of dance, under her guidance. Nautch parties were also held in connection with some other celebration at the Chettinad Palace, Adyar, in honour of MA Muthiah Chettiar. Dr Muthulakshmi Reddy felt that such high profile events meant a resurgence of interest in Nautch and, therefore an encouragement to the Devadasis. Her anger expressed itself in the form of a strongly-worded letter to the city's newspapers in which she attacked the Premier for having associated himself with a Nautch party and the hosts, some of whom had supported her legislations, for having organised such an event. This drew response from E Krishna Iyer, then Secretary of the Music Academy and a man who was not only a talented dancer but also a strong champion of the arts. He agreed with Dr Reddy that dance ought not to be used for immoral purposes, but that did not mean that dance itself was immoral and therefore ought to be banned. Many supported his views and formed themselves under his leadership into a Pro Art lobby. *The Mail*, conducting an opinion survey found that most people agreed that dance ought to be brought out of the closet and that the general public should see its beauty. A new argument emerged that, if the dance could be dissociated from the Devadasis, it would survive.

The Devadasis, led by Nagarathnamma, however were of the view that the art would die if taken away from their caste. The Devadasi Association, of which Nagarathnamma was now the Secretary, issued a statement that the twin arts of singing and dancing had been the community's inheritance and its members knew how best to preserve their divinity. Signatories to this included 'Veena' Dhanam, Salem Lakshmi, Salem Thayi, Meenakshi, the elder daughters of Dhanam – Rajalakshmi and Lakshmirathnam and Mylapore Gowri.[65]

The Music Academy, at the prompting of E Krishna Iyer, began taking steps to showcase dance to the public. It had earlier attempted the same in 1931, when on 15th March, it organised a dance performance of Rajalakshmi and Jeevaratnam, the daughters of Tiruvalaputtur Kalyani, who were therefore billed as the Kalyani Daughters. This had not received much attention. On 3rd January 1932, a dance performance by Mylapore Gowri was organised by the Academy as part of its annual conference and this was very successful. Dance under the auspices of the Music Academy, however, really took off only from January 1933 when, thanks to the ongoing debate between Dr Reddy and E Krishna Iyer, tremendous public interest was generated. Hundreds thronged the Academy's specially erected *pandal* behind the Ripon Buildings to witness the performance of the Kalyani Daughters. Encouraged by this, the Academy began organising many more such performances and soon women from other communities began taking to dance.[66] In this metamorphosis, the Devadasis became facilitators, passing on their inherited knowledge to those who were eager to learn it. It was a break from the stance which Nagarathnamma and some other diehards like her had taken, as per which the arts were the sole preserve of the Devadasis.

Dance was saved, but the Devadasi system was not. The Devadasis' means of livelihood was usurped by women from other communities and ironically, the very songs which, when danced to by Devadasis were considered lewd, became acceptable when presented by others. Prostitution, never the sole preserve of the Devadasis, continued to flourish unabated. Perhaps the only positive aspect of the legislation and the subsequent debates and reforms, was that children were not dedicated and forced into a lifestyle about which they had no knowledge.

The year 1932, was however not a time of disappointments alone for Nagarathnamma, for she had become a successful broadcasting artiste. The radio, which had come to Madras under the auspices of the Madras Presidency Radio Club in 1925, had grown into a popular medium of entertainment.[67] In 1929, the Corporation of Madras took over broadcasting and prominent artistes were invited to perform on Sundays and public holidays between 5:30 and 7:30 pm. Receivers and loundspeakers were installed in public parks and the beach so that people could listen to the programmes. The programmes were broadcast live, from the studios at the Ripon Buildings. Among the first batch of singers were Musiri Subramania Iyer, 'Jalatarangam' Ramaniah Chetty, 'Tiger' Varadachariar, the *Harikatha* exponent C Saraswathi Bai, Chittoor Subramania Pillai, Harikesanallur L Muthiah Bhagavatar and 'Vidya Sundari' 'Gana Kala Visarad' Bangalore Nagarathnamma.[68] She alone was mentioned with her full panoply of titles in the Corporation Commissioner's administration report for the year.

The title *Gana Kala Visarad* had been conferred on Nagarathnamma that year at the Sri Kanyaka Parameswari Devasthanam, a hallowed temple of Madras city belonging to the affluent Arya Vaisya (Telugu) community. At the end of her performance, 'Kaviraja Sarvabhouma'

Krishnamurthy Sastri, a great scholar, gave her the title amidst great applause.[69] This along with the 'Vidya Sundari' received earlier, became a prefix to her name.

Nagarathnamma had however not neglected her Tyagaraja, amidst all these happenings. She found time between 1929 and 1931 to embark on a series of concert tours of the Madras Presidency, the earnings from which were channelled into her Aradhana for Tyagaraja and for the upkeep and maintenance of his Samadhi.[70] Given her dedication and energy, it was not long before her Aradhana eclipsed those of the two Katchis.

## References

[1] Ramanujachari, C; p 114.

[2] Rao, VN Srinivasa & the Editorial Committee; The Madras High Court 1862-1962 Centenary Volume; Madras High Court; 1962; Madras; p 7.

[3] Jordan, Kay K; p 43.

[4] Ibid; p 44.

[5] Ibid.

[6] Ibid; p 48.

[7] Ibid; p 52.

[8] Vijaisri, Priyadarshini; p 142.

[9] Ibid; p 145.

[10] Ibid.

[11] Ibid.

[12] Ibid; p 157.

[13] Jordan, Kay K; p 55-118.

[14] Ibid; p 104-110.

[15] Viswanath, Jaishree; Vazhkai Padagu, Gemini Ganesanin Vazhkai Varalaru; published by Kamala Selvaraj; 2001; Chennai; p 3-4. Dr Reddy's mother was Chandramma, a Devadasi from Pudukottah State.

[16] Narasiah, KRA; Madaraspattinam, (Oru Nagarattin Kadai 1600-1947); Palaniappa Brothers; Chennai; 2006; p 142-144.

[17] Tamilnadu Archives; GO 4079, Law Department; Dec 20, 1927; appeal to The Hon'ble Members of the Legislative Council, Fort St George, signed by T Doraikannammal and others; 3rd November 1927.

[18] Ibid; Further appeal by the Devadasis of Madras Presidency.

[19] Govt. of Madras; Proceedings of the Madras Legislative Council; Vol XXXVIII; p 415.

[20] The Hindu; Swarajya; The Mail.

[21] Tamilnadu Archives; GO 4079, Law Department; Dec 20, 1927;

[22] Ibid.

[23] The Hindu; 6th November 1927.

[24] Tamilnadu Archives; GO 4079, Law Department; Dec 20, 1927; this letter is referred to in T Doraikannammal's reply dated 11th November 1927.

[25] Ibid; Document no 38971; an appeal to abolish the dedication of girls to Temples; 4th November 1927.

[26] Ibid; the letter from the Madras Branch of the Social Hygiene Council dated 20 October 1927 has Dr Reddy's name as a member. The Women's Indian Association, Adyar sent in its letter on 9th November.

[27] The Hindu; 7th November 1927.

[28] Tamilnadu Archives; GO 4079, Law Department; Dec 20, 1927.

[29] Ibid.

[30] Ibid.

[31] Tamilnadu Archives; GO 4079, Law Department; Dec 20, 1927; letter from Parthasarathy Ayyangar on behalf of the Trustees of the Temple; 4th December 1927.

[32] Tamilnadu Archives; GO 4079, Law Department; Dec 20, 1927; letters between T Doraikannammal and Sir CP Ramaswami Aiyar dated 18th November 1927. Interestingly the meeting time was fixed after ascertaining that the traditionally inauspicious hour of rahukalam was avoided!

[33] Tamilnadu Archives; GO 4079, Law Department; Dec 20, 1927; The Humble Memorial of Devadasis of Madras Presidency.

[34] Tamilnadu Archives; GO 4079, Law Department; Dec 20, 1927; note dated 26th January 1928 appended to the Memorials. The signature is not decipherable.

[35] Tamilnadu Archives; GO 4079, Law Department; Dec 20, 1927

[36] The Hindu; 8th November 1927.

[37] The Hindu; 15th November 1927 – 1st December 1928.

[38] The Hindu; 28th November 1927.

[39] The Hindu; 14th & 26th November 1927.

[40] Grihalakshmi; p 19.

[41] Tamilnadu Archives; GO 4079, Law Department; Dec 20, 1927;

[42] Sruti; BNR; p 14.

[43] Arudra; "The Crucial Controversy"; article in Sruti; Issues 27/28; December 1986/January 1987; p 19.

[44] The Hindu; 25th December 1927

[45] The Hindu; 15th, 21st & 23rd December 1927

[46] Report of the All India Music Conference (1927, Madras); December 1927; The Music Academy; Madras.

[47] Ibid; The other four were C Saraswathi Bai (Harikatha), Sundari Bai (Poona), Manoharammal & Mangalammal (Travancore).

[48] The Hindu; 15th December 1927.

[49] Grihalakshmi; p 19.

[50] Ibid.

[51] Report of the All India Music Conference (1927, Madras); December 1927; The Music Academy; Madras.

[52] Bhagavatar, Duraiyappa; "Tiruvayyaru Tiruvizha", Chapter 6 "Adhishtana Kumbhabhishekam"; p 24.

[53] Jordan, Kay K; p 110.

[54] Ibid; p 111-112.

[55] Ibid; p 132-136.

[56] Sundaram, BM; Devadasis and Nattuvanars, A Survey; p 49.

[57] Felton, Monica; A Child Widow's Story; Katha; New Delhi; 2003; p 227, p 241.

58 Tamilnadu Archives; Native Newspaper Reports; 1927-29.

59 Grihalakshmi; p 17-18.

60 Felton, Monica; A Child Widow's Story; Katha; New Delhi; 2003; p 241.

61 Jordan, Kay K; p 135-36.

62 The Hindu; 15th November; 1927.

63 Ibid.

64 Jordan, Kay K; p 115.

65 Arudra; "The Transfiguration of a Traditional Dance"; article in Sruti; Issues 27/28; December 1986/January 1987; p 17-36.

66 Sriram, V; A Brief History of The Music Academy; Ramu Endowments; Chennai; 2006.

67 Thangamani, Pon.; History of Broadcasting in India; Ponniah Padippagam; Chennai; 2000; p 27.

68 Corporation Commissioners Administrative Report; 1931; Courtesy Ms Shobha Menon.

69 Isai Medaikal.

70 The Hindu; 22nd May 1952.

# Chapter 8

*"I have decorated the brilliant mandapam and have installed therein a beautiful golden bedstead overlaid with jasmine flowers. Pray, rest on it"* (Tyagaraja in "Laali Laalayya", raga Kedara gaula, tala Jhampa)[1]

~

"Deep in my heart a thought occurred that I ought to conduct the festival at the site of the grave" wrote Nagarathnamma. "The reason being – women had no access to these festivals. With *Sathguru's* order, in 1927, the festival began at the backyard. *Alparambhaha kshemakaraha* goes the expression (when the beginning is modest, all will be auspicious and successful). Devadasi's songs (then famous in Madras) were sung, *kutcheries* were organised. Tanjavur scholars and women with devotion extended their help to me. I acquired the garden and the land in front of the site through Sri Raja Ram Sahib, relative of the king of Tanjavur. Soon after, a surrounding wall and four rooms were constructed with this servant's hard-earned money. In that spacious site, was celebrated the *Aradhana* with glory."[2] It was a modest précis of what had happened over the years.

Nagarathnamma's life became increasingly centred on Tiruvayyaru, after the building of the temple over Tyagaraja's Samadhi. If she was not travelling and performing concerts in order to collect money for her annual festival at the site, she was in Tiruvayyaru itself often going to the Samadhi and spending time in spiritual communion with Tyagaraja.[3] It also helped that her protégé Banni Bai, had by 1931 come under the patronage of TA Ramachandra Rao, Nagarathnamma's friend and grandee of Tanjavur. Moving over to Tanjavur, Banni Bai had enrolled under a series of tutors, all funded by Rao, to hone her *Harikatha* skills.[4]

Come December, Nagarathnamma would launch into a flurry of activity. Invitations for her *Aradhana* would be printed and a series of minions, whom she paid well and kept happy, would take them to important personages of the area. This would include the Panchayat Board President, the Collector and other Government functionaries, magistrates and the Superintendent of the Police, Tanjavur and the Deputy in charge of the Tiruvayyaru area. She would go in person to invite a few important people who would donate liberally towards her *Aradhana*.[5] She knew the importance of keeping traders and shopkeepers in Tiruvayyaru in good humour and they would all be invited. This last group, always neglected by the two Katchis, became her greatest strength and support. Shops would give her whatever she wanted for the *Aradhana* at reduced prices and extended credit. Among the shopkeepers, Venkatarama Chetty, a goldsmith, was a liberal donor. The establishments of Ponnusami Chetty and Ramachandra Chetty, general provision merchants, supplied all the goods needed for the celebrations. Rice would come from the neighbouring villages of Tillaisthanam, Ganapati Agraharam, Pudu Agraharam, Tiruppazhanam and Ammal Agraharam. From Madras would come the donations of the Nageswara Rao Pantulu family, (owners of the popular Amritanjan balm and publishers of *Andhra Patrika*) and the jewellers Surajmal Lallubhai.[6]

As the day of the *Aradhana* drew closer, activities in Tiruvayyaru would reach feverish pitch. The tension would be palpable as the Chinna Katchi arrived five days prior to the event and began its festivities. Even as this progressed, workers in Nagarathnamma's pay would be clearing the grove behind the Samadhi to erect the *pandal* for her women's festival. On the day of the *Aradhana*, the idol of Tyagaraja and the memorial behind it would be bathed and worshipped, not once but thrice. First, the women led by Nagarathnamma would come in by 4:30 am. Ramudu Bhagavatar would perform the worship even as Nagarathnamma signalled the beginning of the celebrations by singing "Sadguru Swamiki", a song in raga Ritigaula composed in praise of Tyagaraja by her guru, Ramanathapuram 'Poochi' Srinivasa Iyengar. The women would then recite Nagarathnamma's 108 names of Tyagaraja, and then continue to sing the songs they knew.[7] Ramudu Bhagavatar, having washed the idol would offer flowers that had been supplied by a Devadasi, Ammapettai Chellam Ammal as her contribution to the *Aradhana*.[8] The flowers and fruits would be placed on vessels supplied by Padmasini Bai. As the members of the Periya Katchi assembled outside to begin their celebrations at 6:00 am, the symbolic takeover by women would have been obvious to them. The Chinna Katchi would in turn worship at the Samadhi at 9.00 am.[9]

In the evening, even as the Periya Katchi's *Aradhana* began in a blaze of light, for it always electrified and illuminated the Kalyana Mahal for its celebrations, the women's music concerts would begin behind the Samadhi. This area would also be electrified and illuminated.[10] Mysore artistes such as BS Raja Iyengar, by then famous for his 78 rpm recording of the Purandara Dasa song, "Jagadodharana" (raga Hindustani Kapi) would come down to participate in Nagarathnamma's festival.[11] He was a big draw. The high point in the Nagarathnamma-led event would be the *Harikatha* by Banni Bai, always reserved for the sixth and last evening of the festival.[12] Nagarathnamma would introduce each performer with a short speech, in which she would highlight the salient features of the person's art. In this she was following what Soolamangalam Vaidyanatha Bhagavatar did in the

Chinna Katchi and the crowds loved the oratorical skills of the two as much as they did the music.[13] Regular performers at the 'Women's Katchi' as it came to called, included Rajalakshmi and Lakshmirathnam, the two elder daughters of 'Veena' Dhanam, Trichy Neelambal, Tanjavur Ranganayaki, Valadi Rukmini and Kumbhakonam Chellappa Ammal who would sing and play the harmonium simultaneously.[14] Nagarathnamma's faithful violinist, Sivasubramania Iyer would be in attendance on all days of the festival, ready to accompany the women in their singing. The *nagaswaram* for her *Aradhana* was played by Malaikottai Raju.[15] Culinary arrangements for the artistes were under the management of Nagainallur Nataraja Iyer, an expert in the field.[16] The music she offered ensured a large crowd. Proof of this was evident in the attendance of music lovers from the town of Battalagundu, a place close to Madurai from where the ascent to Kodaikanal, the popular hill station begins. The town, on which much of the betel leaf-loving Tanjavur belt depended for its supply, had a set of thickset, rough and ready, but musically knowledgeable patrons who would attend most of the *Aradhana* concerts. They were experts in identifying slips and errors and if any musician was found wanting they would begin a non-stop derisive applause in slow speed and keep on at it till the musician's voice or instrument was drowned in the noise. They would stop only when the musician stopped his performance and got off the stage. This group shifted allegiance to Nagarathnamma from the Periya Katchi and generally behaved itself during the performances she organised.[17]

Despite her success in dealing a powerful blow to male chauvinism in the field of performing arts, Nagarathnamma never accepted its existence in the domestic sphere. In her view, domestic women, as opposed to women in the public field such as herself, did not need liberation or autonomy. She thus entered into a debate on the subject in the columns of *Grihalakshmi*, the magazine begun in Madras in 1929, by Dr KN Kesari. V Saraswathi, a correspondent of the magazine had written about the selfishness of the Indian man in the domestic sphere. Hotly contesting this Nagarathnamma wrote:

"You have written that *Bharata Purushudu* (Indian man) is selfish. *Bharata Purushudu* has accepted his woman as his better half; and continues to accept in the present and will do so in the future. And in this he has been directed by the *Puranas*. For the maintenance of the family, (he) seeks help from those one cannot, worship those who don't deserve to be, and by earning money, he fills the house with material necessities. And isn't it the woman who reigns as the queen? And now what is the loss that men are causing to women? How can one justify by generalising and exaggerating about the weakness of one man as a common phenomenon? There are a few women (whom I know) who are ignorant of the difficulties faced by their husbands and pester them for new clothes. On failure to gain new clothes they seek refuge in their mother's place. Taking such women as an example and arguing that Indian women are all the same would not be fair. Good and bad exist among both the *jatis* (male and female). In this case it is wrong to accuse one and praise the other. I plead that you think about it and I expect a response."[18] Perhaps her inability to recognise male chauvinism or her ability to deny its very existence was responsible for her success.

Both the Periya and Chinna Katchis viewed Nagarathnamma's *Aradhana* with misgivings. It however hit the Periya Katchi harder than the Chinna Katchi. Firstly, her festival coincided with theirs and depleted their audience, despite their high expenditure.[19] Secondly, by 1930, there were protests from the *nagaswaram* community, which began questioning the denial of performing rights during the *Aradhana* proper. In this it was probably encouraged by the success of the women. Consequently, a group of *nagaswaram* artistes broke away from the two Katchis and began conducting an *Aradhana* by itself.[20] The biggest blow however, was the stroke that laid Malaikottai Govindasami Pillai low.

Pillai, who had long been the kingpin of the Periya Katchi, was an artiste in the old style who never believed in saving for a rainy day. The illness forced him to give up performing and he began facing severe hardships, alleviated only by the patient nursing of his faithful disciple 'Papa' KS Venkataramiah.[21] By the middle of the year 1930, he had however staged a recovery of sorts. Working with manic energy and despite having to be helped while walking, he embarked on a major fund collection drive for the *Aradhana* of 1931. This included a series of concerts at the Gokhale Hall in Armenian Street, Madras. Pillai himself accompanied artistes during the series, keen as he was to contribute his mite towards the proceedings. On the last day, he had to be carried on to the stage.[22] It must have been a poignant moment for the man who had once strode that very stage like a colossus. He must have remembered the time in 1918, when he, along with Dakshinamurthy Pillai and Azhagianambi Pillai, had introduced the young Chembai Vaidyanatha Bhagavatar to Madras audiences at the very same venue.[23] Now he was a mere shadow of his former self. Dragging himself to the mike, Pillai thanked the main artiste, Palghat Rama Bhagavatar for having accepted his invitation and agreed to perform. The singer burst into tears, even as the audience silently wiped its eyes.[24]

Back in Trichy after the series of concerts, Pillai requested the Tanjavur-based drama company Sri Sudarsana Sabha to perform plays and collect money for the Periya Katchi's *Aradhana*. This was a moribund organisation which had attained affluence only due to the generosity of Pillai, who being an avid lover of theatre, had helped it in many ways when he was at the peak of his success. The drama troupe responded to his request and soon collected a good amount of money for the *Aradhana*.[25]

The *Aradhana* of 1931 was Pillai's swansong. He organised the debut of Papa on stage at Tiruvayyaru that year as an accompanist to

Semmangudi Srinivasa Iyer[26], who in 1930 had made an enormous impact on the audiences at the *Aradhana*.[27] Realising full well that he would not live to see another *Aradhana*, Pillai called for the *nagaswaram* duo, the Tiruvizhimizhalai Brothers and handing over the portrait of Tyagaraja that he had received from Narasimha Bhagavatar in 1911; he symbolically entrusted the responsibility of the Tyagaraja *Aradhana* to them.[28] Moving over to Kumbhakonam for medical treatment, Pillai passed away there on 13th March 1931.[29] Musicians mourned his passing, notwithstanding the differences between the Katchis. Mangudi Chidambara Bhagavatar, despite being a pillar of the Chinna Katchi wrote a long and heartfelt tribute in his praise in *The Hindu*.[30] Nagarathnamma too felt his passing for she knew that despite his rigid views on women, he was a noble soul who had worked hard for the success of the *Aradhana*. The year 1931 also brought another sorrow to her. Bidaram Krishnappa, her famed guru, passed away in Mysore on 30th July, after a life of honours and achievements.[31] Like her, he too had been obsessed with building a temple, to his and Tyagaraja's favourite deity Rama, in Mysore. Like her, he too donated most of his life's earnings to the Sitarama Mandiram which stands testimony to his faith even today in Mysore.[32] Perhaps it was appropriate that while the guru built a temple to Rama, the disciple should build a temple for Rama's greatest devotee, Tyagaraja.

With Pillai's passing, the Periya Katchi's *Aradhana* became the responsibility of the Tiruvizhimizhalai Brothers. A grand programme was organised in Tanjavur's Rao Bahadur Ramanathan Chettiar Hall to formally signify their taking over.[33] The chief guest was Mangudi Chidambara Bhagavatar, who was then temporarily estranged from Soolamangalam Vaidyanatha Bhagavatar.[34] The Periya Katchi had perhaps hoped to entice him into their fold. Bhagavatar, though he did not cross the floor and soon made up with the Chinna Katchi, attended the programme and handed over once again the portrait of

Tyagaraja that had been in Pillai's possession to Tiruvizhimizhalai Subramania Pillai, the elder of the duo. He also gave him a gold bracelet that had once been gifted by Gopinath Tawker, the famed jeweller of Madras to Govindasami Pillai.[35] Despite this fanfare the Periya Katchi's *Aradhana* declined steadily in attendance and enthusiasm.[36] Azhagianambi Pillai passed away sometime later, thereby robbing the group of a powerful supporter. Kanchipuram Naina Pillai kept it going for two more years, but in 1933 he fell ill with tuberculosis and diabetes and remained bedridden in his hometown, passing away there in 1934.[37] Marungapuri Gopalakrishna Iyer, the famed violinist and close friend of Govindasami Pillai also contributed for a few years. But he began conducting a festival by himself in Srirangam and stopped attending the Tiruvayyaru festivities thereafter.[38] The famed dramatist 'Nawab' Rajamanikkam Pillai, contributed money to the group by staging plays for its benefit.[39]

The Chinna Katchi's festival however continued in its usual fashion with Soolamangalam Vaidyanatha Bhagavatar ensuring that the celebrations ran entirely as per his wishes. He remained adamant in not allowing *nagaswaram* artistes on to the *Aradhana* stage.[40] He also ensured that feeding of the poor was organised on caste lines. Electricity at the celebrations was eschewed as a modern development and the events took place as earlier, under gaslights.[41] Aspiring musicians had to be approved by him before they were given a chance to perform at the festival. He grudgingly gave Musiri Subramania Iyer his approval and allotted him 1½ hours as opposed to the usual three. The slow-paced and emotional style of Musiri did not make an impact on the audience in that short duration.[42] Bhagavatar rather sarcastically remarked that Musiri would do better as a theatre artiste. Musiri stayed away from the *Aradhana* after that.

Yet another of those who Bhagavatar felt was not yet ready to perform was his own disciple, Swamimalai Janakiraman, who was a student in residence during 1935-36. Despite several entreaties from the disciple the guru would not budge. Frustrated, Janakiraman approached Nagarathnamma one afternoon, while she was relaxing at her place of stay. On ascertaining that he was Bhagavatar's disciple, Nagarathnamma asked him to sing. Having heard him, she asked him to come to the celebrations she conducted in the evening and promised to give him a chance. That evening, Janakiraman was asked to perform a full concert on Nagarathnamma's stage. She sat through the entire performance and at the end, introduced him to the audience as Soolamangalam Vaidyanatha Bhagavatar's disciple and asked them to applaud him. The next day Bhagavatar came to know of what had happened. He refrained from commenting, but the cheekiness of Nagarathnamma must have rankled.[43] He never warmed to her and often spoke derisively of her efforts in conducting an *Aradhana*. Nagarathnamma however, came to appreciate the difficulties Bhagavatar overcame, despite advancing age, to keep the Chinna Katchi's celebrations going. She often referred to him as the living image of Tyagaraja.[44]

Between 1933 and 1935, Nagarathnamma began acquiring the lands surrounding the Samadhi.[45] This was a difficult and slow process, for her income as an artiste had begun to dwindle, partly because she had reduced her concert opportunities in order to concentrate on her mission of building a temple for Tyagaraja. The arrival of talking and singing cinema had begun to demand a new kind of music and Nagarathnamma was not one to give up her ideals so easily. The gramophone boom left her cold, for her independent nature would not allow her to submit to the tyranny of the recording engineers and sing as per their direction.[46] Her immense bulk made it difficult for her to travel long distances and so she began refusing outstation concerts.

Mannappa Saheb, the old aristocrat who had transferred the Samadhi to Nagarathnamma was no more and his son Rajaramannaji

Soorvey was now the trustee. Heeding his father's last wishes he now came forward to exchange the lands surrounding the Samadhi. As in the earlier purchase, Nagarathnamma bought fertile land elsewhere and transferred it to Soorvey in exchange for the Samadhi lands. CV Rajagopalachariar, the Government pleader of Tiruvayyaru and by now, an ardent admirer of Nagarathnamma helped in the documentation and transfer of title deeds.[47] The entire transaction cost Rs 2000 and in order to fund it, Nagarathnamma began selling her jewels.[48] The doors of Surajmal Lallubhai were now opening to a seller and not a valued customer. But such was the mutual respect between the ageing singer and the old businessman that he ensured that a fair deal was struck for each item.[49] The *Zamindarini* of Chikkavaram, Saraswathi Devi remembered till her last days a choker of uncut diamonds which alone fetched Nagarathnamma Rs 3500. Then there was a ring with a diamond as big as a soap nut. The sheer detachment with which Nagarathnamma watched the sale was amazing to those who knew her passion for jewels and diamonds in particular.[50] Using the surplus cash she also purchased in her own name, fertile lands in Tiruvayyaru, spanning around an acre.[51] She also used the funds for charitable purposes. Any enterprise associated with Tyagaraja was enough to make Nagarathnamma come forward with donations. Thus it was that, when KK Ramaswami Bhagavatar, the son of Tyagaraja's disciple Wallajahpet Krishnaswami Bhagavatar, thought of writing a biography of Tyagaraja, he turned to Nagarathnamma, among others, to help with funding the printing of the book. The work titled *Sri Tyaga Brahmopanishad*, came out in 1935 and acknowledged Nagarathnamma as one of the munificent donors.[52]

When the purchase of the lands surrounding the Samadhi went through, Nagarathnamma and her women shifted their *Aradhana* celebrations from the rear of the shrine to the front.[53] Members of the two Katchis had to go past her celebrations each time they went into the shrine. Her conquest now appeared complete to most, but not to Soolamangalam Vaidyanatha Bhagavatar. While reluctantly conceding that she had made women an integral part of the *Aradhana* and had outwitted him in every way on Samadhi matters, he pointed out that there was one aspect of the annual ceremonies which women could never perform. That was the *shraddha* or annual rite which formed the core of the *Aradhana* and which involved the worship and ceremonial feeding of 16 Brahmins as representatives of the dead soul. It also involved the *Uncchavritti* procession which was never performed by women.

Nagarathnamma, when she came to know of it, felt that Bhagavatar had challenged her. She sent for Seethapathi, the young nephew of violinist Sivasubramania Iyer and asked him to identify Brahmins who would come to her house and participate in the *shraddha* that she would organise for Tyagaraja. Not one man would accept. The chief objection was that they could not partake of a meal cooked by Nagarathnamma as she was a Devadasi. Nagarathnamma then gave a solemn assurance that the cooking would be done by a Brahmin and that she herself would not come out of her room till the *shraddha* and the feeding of Brahmins were completed. All that the Brahmins needed to do was to bless her when the ceremony was over by showering grains of rice on her head, thereby transferring the fruits of conducting the *shraddha* to her. The Brahmins agreed to this. Nagarathnamma wanted the ceremony to be complete in all respects and therefore organised the *Uncchavritti* as well. With Ammapettai Balasubramania Iyer and Pattukottai Rajagopala Bhagavatar singing, Kizhparur Lakshminarasimhan playing the *mridangam* and another person keeping the drone, the procession left the Tuesday Ghat Chattram, Nagarathnamma's place of stay on *Aradhana* day, with Neelakantha Bhagavatar collecting rice from all the houses. Soolamangalam Vaidyanatha Bhagavatar watched in amazement as the singing group wended its way around Tiruvayyaru and returned in time for Annadurai Bhagavatar to cook the food in ritual fashion for the *shraddha*. True to her word, Nagarathnamma made herself scarce during the rites, returning in time only for the benediction. The Brahmins were delighted with the clothes and vessels she gifted them and promised to return year after year for the ceremony. With this Nagarathnamma's *Aradhana* was complete in all respects and none could pinpoint any lacunae in its observance.[54]

Despite this, Nagarathnamma grieved over the lack of unity among musicians which made it necessary for three separate *Aradhanas* to be conducted, thereby making a mockery of the very spirit of Tyagaraja's songs. The decline of the Periya Katchi was evident to everyone and it was an open secret that the Tiruvizhimizhalai Brothers were spending more and more out of their own pocket to keep the event going.[55] A word from her regarding unification was all that was needed. But the Chinna Katchi, led by Vaidyanatha Bhagavatar was adamant on its stance of not allowing women to perform at the Samadhi. Given this condition, Nagarathnamma chose not make any overt moves for unification.[56]

Between 1937 and 1938, Nagarathnamma sold more of her assets and funded the construction of a circumambulatory passage around the shrine proper. She named the area comprising the Samadhi and surrounding lands as Tyagaraja Ashrama (the hermitage of Tyagaraja).[57] The beauty of the spot, with the river Kaveri flowing by it, began powerfully attracting her and she found that life in Madras had no meaning. She seriously began contemplating the sale of her home in Madras and relocating to Tiruvayyaru. Perhaps the one thing she would miss would be the company of 'Veena' Dhanam, her beloved friend with whom she had spent many a pleasant afternoon. But Dhanam herself did not have long to live.

In the years when Nagarathnamma was away fighting her battles in Tiruvayyaru, Dhanam had become increasingly withdrawn and yet this very reclusive nature, combined with the most exquisite of music formed the lifeblood of an ardent band of admirers that included newspaper baron Kasturi Srinivasan, businessman TT Krishnamachari, the lawyer ND Varadachari and the ICS officer SY Krishnaswami.[58] To them, the Friday evening chamber concerts of Dhanam were like weekly visits to a shrine. Blind by then and subject to many ailments, Dhanam was kept going by the munificence of these admirers and the patrons of her daughters.

In mid 1938, Dhanam left her home in Ramakrishna Chetty Street, in order to stay with her granddaughter T Balasaraswathi, by then a well-known dancer, at her Aravamudu Gardens residence in Egmore. The festival of Navaratri came about in end September and as was her wont, Dhanam despite severe ill health celebrated it the usual way. This involved bathing every evening in rose water and then having seated herself under a bower of jasmine, she would play the veena. The entire family would gather and first worship the goddess of learning, Saraswathi, by singing the Muttuswami Dikshitar song "Veena pustaka dharinim" in raga Vegavahini. To many onlookers it was the worship of Dhanam herself. The monsoons had broken early that year and the strain of the celebrations made Dhanam take to her bed after the Vijaya Dasami festival.[59] She passed away on 15th October, her passage eased by the voices of her daughters as they sang her favourite songs in chorus.[60] Her funeral was a grand affair with many of the city's leading lights in attendance, despite the pouring rain.[61]

Condolence meetings were held at many places with perhaps the most befitting one being held at the Senate House, Madras University on 3rd November.[62] A smaller meeting had been held on 24th October under the auspices of the Tyaga Brahma Bhakta Jana Sabha at 20, Ekambreswarar Agraharam, Park Town with Ariyakkudi Ramanuja Iyengar presiding. Nagarathnamma participated in the event and in her speech said that "Dhanammal had left an indelible impression in

the minds of music lovers of South India." By then everyone and
everything for her had to be seen in the context of Tyagaraja and so
she also said that the music of Dhanam was testimony to her "love
and regard for Tyagaraja and his compositions."[63]

With the death of Dhanam, Nagarathnamma moved quickly to sell
her own house at Srinivasa Iyer Street, George Town. The shift to
Tiruvayyaru was done with Nagarathnamma taking only the bare
essentials with her and preferring to dispose of the rest. The daily
items of *puja* were taken to Tiruvayyaru with due reverence and placed
inside the Tyagaraja Samadhi shrine, to the left of the idol. They would
henceforth be worshipped by Ramudu Bhagavatar. The lamp that
burned all the while in her *puja* room was taken with great care to
Tiruvayyaru, with Nagarathnamma filling oil en route and ensuring
that the flame was not extinguished.[64]

The proceeds from the sale of the house were invested in the
completion of the circumambulatory passage around the Samadhi and
in the purchase of some more fertile land adjoining Tiruvayyaru. [65]
The constructions around the Samadhi were completed in November
1938 and the culmination was marked by the placing of a
commemorative marble slab at the entrance, engraved by the Madras-
based engravers and tombstone makers, J Leese and Co. It read as
follows:

SRI RAMA JAYAM
*This shrine and the Asram*
*Are the offerings*

*To*
*Sri* **Thyagaraja Swamigal**
*The Great Saint and Musician*

*By*
His Humble Devotee

*Vidyasundari*
## Bangalore Nagarathnammal
*Daughter of*
## Puttalakshmi Ammal
*of Mysore*

*Kumbhabhishekam*          *Completion of the Building*
*7-1-1925*                      *November 1938*

With that, Tyagaraja's remains had a roof. Ironically, the woman who made it possible did not and chose to live in the Tuesday Ghat Chattram premises and later at a rented house on the main street of Tiruvayyaru.

Here, she kept herself occupied by singing songs of Tyagaraja and many began to flock to her house to listen. The highpoint of these performances was that when she was deeply involved in the song, Nagarathnamma's *abhinaya* talents would come to the fore. Forgetting the presence of others, she would mime the meaning of the song using her eyes, face and hands for expression even as she sang. Her perfect knowledge of Telugu ensured that she never faltered in her interpretations.[66] There were also occasions when overcome with emotion she would be unable to continue with the song. She would then expound the import of the lyrics and explain them to the audience, always concluding with a sentence or two on the greatness of Tyagaraja.[67] Tiruvayyaru had a women's association and the leading lights were Shakuntala (Juju Mami to friends), the wife of the village doctor, Sethurama Iyer and Kamala Mami, of whom all that is remembered today is that she lived opposite Nagarathnamma's house. These two women formed a trio with Nagarathnamma and became inseparable companions. Shakuntala's younger sister, Janaki was then all of seven and became very dear to Nagarathnamma, who taught her many songs.

Janaki, now living in Bangalore, can truly claim to be Naga-rathnamma's disciple and in 1939, she was given an opportunity to sing at the *Aradhana* organised by the women. Nervous at the prospect and in particular of the men from Battalagundu, Janaki was encouraged and emboldened by Nagarathnamma. Others who were active members of the women's association and so regulars at Nagarathnamma's beck and call were Shambu Mami, Abhayam and Vishalam.[68] Among the men, CV Rajagopalachariar was constantly at Nagarathnamma's service, not hesitating to even remove the leaves from which the Brahmins had eaten after her *Aradhana* was concluded. Appreciating his dedication and sense of service Nagarathnamma would pun on his name and refer to him as Tyaga Rajagopalachari.[69] Yet another man who did much to organise her *Aradhana* was TA Ramachandra Rao, The scheduling of concerts and arrangements associated with them were left to him.[70]

Having settled down thus, Nagarathnamma rarely stirred out of Tiruvayyaru. Invitations from the Rajah of Venkatagiri were however, commands to her and she always made it a point to travel there whenever called. She was on close terms with the family members of that royal household, and they could never imagine any auspicious event in their palace being held without a concert by her. She had become a court musician, early in life, at Venkatagiri and for rendering musical service received a hefty annual payment of Rs 1500, in addition to gifts and rewards whenever she visited. She was expected to sing each year on Vijaya Dasami day in addition to performing during weddings and other auspicious occasions. An invitation to Venkatagiri also held the attraction of a visit en route to Madras where Nagarathnamma would stay with her favourite, Banni Bai, who had by then relocated to that city. A car from Venkatagiri would meet her at the station and drive her to Banni Bai's George Town residence. From here, Nagarathnamma would set out for Venkatagiri, accompanied by Sivasubramania Iyer, the violinist.

At the Venkatagiri palace, the Rajah always had a fixed set of songs which were his favourites. "Vachamagochara", a composition of Mysore Sadasiva Rao, in raga Athana was a must. Nagarathnamma would render it in a slow pace as made famous by 'Veena' Dhanam. After the formal concert, Nagarathnamma would regale the other members of the family with jokes and stories of her career. Once she translated "Ni matale mayanura", the *javali* of Pattabhiramayya in raga Purvikalyani into English and sang it much to the amusement of everyone. The song "Mathuranagarilo" of Chittoor Subramania Pillai, her one-time paying guest, set in raga Anandabhairavi was yet another favourite. She would also mimic well-known artistes such as 'Tiger' Varadachariar and Maharajapuram Viswanatha Iyer, copying their mannerisms while singing. Such sessions would always end with an admonition that all these greats were not to be taken lightly when it came to their talents in music. Once in a while Nagarathnamma would take a dig at Tamilians singing Telugu lyrics and would transform the Tyagaraja kriti "Ne pogadakunte" (raga Desika Todi) into "Ne pakoda tinte nikemi kodava" (what do you lose if I eat pakodas) and sing it. When her visit ended, Nagarathnamma would invariably depart with numerous Venkatagiri saris gifted by the women of the *zenana*.[71]

In Madras city, a visit to Dr KN Kesari at his Royapettah home, Kesari Kuteeram was a must. There, after having discussed her numerous ailments and receiving medication, Nagarathnamma and the learned doctor would discuss Telugu literature and poetry. Dr Kesari was firmly of the view that Nagarathnamma brought prosperity to any enterprise she was involved with and had her sing for the house-warming ceremony at Kesari Kuteeram and also for the wedding of his daughter, Seshagiri. He contributed regularly to Nagarathnamma's *Aradhana* and when a friend of his in Bangalore built Sastry's Hotel, he recommended that Nagarathnamma be asked to inaugurate it. She did so with a concert and later Dr Kesari was to recall with justifiable pride that the owner made lakhs out of his enterprise.[72]

Back in sylvan Tiruvayyaru, in the evenings, she would have Krishnan, the young and burly coachman of Tiruvayyaru escort her to the Samadhi. There she would sit in silent meditation. Sometimes she would be seen to be speaking in Telugu. The sentences and words were structured as though she was having a conversation with someone. When once asked respectfully as to whom she spoke to in the deserted Samadhi, she claimed that Tyagaraja often engaged her in conversation. She sang to him, spoke endearingly to him, offered him food and even entertained him by means of *abhinaya*.[73] He dominated her thoughts all the time and she had dedicated everything she possessed to him. In the evening of her life, the last of the great Devadasis had found her final patron.

## References

[1] Ramanujachari, C; p 545.

[2] Grihalakshmi; p 17.

[3] Bai; C Banni; p 14.

[4] Gurumurthy, Dr Premeela; Kathakalakshepa, A Study; International Society for the Investigation of Ancient Civilsations; Madras; 1994; p 139-40.

[5] Bai, C Banni; p 13.

[6] Interview with Seethapathi, assistant to Bangalore Nagarathnamma at Tiruvayyaru, May 2006.

[7] Interview with Janaki Subramaniam, disciple of Bangalore Nagarathnamma in Bangalore, July 2007.

[8] Interview with Seethapathi, assistant to Bangalore Nagarathnamma at Tiruvayyaru, May 2006.

[9] Soolamangalam ;p 43-44.

[10] Ibid; p 51-52.

[11] Isai Medaikal.

[12] Bai, C Banni; p 13.

[13] Soolamangalam; p 51-52.

[14] Facts given by scholar BM Sundaram; July 2007.

[15] Soolamangalam; p 51.

[16] Interview with Seethapathi, assistant to Bangalore Nagarathnamma at Tiruvayyaru, May 2006.

[17] Interview with Janaki Subramaniam, disciple of Bangalore Nagarathnamma in Bangalore, July 2007.

[18] Vijaisri, Priyadarshini; p 267-268.

[19] Bhagavatar, Duraiyappa; "Tiruvayyaru Tiruvizha", Chapter 7 "Sri Govindasami Pillayin Erpadugal"; p 70.

[20] Soolamangalam; p 48.

[21] Carnatic Summer; p 232.

[22] Sankaran, T; "Who was Oho in Carnatic Violin?"; article in Sruti; Issue 19; October 1985; Hereinafter referred to as Sruti; Violin; p 22-23.

[23] LRV; Chembai Chelvam; Amuda Nilayam; Madras; 1954; p 110-111.

[24] Sruti; Violin; p 22-23.

[25] Bhagavatar, Duraiyappa; "Tiruvayyaru Tiruvizha", Chapter 7 "Sri Govindasami Pillayin Erpadugal"; p 69.

[26] Carnatic Summer; p 232.

[27] Soolamangalam; p 49.

[28] Bhagavatar, Duraiyappa; "Tiruvayyaru Tiruvizha", Chapter 8 "Katchigal Ondrupattana"; p 78.

[29] The Hindu; "Famous Violinist Dead"; 14th March 1931.

[30] Bhagavatar, Mahakathaka Kanteerava Brahma Sree Chidambara; "The Late Mr Govindaswami Pillai"; article in The Hindu; Madras; 18th March 1931.

[31] The Hindu; "Death of a Famous Musician"; 31st July 1931.

[32] Ibid.

[33] Sundaram, BM; Mangala Isai Mannargal; Meyyappan Tamizhaivagam; Chidambaram; 2001; p 163.

[34] Bhagavatar, Duraiyappa; "Tiruvayyaru Tiruvizha", Chapter 7 "Sri Govindasami Pillayin Erpadugal"; p 71.

[35] Sundaram, BM; Mangala Isai Mannargal; Meyyappan Tamizhaivagam; Chidambaram; 2001; p 163.

[36] Bhagavatar, Duraiyappa; "Tiruvayyaru Tiruvizha", Chapter 8 "Katchigal Ondrupattana"; p 73.

[37] Ibid.

[38] Bhagavatar, Duraiyappa; "Tiruvayyaru Tiruvizha", Chapter 7 "Sri Govindasami Pillayin Erpadugal"; p 70.

[39] Bhagavatar, Duraiyappa; "Tiruvayyaru Tiruvizha", Chapter 8 "Katchigal Ondrupattana"; p 73.

[40] Soolamangalam; p 50.

[41] Ibid; p 51-52.

[42] Ibid.

[43] Sriram, V; "Swamimalai Janakiraman: Bhagavatar's Student"; article in Sruti; Issue 233; February 2004; Chennai; p 35.

[44] Soolamangalam; p 47-48.

[45] Nagarathnam, Bangalore; Last Will and Testament; 5th January 1949.

[46] Interview with VAK Ranga Rao in 2007.

[47] Nagarathnam, Bangalore; Last Will and Testament; 5th January 1949.

[48] Interview with Seethapathi, assistant to Bangalore Nagarathnamma at Tiruvayyaru, May 2006.

[49] Ibid.

[50] Interview with VAK Ranga Rao in 2007.

[51] Nagarathnam, Bangalore; Last Will and Testament; 5th January 1949.

[52] Jackson, William J; p 81-82.

[53] Bhagavatar, Duraiyappa; "Tiruvayyaru Tiruvizha", Chapter 8 "Katchigal Ondrupattana"; p 73.

[54] Interview with Seethapathi, assistant to Bangalore Nagarathnamma at Tiruvayyaru, May 2006.

[55] Bhagavatar, Duraiyappa; "Tiruvayyaru Tiruvizha", Chapter 8 "Katchigal Ondrupattana"; p 73.

[56] Soolamangalam; p 47-48.

[57] Nagarathnam, Bangalore; Last Will and Testament; 5th January 1949.

[58] Sampath, NV; Rangaswami Malathi; Kasturi, NV; The Kasi Diaries, Excerpts from the diaries of ND Varadachariar; East West Books (Madras) Pvt. Ltd.; Chennai; 2004.

[59] Isai Medaikal.

[60] Isai Medaikal.

[61] Carnatic Summer; p 233.

[62] The Hindu; 4th November 1938.

[63] The Hindu; 25th October 1938.

[64] Bai, C Banni; p 15.

[65] Nagarathnam, Bangalore; Last Will and Testament; 5th January 1949.

[66] Interview with Seethapathi, assistant to Bangalore Nagarathnamma at Tiruvayyaru, May 2006.

[67] Interview with TS Parthasarathy, eminent music historian; 2004.

[68] Interview with Janaki Subramaniam, disciple of Bangalore Nagarathnamma in Bangalore, July 2007.

[69] Bai, C Banni; p 16.

[70] Interview with Seethapathi, assistant to Bangalore Nagarathnamma at Tiruvayyaru, May 2006.

[71] Interview with Gopalakrishna Yachendra, younger son of the last Rajah of Venkatagiri in Chennai; June 2007.

[72] Grihalakshmi; p 54-58.

[73] Interview with coachman Krishnan in Tiruvayyaru; June 2006.

# Chapter 9

*"Is there any bliss greater than this- to deem it sufficient to dance, to sing divine music, to pray for His presence and to be in communion with Him in mind?"* (Tyagaraja in "Intakannaanandamemi", raga Bilahari, tala Rupakam)[1]

~

During the years 1935-37, attacks on what remained of the old Devadasi system continued. In 1934, the Bombay Presidency passed an act which made it illegal for women to be dedicated to temples. In 1937, the newly constituted Madras Legislative Assembly saw the introduction of a Bill banning Devadasi dedication. This was referred to a Select Committee and before it could table its report, the Second World War broke out in 1939. The Viceroy, Lord Linlithgow announced the decision of the Indian Government to join the war without consulting the provincial ministries, as a result of which they resigned in protest. The Bill was pigeon-holed for the time being.[2] There was however no reaction from the Devadasis to these moves. Nagarathnamma herself appears to have not made any statement on the subject, though the gradual disappearance of her kind must have caused her immense sorrow. She channelled all her energies into the conduct of the *Aradhana*.

The year 1939 saw the arrival of a music-loving government official in Tanjavur. This was SY Krishnaswami, ICS, who was appointed as

Special Officer of the Kaveri Delta Region.[3] He had been a great patron of the 'Veena' Dhanam family and knew all the musicians well. Being an acceptable mediator to all, his efforts in bringing about unity among the musicians with respect to the *Aradhana* began to bear fruit. Circumstances were also favourable to unification. The Periya Katchi was eager to throw in the towel. Even within the Chinna Katchi there were signs of revolt. Ariyakkudi Ramanuja Iyengar was under pressure from his life companion, KS Dhanammal, a Devadasi, to give women an opportunity to perform at the *Aradhana*. Maharajapuram Viswanatha Iyer could harbour no ill will towards anyone and was happy as long as the *Aradhana* was conducted each year for Tyagaraja, no matter who did it. The flautist Palladam Sanjeeva Rao, for long a senior member of the Chinna Katchi, with whose rendition of Tyagaraja's "Chetulara" (raga Bhairavi), the group's *Aradhana* would begin, was also feeling the strain. Soolamangalam Vaidyanatha Bhagavatar would possibly have carried on despite all these signs, had it not been for the sudden death in 1938 of Mangudi Chidambara Bhagavatar. The passing away of a junior contemporary shook Vaidyanatha Bhagavatar and he was now somewhat unsure of himself. Still, by end 1939, he had begun making plans for the Chinna Katchi's *Aradhana* of 1940 and orders were given to the printers to prepare the invitation cards and handbills.

It was at this time that Musiri Subramania Iyer, by then a close friend of SY Krishnaswami, pressed for a meeting of all the factions in Madras. This took place on 10th January 1940 at the latter's residence, with Ariyakkudi Ramanuja Iyengar attending on behalf of the Chinna Katchi. The Tiruvizhimizhalai Brothers represented the Periya Katchi and Bangalore Nagarathnamma along with CV Rajagopalachariar represented her group. Musiri Subramania Iyer and Semmangudi Srinivasa Iyer too attended. The meeting concluded with an agreement in principle to conduct a unified *Aradhana*. The invitation and handbills were then drafted out and these were sent through

CV Rajagopalachariar to Vaidyanatha Bhagavatar for his approval. A letter, signed by Ariyakkudi, Musiri and Semmangudi accompanied these drafts. The three musicians appealed to Vaidyanatha Bhagavatar to withhold the invitations of the Chinna Katchi and to go through the draft invitations enclosed, to satisfy himself about the sincerity of their motives.

A second meeting was held at Trichy a few days later in which Soolamangalam Vaidyanatha Bhagavatar too participated. Here he laid down his conditions for unification.

The first was on the rights of the disciples belonging to Tyagaraja's lineage to worship at the Samadhi, which was done by Rajagopala Bhagavatar as their representative. Vaidyanatha Bhagavatar stated that he would never agree to worship by Ramudu Bhagavatar and that even post-unification, a separate *puja* by Rajagopala Bhagavatar, representing the Chinna Katchi ought to be allowed. This was agreed to.

The second was that the *shraddha* or annual rite ought to be done as per the *Sastra*s and food for the same must be cooked in the ritually pure fashion. This food must only be offered to the 16 Brahmins representing the soul of Tyagaraja and none else could partake of it. This was also agreed to. Bhagavatar however agreed that the *shraddha* would henceforth be a common rite to all Katchis and could be conducted at Ramudu Bhagavatar's residence.

The last condition was that under no circumstances could the *nagaswaram* artistes be allowed to perform from the dais. They had to stand outside the Samadhi and perform as per tradition. Surprisingly, the Tiruvizhimizhalai Brothers agreed to this also without any argument.[4]

Amidst all these negotiations and parleys, Musiri Subramania Iyer emerged as a key player. He was fluent in English, had friends in high places and could charm his way into the heart of the most recalcitrant and hidebound musician. Assisting him in every way, giving indications of the smooth operator that he was to become later on in life, was Semmangudi. Musiri, given his experience at the Music Academy, of which he was a key member, felt that musicians ought to band together into an organisation on the lines of the Academy to celebrate the *Aradhana* each year. The Sri Tyagabrahma Mahotsava Sabha was thus registered and rather like the coalition ministries of today, a truly enormous and unwieldy committee was put together in order to accommodate all factions. Significantly, the *Sabha* was registered with its head office in Madras and not Tiruvayyaru, indicating that it was the city that was going to be the centre of action rather than Tyagaraja's village. Also, as in the case of the Music Academy, the top office-bearers were not from the music fraternity. Raja Sir Annamalai Chettiar, the business baron of Chettinad was made President. The Trustees were the Yuvarajah of Pithapuram, Sir RK Shanmukham Chetty, Dewan of Cochin and by then the patron of dancer T Balasaraswathi, K Srinivasan of *The Hindu*, the well-known lawyer of Mylapore KS Jayarama Iyer, the business and landholding magnate VS Thyagaraja Mudaliar and CVCTV Venkatachalam Chetty, a businessman.

This list merits scrutiny. For by then the music world was in the throes of what was known as the Tamil Isai Movement, with one group demanding that Tamil songs ought to be given importance in concerts and the other claiming that Tamil was a non-musical language. The President of the Sabha was an avid supporter of the Tamil Isai lobby. Among the trustees, three (Sir RK Shanmukham Chetty, VS Thyagaraja Mudaliar and CVCTV Venkatachalam Chetty) were of the same faction while the Yuvarajah of Pithapuram belonged to the anti-Tamil faction. KS Jayarama Iyer, the lawyer and K Srinivasan of the Press were probably neutral. Yet they had all come together in supporting an organisation that was meant to commemorate Tyagaraja, a Telugu composer. While this could be attributed to the greatness of Tyagaraja, it was also equally due to the man whose name followed immediately below the

Trustees, in the list of office- bearers, as Secretary- Treasurer, that of Musiri Subramania Iyer. In a period of one month he had pole-vaulted from being a rank outsider to becoming the prime mover of the *Aradhana*. S Subramania Pillai, one of the Tiruvizhimizhalai Brothers was another Secretary. There were two Assistant Secretaries of whom Nagarathnamma's devoted assistant CV Rajagopalachariar was one.

The names of 38 musicians as members of the Governing Body came below them. This included names of several musicians who had been involved in the conduct of the *Aradhana* in past years. Significantly, there were five women comprising Alamelu Jayarama Iyer (wife of KS Jayarama Iyer and a singer and patron of the arts in her own right), Bangalore Nagarathnamma, C Saraswathi Bai, T Balasaraswathi and KB Sundarambal, the singer and drama/cine artiste. Lording it over the entire list of office- bearers were four royal patrons, the Maharajahs of Mysore, Gwalior and Travancore and the Junior Maharani of Travancore, Sethu Parvathi Bayi. In a matter of few days the *Aradhana* had transformed itself from a simple musical and religious tribute into a huge social event with participation becoming a matter of social prestige. Such a star-studded event needed finance and for the first time the *Aradhana* needed a bank for handling funds. The Chettiar dominated Indian Bank became the banker for the event. It was also decided that souvenirs would be brought out each year, which would not only be a record of what had happened during the *Aradhana* but also a vehicle to carry advertisements from sponsors. These advertisements would bring in the much-needed money, for a mega event needed a mega budget as well.[5]

A formal programme for the conduct of the *Aradhana* was put together. For it was no longer simply a question of a few musicians banding together, observing a religious rite and then singing a few songs. The committee of office-bearers now felt that the event needed a formal inauguration just like it was done during the annual conferences of the Music Academy and other city-based *Sabhas*. A proper schedule of concerts was put together, as was the practice in the December Music Season in Madras. A clear listing of who would sing after whom and be accompanied by which artistes was compiled. The earlier system where a Soolamangalam Vaidyanatha Bhagavatar or a Bangalore Nagarathnamma could simply ask someone to come forward and sing was not feasible any longer. The presence of bigwigs on the committee also meant that their favourites had to be accommodated on the concert platform as well. Musical merit was no longer the sole consideration.

The *Aradhana* of 1940 was a grand event. The programmes were held in a specially erected, electrically illuminated pavilion in front of the Samadhi. All musicians worked hard to ensure that everything went through without a hitch. C Rajagopalachari (Rajaji), the well-known Congressman and ex-Premier of Madras Presidency, though a personality not known for his musical inclinations, inaugurated the celebrations. It was a five-day event with the third day being the *Aradhana* proper. Harikesanallur Muthiah Bhagavatar, who had, true to his word, stayed away as along as the *Aradhana* was being observed separately by the factions, attended the celebrations and participated with gusto. Embracing Soolamangalam Vaidyanatha Bhagavatar in Tiruvayyaru's main street, he remarked that it was like the coming together of the northern and southern spires of the Panchanadeeswara Temple of Tiruvayyaru.[6]

But Vaidyanatha Bhagavatar was far from happy. The unthinkable had happened. Two days prior to the commencement of the festivities, TN Rajarathinam Pillai, the leading *nagaswaram* performer had chided his fellow artiste Tiruvizhimizhalai Subramania Pillai over his agreeing to Bhagavatar's condition that no *nagaswaram* artiste would be allowed to perform from the dais. In characteristic fashion Rajarathinam had told Subramania Pillai that it was better he resigned from the committee if he could not look after the interests of his own community. Musiri Subramania Iyer intervened and the committee went into a huddle. At the end of the meeting it was announced that *nagaswaram* artistes would be allowed to perform from the dais.[7] There was jubilation among the pipers but for an orthodox man like Vaidyanatha Bhagavatar the about-turn was shocking.

· The first day of the celebrations witnessed several musical performances culminating with that of Semmangudi Srinivasa Iyer, which went on till late in the night. The highlights of the second day included performances by Madurai Mani Iyer, the flautist Palladam Sanjeeva Rao and Musiri Subramania Iyer. The third day being the *Aradhana* proper, witnessed two separate *puja*s at the Samadhi, one by the group led by Rajagopala Bhagavatar representing the Chinna Katchi, thereby respecting Vaidyanatha Bhagavatar's wishes and the second by Ramudu Bhagavatar representing the entire music community. The *nagaswaram* artistes, as per the recent changes, performed and then followed musical homage by various singers and instrumentalists, with each man or woman rendering one song. The *shraddha* ceremony was performed at the residence of Ramudu Bhagavatar at 1:00 pm, in the presence of Soolamangalam Vaidyanatha Bhagavatar and others.

What of Nagarathnamma in the meanwhile? Nothing could describe her delight as she went about the village seeing the grandeur with which the event was being celebrated. True she was no longer the prime mover of an *Aradhana* for her patron saint. But all that mattered to her was that Tyagaraja's annual rite had received enormous public attention and that all musicians were now united in their homage to the personality on whom their profession largely depended. "All my wishes are fulfilled", she wrote. "The two factions have united with me and what more can I ask for when the celebrations took place without any problems at the Samadhi itself?"[8]

Music concerts began at 3:30 pm on *Aradhana* day and Naga-rathnamma sang from 6:00 to 8:30 pm and was followed by Ariyakkudi Ramanuja Iyengar.

Soolamangalam Vaidyanatha Bhagavatar's *Harikatha* was scheduled at 10:30 pm. Just as he was about to begin, Nagarathnamma arrived and slowly climbed up to the dais. The vast crowd applauded her as she took the mike and addressing Bhagavatar said that it had long been her wish to sit by his side when he performed and with his permission her desire could be fulfilled that day. She then spoke a few words in praise of Bhagavatar. The audience cheered her repeatedly. Bhagavatar nodded acquiescence and Nagarathnamma sat by his side and heard his discourse. Even though she did not say it, it was clear to the audience that she had emerged the winner in the struggle for equality.

The highlight of the fourth day was the *Harikatha* performance by Banni Bai. On the morning of the fifth day, Harikesanallur Muthiah Bhagavatar performed a *Harikatha*, at the end of which Soolamangalam Vaidyanatha Bhagavatar rose to address the audience. In his speech he said that he had often been blamed for preventing a unified *Aradhana*. He was glad, he said, that he had been able to witness the common celebration in his own lifetime. That night, a grand procession was taken out with Tyagaraja's portrait being carried in a palanquin. *Nagaswaram* artistes performed en route and the procession returned to the Samadhi at 6:30 the next morning. The celebrations concluded with a speech by Vaidyanatha Bhagavatar summarising the *Aradhana* festivities. Outwardly he lavished praise on the event but he had made up his mind to stay away from the celebrations in subsequent years.[9] He realised that he was ploughing a lonely furrow, with his stance on women, *nagaswaram* artistes and other issues. At the same time, he felt that his role in the *Aradhana* was largely over and that it was now in other hands which would carry it forward in the years to come. Bhagavatar retired to Soolamangalam village where he continued conducting the Bhagavata Mela, a dance drama that was famous in the region and held in several villages.

In the meanwhile, plans were already afoot for the Tyagaraja *Aradhana* of 1941. Many meetings among musicians and music lovers were held and a series of concerts was planned in Madras city to raise funds. The programmes were held at the Rasika Ranjani Sabha premises, Mylapore with a grand inauguration on the 22nd of September with the eminent advocate S Srinivasa Iyengar as Chief Guest and the music-loving Mayor of Madras, S Sathyamurthy presiding. Nagarathnamma was an honoured invitee and was asked to propose a vote of thanks. In her speech she said that Tyagaraja, in his song "Sadhinchene" (raga Arabhi) had sung of Rama always having his way with people. Similarly Tyagaraja too had had his way and she was glad that the *Aradhana* had become a matter of interest to many.[10] The highlight of the series, with the maximum gate collections was the concert of MS Subbulakshmi (MS), who as was her wont, sang gratis for the event. "Pronunciation faulty", had been the terse judgement of Nagarathnamma in the 1930s when someone had asked her opinion on the music of MS.[11] All that had changed by 1941. MS was known for excellence in every aspect of music. Her success in the fund-raising series pleased Nagarathnamma no end. Clearly women had come to stay as far as the *Aradhana* was concerned. On 23rd December, the last day of the series, Tyagaraja's portrait was taken out in procession on an elephant, with musicians singing along. It must have amused the composer who had eschewed such grand modes of conveyance and had largely, walked all his life. But to his devotee, standing at a doorstep nearby, with tears of joy blurring her vision, it was a dream come true.

Nagarathnamma did not raise funds for the *Aradhana* by performing concerts. Her own reserves were now reduced to what she needed to lead a life of dignity in her remaining years. She therefore went about requesting her highly-placed patrons and friends to donate money for the *Aradhana*. Through Dr KN Kesari she obtained an introduction to Jayachamaraja Wodeyar, the Maharajah of Mysore. She proceeded there for a command performance and was rewarded at the end with not one but two gold bracelets. This was a departure from custom at the Mysore Court and was remarked upon by several people. The Maharajah, who was a man of erudition, had been moved by her learning and her devotion to Tyagaraja.[12] Unhesitatingly Nagarathnamma donated both the bracelets as her contribution towards the *Aradhana* celebrations.

Not that she was received with equal warmth everywhere. Visiting Nellore during these years with CV Rajagopalachariar in tow, she experienced a different reception. The arrival of a Devadasi was not looked upon with favour by those whom she had planned to tap for donations and while Rajagopalachariar stayed at the potential donor's house, Nagarathnamma was made to stay at a guest house that belonged to the TVS Group of Companies. The next morning, Nagarathnamma called on Rajagopalachariar's hosts to seek donations. Coffee was served in a brass tumbler for Nagarathnamma, while silver was used for the house guest. The women remained indoors. She was asked to sing. Stung to the quick at the treatment, Nagarathnamma sang Tyagaraja's "Edutanilicite" (raga Shankarabharanam). The refrain of the song went thus:

*"If you come and stand before me, will you lose all your wealth? Is it possible for me to transgress my fate? Should I, knowing this, sit quiet and be deceived?"*

It was a well-deserved rebuke and one that the Telugu-knowing audience understood only too well. The donation that came was handsome and Nagarathnamma took it, but not before remarking at the backwardness of her hosts.[13]

The 1941 *Aradhana* exceeded the previous years in grandeur and scale. The festival was inaugurated by Sir RK Shanmukham Chetty.

There were over a 100 principal artistes to be accommodated in concert slots during the five-day celebrations and the programmes, which in earlier years used to begin only after midday, now began in the morning hours and went on till late at night. Artistes were given time slots, according to seniority, as in the Music Academy with the senior-most, performing for 45 minutes in the night. The others were placed in 15, 20 and 30 minutes categories, depending on seniority and were scheduled during the day. Nagarathnamma's performance was scheduled on *Aradhana* day and she performed in the senior slot, accompanied by Sivasubramania Iyer on the violin and Ramamritham Iyer on the *mridangam*. There was just one disappointment. Soolamangalam Vaidyanatha Bhagavatar had resolutely refused to attend, despite the entreaties of Musiri Subramania Iyer. Harikesanallur Muthiah Bhagavatar, on coming to know of Vaidyanatha Bhagavatar's decision to abstain had refused to participate as well.[14] The Trichy station of All India Radio broadcast sections of the music concerts. This was open only to graded artistes and Nagarathnamma being one was also recorded. As she mounted the stage, memories of the years of struggle must have surged inside her. She, a woman and a Devadasi was being given a status equal to that of many men. "I am a *Devar Adiyal*" she announced into the mike and then began her concert.[15] The war cry of the last Devadasi was broadcast all over the network. The assembled crowds gasped and then broke into wild applause. It was a moment of victory for all that Nagarathnamma had fought for.

The 1942 *Aradhana* too followed the same pattern of fund-raising concerts in Madras, the opening of the *Aradhana* by a bigwig and a series of crowded programmes right through the five-day festival. Once again the festivities opened with Nagarathnamma singing the first prayer in praise of Tyagaraja at the Samadhi.[16]

A challenge of a different nature faced Nagarathnama in 1942. Despite her reduced circumstances and the sale of most of her jewels, tales abounded about her wealth. She was the victim of an attack by thieves one night, when they not only decamped with some jewels but also inflicted injury on her person. Nagarathnamma was shaken and for some time did not have the courage to sleep alone at her house. In that hour of insecurity, she wanted someone who could speak her mother tongue, Kannada. Suddenly, Tiruvayyaru, with its Tamil and Telugu-speaking peoples appeared alien. But at the same time, the call of Tyagaraja was so powerful that she could not leave the place. She sent word to Rama Rao, a Kannada gentleman who lived a few streets away. Would he and his family have any objection if she came and stayed with them for a few months? Rao and his wife Saguna Bai, a descendant of one time Mysore *Dewan* VP Madhava Rao, welcomed her with open arms. The residence, well known as Bhat Goswami House in the village, was a large one that spanned an entire street. The Rao family had vast lands in the area and had at one time so many horse carriages in their possession that the place was called Gadi Khana (storeroom for coaches). Nagarathnamma stayed at their house for six months, during which time she taught the Rao children Tyagaraja's songs. She maintained a separate kitchen but gradually barriers were broken and it became one house. [17]

Madras was being evacuated owing to war-time scares and several people were moving to the Tanjavur district. Among them was young Janaki, Nagarathnamma's disciple and sister of Shakuntala Sethuraman, her close friend. Janaki and her parents too lived as tenants of Rama Rao and she came to learn many songs from Nagarathnamma. [18]

In the meanwhile, Sivasubramania Iyer the violinist came to know of the attack on Nagarathnamma. He immediately came to Tiruvayyaru and made arrangements for Seethapathi, his nephew to sleep in the verandah of Nagarathnamma's house every night, in order to provide her security. Emboldened by this, Nagarathnamma returned home. A good six months had passed since the burglary, but neither the thieves nor the stolen goods could be traced. The old lady bore her loss with equanimity. The jewels she said had been given her by Tyagaraja and now he had taken them away.[19]

A cholera epidemic broke out in early 1943. The District Collector forbade the conduct of the *Aradhana* as the gathering of large crowds would only exacerbate the problem. There was disappointment in Tiruvayyaru as musicians who had come down to celebrate the festival whiled away their time. The *Aradhana* Committee made repeated representations to the district administration only to be turned down. Nagarathnamma alone remained unperturbed. She predicted that Tyagaraja would ultimately have his way and that she was certain that the Collector would relent. And miraculously that is what happened. The administration allowed the conduct of a three-day *Aradhana* and realising that it was the glamour of the radio broadcast that attracted musicians and so the crowds, forbade the AIR from relaying the performances. The *Aradhana* that year was therefore rather subdued. To Nagarathnamma what mattered was that it was conducted.[20] Rumours abounded that Soolamangalam Vaidyanatha Bhagavatar had relented after many letters from Musiri and would be attending the *Aradhana*. But the old man, by then ill with diabetes had become quite frail. He was advised by his sons not to make the journey.

In October 1943, Vaidyanatha Bhagavatar realised that he did not have long to live. He took holy orders and became a *sanyasi* just as Tyagaraja had done. He lived for three days after the event and passed away on 24th October that year. He was buried with due honours near his village and a Samadhi was erected at the spot.[21]

Among the three who had conducted the Tyagaraja *Aradhana*, it was Nagarathnamma who was the sole survivor. And she became one of the attractions of Tiruvayyaru. Every visitor made a beeline to her house after visiting the village temple and Tyagaraja's Samadhi. If she was not speaking to them, she was teaching music to the village children. By then, the propagation of Tyagaraja's songs had become her greatest ambition. Knowing full well, that children needed some enticement, she hit upon a winner of a plan. She would sit in a specially made reclining chair, commodious enough to accommodate her large frame and sing with them. Hanging from her right hand would be a string bag from which at the end of the lessons, she would pull out handfuls of coins and distribute them among the children. This made her lessons a great success and in time, made the children love music. She was adored by the people of the village and when her assistant Seethapathi set out shopping on her behalf, shopkeepers would vie with one another to give him whatever she had ordered, at greatly reduced prices. Many vegetable vendors gave freely from their wares. Women thronged her doorstep to receive the *kumkum* and turmeric that she distributed as though they were gifts from the gods.[22]

The legend of Tyagaraja had always been a powerful subject for *Harikatha* performances and plays. So the medium of cinema too was attracted by it. Even in the silent film era, rather incredibly, a film had been made on Tyagaraja. When the talkies came, yet another film was attempted which was not successful. Then in 1944, Chittoor V Nagaiah, the well-known actor began working on 'Thyagayya' in Telugu. The film was shot extensively in Tiruvayyaru and assisting Nagaiah in the musical aspects of the film were many musicians. Nagarathnamma was an honoured advisor.[23] When the film was released in 1946 it was a great success and Nagaiah, ever the soul of generosity asked Nagarathnamma as to what she wanted as a gift. The singer replied that she needed nothing, but Nagaiah realising that she was still living in rented accommodation, offered to help her in buying a house. Thus 'Tyagaraja Nilayam', a modest house on Tiruvayyaru's South Main Street was acquired and became Nagarathnamma's home. She however made it clear that it was more of a guest house attached to the Samadhi and that it was open to any pilgrim who came to Tiruvayyaru to pay homage to Tyagaraja. It was also open to anyone who wished to learn the composer's songs from her.[24]

The *Aradhana* became an even more popular event thanks to the film. Larger and larger crowds began descending on Tiruvayyaru, putting the organisers' capabilities to severe stress. The musical offerings by each musician became further reduced in duration of time, with the result that it appeared to writer Kalki Krishnamurthy that a musician had hardly ascended the dais when he was ordered off it, to make way for the next. The quality of music too had deteriorated according to many, with juniors and amateurs making it to the stage by exerting influence on the organisers.[25] Nagarathnamma and a few other musicians were disappointed. They decided to voice their disenchantment with the conduct of the *Aradhana*.

The venue for their meeting was highly symbolic, for it was the home of Vaidyanatha Bhagavatar in Soolamangalam. They had all now realised what the old man had meant when he had worried about dilution in standards and had expressed sorrow over a musical event becoming an "official function".[26] The meeting, held on 24th February 1947, elected Palladam Sanjeeva Rao as its leader and demanded that the practice of having political and industrial bigwigs to inaugurate the *Aradhana* be discontinued forthwith. Yet another resolution was that the *Aradhana* Committee ought to have only musicians in it. A third, decried the practice of indiscriminately organising concerts of very short durations during the festival.[27] These resolutions were duly conveyed to the organising committee but fell on deaf ears. The *Aradhana* continued much the same way in subsequent years.

There is no record of Nagarathnamma expressing her opinion on the struggle for Indian independence about which she could not have been unaware. Many of her community had participated in it. Madras Lalithangi had been the first Carnatic artiste to record a song with freedom as it's theme.[28] Tanjavur Kamukannammal was an ardent champion of the Congress party.[29] Padmasini Bai had given up a flourishing career in Harikatha to participate in the freedom struggle.[30] But an article Nagarathnamma wrote later, gives her opinion about colonial rule.

"Around 300 years ago, men from the East India Company of England arrived here and through intoxicating drinks and other temptations subdued all the local rulers and enticing our people by their language, strange dress and alien food habits, stole away our precious gems. They gave us in return cheap porcelain dishes, cigarettes and other narcotics and many types of worthless biscuits and enslaved our people and made them commit sins."[31] Given this strongly-worded indictment, it is reasonable to assume that she must have rejoiced when India became free in 1947. However, to artistes of her generation it also spelt the end of the princely order as a strong source of sustenance and support.

Whatever be her disappointment over the conduct of the festival, Nagarathnamma's devotion to Tyagaraja was as strong as ever. It was her dearest wish that a *Choultry* bearing the name of Mysore ought to come up in Tiruvayyaru. She therefore planned one last visit to her native state. The timing could not have been worse. Nagarathnamma herself was not keeping well. The state had acceded to the Indian Union in August but Mysore Congressmen feared that princely rule would continue, thereby denying them a share in power. There were consequently *hartals*, protests marches and large scale arrests.[32] It was not the peaceful Mysore that Nagarathnamma knew. The *Dewan*, Sir A Ramaswami Mudaliar, with great difficulty, organised a few performance opportunities for her. The collection was meagre and Nagarathnamma was disappointed. Someone suggested to her that she could have collected much more by performing in Madras. But Nagarathnamma disagreed. She wanted *Kannadigas* to build a *Choultry* in Tiruvayyaru and she did not want to be obliged to non-*Kannadigas* for this.[33]

On her way back Nagarathnamma stayed in Bangalore at the residence of singer, Tarabai. Even during that short stay she wanted to impart lessons in music and gathered a few students. DV Gundappa, the eminent writer called on her. She was teaching a particularly difficult song of Mysore Sadasiva Rao, to a few students and was splitting the syllables so that they could grasp the words easily. Why bother with such difficult songs asked DVG. "Our gurus have composed these and it is our duty to pass them on to the subsequent generations. If we concentrated on the simple songs alone, what will happen to the masterpieces?" she replied.

DVG, who, when young, had been a staunch Anti-Nautch lobbyist, was clearly fascinated by her personality. He became a frequent visitor. On one occasion, he found her suffering from headache. With a view to alleviate her suffering he tried to get her to talk of her past triumphs. "Why bother about that?" she asked. "I was named Nagarathnam, then I became a *Bhoga Ratnam* (a gem among worldly pleasures) and now I am merely *Roga Ratnam* (a storehouse of illnesses)". Not to be outwitted, he reminded her that she was also *Raga Ratnam* (an expert in singing ragas) and a *Tyaga Ratnam* (an epitome when it came to sacrifices). He asked her to demonstrate her skills in *abhinaya*. What followed was a half hour demonstration which moved DVG. Remaining seated all the while, Nagarathnamma displayed her skills in mime for the Jayadeva song "Yahi Madhava".[34]

The year 1947 brought joys and sorrows to her. The *Radhika Santwanamu* was brought out of the closet, when T Prakasam, Premier of Madras Province ordered the lifting of the ban on the work and Vavilla Press brought out new editions.[35] If this vindicated her stance on the capabilities of Devadasi women, her fight against the banning of the system, met with defeat. The Madras Legislative Assembly on 26th November passed the Madras Devadasi (Prevention of Dedication) Bill 1947. It became illegal for any woman to be dedicated to a temple and performing of the *Kumbharati*, was banned in all temples.[36] By then, there were hardly any practising Devadasis. Brahmin women had taken to classical dance, which was now portrayed as religious, holy and a form of prayer. The songs were however, largely, the very same ones to which Devadasis had once danced. A far more corrupting influence by then was cinema, but nobody had noticed that. The handmaidens of God had been outlawed forever. Very few like T Balasaraswathi had the courage of conviction to continue dancing in the traditional way. But then women like Balasaraswathi, very much in the Nagarathnamma mould, were rare. The majority chose to deny that they were Devadasis and with them several precious music and dance pieces vanished. It was a grievous loss to the world of art.

In 1949, it was decided by the *Aradhana* committee that musicians ought to sing together by way of homage to Tyagaraja, when worship was offered at the Samadhi on *Aradhana* day. Five songs of the composer in the ragas Nata, Gaula, Arabhi, Varali and Sri, now called the *pancharatnams* were rendered for the first time at the *Aradhana* by all the musicians. Prior to this, Nagarathnamma was given the honour of singing as verse, the 108 names of Tyagaraja that she had composed and as she sang, she performed the *kumbharati*.[37] It was exactly what a Devadasi would do at the temple to which she was dedicated and Nagarathnamma, who had never been dedicated to any shrine, was now performing the same ritual at Tyagaraja's shrine. The Government had banned the custom, but in a temple that was owned by her nobody could object to what she was doing. Immediately after her performance, the flautist Palladam Sanjeeva Rao rendered Tyagaraja's "Chetulara" (raga Bhairavi) and then the musicians sang the five songs in chorus.

## References
[1] Ramanujachari, C; p 589.

[2] Jordan, Kay K; p 143-5.

[3] Krishnaswami, SY; Memoirs of a Mediocre Man; Bhamati Books; Bangalore; 1983; p 194.

[4] Soolamangalam; p 56-59.

[5] Saint Thyagaraja Festival Souvenir; Sri Thyagabrahma Mahotsava Sabha; Madras; p 5.

[6] Soolamangalam; p 56-59.

[7] Sundaram, BM; "Quest for Self Respect and Equity"; article in Sruti; Issue no 171; December 1998, Chennai; p 38.

[8] Nagarathnam, Bangalore; article in the souvenir of the Sri Thyagabrahma Mahotsava Sabha; Tiruvayyaru; 1951; p 11.

[9] Soolamangalam; p 56-59.

[10] The Hindu; 23rd September 1940.

[11] Nayudu, WS Krishnaswami; My Memoirs; Madras; 1977; p 449.

[12] Grihalakshmi; p 54.

[13] Anecdote related by social historian Randor Guy.

[14] Soolamangalam; p 56-59.

[15] Sruti; BNR; p 14.

[16] The Hindu; October 5th, 22nd, November 30th, December 23rd, 25th 1941 and January 6th 1942.

[17] Interview with Saguna Bai, friend of Nagarathnamma; Madras; 2007.

[18] Interview with Janaki Subramaniam; Bangalore; July 2007.

[19] Interview with Seethapathi, assistant to Bangalore Nagarathnamma at Tiruvayyaru, May 2006.

[20] Rasikan; "Adal Padal"; article in Ananda Vikatan; Madras; January 31st, 1943; p 22-24.

[21] Sriram V; "Soolamangalam Vaidyanatha Bhagavatar (1866-1943), A Katha"; article in Sruti; Issue 233; February 2004; Chennai; p 21-36.

[22] Interview with Seethapathi, assistant to Bangalore Nagarathnamma at Tiruvayyaru, May 2006.

[23] Sastry, KNT; Chittoor V Nagaiah, A Monograph; Publications Division, Ministry of Information and Broadcasting, Govt. of India; New Delhi; p 78-89.

[24] Sruti; BNR; p 16

[25] For a detailed discussion on the deterioration of the Aradhana see "Thinnai Pecchu"; article in Ananda Vikatan; Madras; 15th January 1950; p 30-32.

[26] Soolamangalam; p 56-59.

[27] The Hindu; 18th March; 1947.

[28] Carnatic Summer; p 175.

[29] Sundaram, BM; p 98.

[30] Rajam, S; "Master in the Art of Story Telling", article in Sruti; Issue 263, August 2006; p 37.

[31] Nagarathnam, Bangalore; article in souvenir of Sri Thyagabrahma Mahotsava Sabha; Tiruvayyaru; 1951; p 12.

[32] Manor, James; "Gandhian Politics and the Challenge to Princely Authority in Mysore, 1936-47"; article in Congress and the Raj; DA Low (Ed); Heinemann; London; 1977; p 421-24.

[33] Vasudevachar, Mysore; p 72.

[34] DVG.

[35] Women Writing In India; p 5.

[36] Jordan, Kay K; p 145-6.

[37] Rasikan; "Adal Padal"; article in Ananda Vikatan; Madras; 30th January 1949; p 33-35.

# Chapter 10

*"I feel blessed to hear people say that I am your own. It is
probably the result of my worship in the past, or it may be the
effect of your own grace."* (Tyagaraja in "Sita Manohara", raga
Manohari, tala Adi)[1]

∼

By 1948, Nagarathnamma had visibly declined in health. There was
considerable speculation as to who would be the beneficiary of her
properties and jewellery. The Tyagabrahma Mahotsava Sabha was keen
to be given the Samadhi and the surrounding lands. It had already
acquired the house where Tyagaraja lived. But Nagarathnamma thought
differently.

The will was presented at the Sub Registrar's office in Sowcarpet,
Madras on 4th January 1949 and registered the subsequent day. Though
the legalese had been taken care of by her friend CV Rajagopalachariar,
it was clear that the thoughts and actions dictated in the document
were all Nagarathnamma's.

The will begins with the proud declaration that she was the daughter
of Haggada Devanna Kotha Putta Lakshmiammal Vaishnavi. It then
gives the history of the *Aradhana* in brief and Nagarathnamma's own
role in renovating the Samadhi and the sacrifices she had made to
ensure that it became an edifice worthy of Tyagaraja. The account
ends with the unification of the factions into the Sri Tyagabrahma

Mahotsava Sabha and the commendation that "the *sangeetha vidwans* have got to be congratulated for their cooperation in a great cause". It was her wish and prayer she said, that "they will continue to show the very same spirit of cooperation and help also in future in celebrating this great national music festival of our country".

However the *Sabha* was not to be the owner of the Samadhi premises, after her death. She dedicated all her immovable and movable properties "all purchased by me with my own self earned money" to a trust which would become the absolute owner on her demise. The body was to be named as the Vidyasundari Bangalore Nagarathinam Trust and it was to have three Trustees, CV Rajagopalachariar, TA Ramachandra Rao and V Meenakshisundaram Iyer, the teacher at the Tondaimandalam School, Madras, who had been her factotum during her lonely years in Madras.

The Trust, declared Nagarathnamma, should ensure that the site of the Samadhi be always made available to the Tyagabrahma Mahotsava Sabha to celebrate the *Aradhana* festival and if that Sabha ceased to exist then the area must be made available to any other individual or institution willing to celebrate the event. There was however one proviso – permission to observe the *Aradhana* at the premises may be refused or withdrawn if the Sabha tried to "debar lady artistes and singers including Devadasis to give their performance at the dais".

Perhaps anticipating a time when land would become dear and the open space in front of the Samadhi put to commercial purposes, Nagarathnamma clearly forbade any permanent construction, as it would mar the beauty and pious atmosphere of the place. The Samadhi, she declared must always be open to public worship with people coming in to offer "pious recitations, *bhajans* and similar musical performances in tune with Hindu religion and *dharma*". Ramudu Bhagavatar and his descendants, Nagarathnamma stipulated, should continue the daily *puja* at the premises, but could be removed for misconduct, insubordination or incompetence. In such an event she wanted the rights of worship to be assigned to another Telugu Brahmin family and if that was not available, then a Tamil priest ought to be found.

The will then listed out the various charities and annual *pujas* that Nagarathnamma was supporting in various parts of Madras Presidency. This included worship on special days at temples in Madras city and Mysore and the observance of her mother's day of passing. The budget for each of these was specified and the Trustees were instructed to carry out these tasks year after year. The icons in her own *puja* together with the pictures of Gods and Goddesses she had acquired in Mysore, Nagarathnamma made over to the Samadhi and left behind clear instructions as to the mode of worship and the offerings to be made.

The document ends with a listing of all her savings, properties and jewels all of which she made over to the Trust founded in her name which would administer the Samadhi after her death.[2]

Having made out her last will and testament, Nagarathnamma spent her remaining days in peace in Tiruvayyaru. To be able to walk around the streets where Tyagaraja had conducted his *Uncchavritti*, to be able to see the house where he lived, to watch the same river in which he had bathed, to sing his songs and to worship at his Samadhi was enough. Life held no other attractions. She made the occasional trip to Madras and the annual *Navaratri* journey to Venkatagiri, but otherwise she remained homebound. But any activity associated with Tyagaraja would energise her and she would set forth without delay. Thus it was that she visited Madurai despite being in indifferent health to preside along with T Chowdiah, the famed violinist and fellow disciple of Bidaram Krishnappa, at a modest Tyagaraja *Aradhana* festival in 1948. A music competition was held on that occasion and both of them selected a young lad as the winner and gifted him a *tambura*.[3] The winner, Madurai GS Mani, would become a well-known name in music, in later years.

Musicians and devotees continued coming home. To them, her gifts were portraits of Tyagaraja. One of the recipients was Janaki, her disciple. PR Thilagam, the last of the Kondis, whose hereditary rights to dance before the deity in Tiruvarur, Nagarathnamma had once challenged in her hot-headed days of youth, was another. It was with some trepidation that Thilagam introduced herself as the granddaughter of Kutti Ammal who had spiritedly opposed and won over Nagarathnamma in that tussle. But she need not have worried. Nagarathnamma was filled with peace in her last days and harboured no ill will towards anyone. She merely remarked admiringly that Thilagam came from a glorious ancestry.[4]

Any achievements by women gave her special joy. She would bless young girls who sang well and when KM Soundaryavalli, a housewife, sent in a few compositions which she had created on Tyagaraja, Nagarathnamma's joy knew no bounds. She sent a letter in reply warmly praising the woman for her work.[5] The compositions of Ogirala Veeraraghava Sharma, then a young composer, were also commended by her.

It was time for her work in connection with the Samadhi also to be recognised. For many years it was the annual practice of Dr KN Kesari, the founder of the women's magazine *Grihalakshmi* to reward accomplished women of arts and letters with a gold bracelet. The *Grihalakshmi Swarna Kankanam* award was highly regarded in the fields of literature and culture. In 1949, Nagarathnamma was selected for it and the event was held on 16th March that year, at Dr Kesari's residence, Kesari Kuteeram in Royapettah. The Maharani of Vizianagaram, Vidyawati Devi presided over the event. What perhaps gave greater joy to Nagarathnamma than the golden bracelet was the title *Tyaga Seva Saktha* (one who is unshakeable in service and sacrifice) conferred on her on the same occasion by the women of Madras. It was a day of nostalgia for her, for Dr Kesari and other speakers touched on the various significant events of her life in their speeches and praised her manifold achievements. Vai Mu Kothainayaki, the girl whom she had encouraged to take to a concert career and who was by then a celebrity in her own right as a publisher and editor of the women's magazine *Jaganmohini* was present. The prayer song was sung by ML Vasanthakumari, then a young artiste who was rapidly making it big as a Carnatic musician and a playback singer in films.

Her women friends from Tiruvayyaru had sent a message which read "No one has seen the Gods, Sri Rama & Krishna. Few have seen their devotee, Sri Thyagayya. Through Nagaratnamma, we were able to view the significance of his devotion."

Departing from her usual practice, Nagarathnamma did not donate the gold bracelet to the Tyagaraja Samadhi. It was given away to the Sarada Niketan, a home for the rehabilitation of widows. The *Grihalakshmi* issue of March 1949 carried many articles on her.[6]

Back in Tiruvayyaru, life resumed its normal routine except for one journey to Madras to attend the wedding of her disciple Janaki who after marriage would depart to far away Bihar. Nagarathnamma sang Tyagaraja's 'Dinamani Vamsa' (raga Harikamboji) and blessed the newly-wedded couple.[7]

The *Aradhana* of 1951 came and went. She did not perform in it, but offered her musical obeisance as usual, before the choral rendition of the *pancharatnam*s. C Rajagopalachari, then Home Minister, Government of India, inaugurated the festivities and during the course of his speech remarked that Nagarathnamma was a *sanyasini* and a saint whose ideals were worth emulating. He also said that even during his 1940 visit he had noticed musicians approaching her with awe and trepidation.[8] When she came to know of it, Nagarathnamma smiled wryly. After all it was the same Congress party of which he was a member which had all along fought for the abolition of the Devadasi system and had equated them with prostitutes. "Tell him," she said, "I am a mere *Devar Adiyal*".[9] The correspondent of *The Hindu* who was covering the event engaged her in conversation and during the course of it, she stated that though the celebrations had been spectacular, the element of piety was lacking. She was of the opinion that there was more of pomp and show than a feeling of simple offering and dedication. It appeared to her that many musicians missed the real significance of the occasion and attempted to convert it into a forum for exhibiting their learning. A clear distinction ought to have been made between Sri Tyagaraja's shrine and a music *Sabha*. She objected to the use of public address systems, which amplified the volume to such an extent that the peace and quiet of the Samadhi was disturbed. She desired that opportunities be given to people to sing for at least two hours in the sanctum. Her dream was that more and more women would come forward to propagate Tyagaraja's music. She also wanted music schools, *ashrams*, *bhajana mandirams* and libraries in Tiruvayyaru so that the place would become a centre for learning.[10] Clearly, she was now at odds with what was happening in the village, in the name of the *Aradhana* and perhaps even regretted the unification that had resulted in such cacophony and chaos.

Once the *Aradhana* was over, peace descended on Tiruvayyaru and as a wag once commented, Tyagaraja too returned to his Samadhi, having wisely stayed away while the festivities were going on. Nagarathnamma was the sole devotee in attendance and she was able to spend as much time as she wanted, singing the songs of the composer at his Samadhi. Her voice was as powerful as ever. To passers-by who stopped to listen to her music, it was an idyllic experience, with the coconut fronds swaying in the breeze, even as the river rippled by as though keeping time to her song.

Then one night, in Tiruvayyaru, she had yet another vision, rather like the one in 1921 which had altered the course of her life. Waking up, she dashed off a letter to her patron, the Rajah of Venkatagiri.

"Mahaprabhu," it said. "My Lord Sri Tyagaraja gave me *darshana* (vision) in a dream and commanded me to go to Venkatagiri, in order to be blessed by *Darshan* of Bhagavan who has come to *Bhuloka* (earth) and who is soon reaching Venkatagiri, in His travels. My lord told me that Bhagavan has assumed the name of Sri Sathya Sai. I shall come to Venkatagiri as soon as I hear from you."[11]

Members of the Venkatagiri family had become ardent devotees of the young seer and he was staying in the palace as an honoured guest. Nagarathnamma reached the town on *Janmashtami*, the day when the birth of Krishna is celebrated. *Bhajan*s were in full swing in the room in which the Baba was staying and a silence fell as Nagarathnamma walked in. She was introduced to the Baba, who having asked her to sit, requested her to sing. She asked him to suggest a song and he asked for Tyagaraja's "Sri Raghuvara Aprameya" (raga Kamboji). Nagarathnamma began the song and was soon lost in its melody. Those who were soaking in the musical atmosphere, soon realised that two voices were singing. The Baba had joined Nagarathnamma in the song. As the devotees gaped in wonder the song came to a close. Baba requested her for yet another song and joined her in it. What followed was a concert for over two hours with the Baba singing most of the songs with her. At the end of the performance, a pleased Baba asked Nagarathnamma if she desired anything.

There was nothing she wanted in this life she replied boldly, but she had two requests to make regarding her last moments on this earth. She wanted her end to be peaceful and she wanted to die fully conscious of her own passing so that she would have the time to chant the name of Rama as she drifted away. The Baba assured her that it would be so and then gifted her an idol of Lord Rama. Receiving the idol Nagarathnamma went into a trance. Baba signalled to everyone to get up and leave silently and he too went with them, leaving her alone in her experience of bliss. Nagarathnamma came to after a full 24 hours.[12]

Feeble in health, but happy in mind, Nagarathnamma spent the last days of her life in communion with Tyagaraja in Tiruvayyaru. One of her last visitors was AR Sundaram who called on her in April 1952. Sundaram, a talented singer, was asked to sing Tyagaraja's "Upacharamulanu" (raga Bhairavi) and as she sang, Nagarathnamma seated all the while, performed *abhinaya* for it. Sundaram was to later recall that it was one of the most thrilling experiences of her life.[13]

The summer of 1952 was intense and Nagarathnamma hated it as much as she had her first summer in Madras. She remained largely indoors, reclining in her special chair and watching the happenings in the street. There was always something of interest going on there. On 19th May, it was a funeral procession wending its way to the burning ghat. Someone came in and informed her that Ramudu Bhagavatar's young son had drowned in the Kaveri and it was his body that was being taken for cremation. The young lad had been very dear to Nagarathnamma and the shock of his demise brought on searing chest pain. As she staggered under its impact and fell back on attendants, who rushed to support her, it was clear to everyone that her last moments had come. A doctor was summoned urgently and word was sent to TA Ramachandra Rao and CV Rajagopalachariar. When they came in, they found her calmly preparing herself to meet her maker. Despite being in intense pain she refused an injection to ease it. Her body, she said, was filled with the name of Rama and piercing it would be a sin. She asked for a mat to be spread on the ground and lay on it. Placing her head on the lap of Pacchayi, a friend, she chanted the names of Rama and Anjaneya. The Baba had promised her a peaceful end and with sufficient consciousness to chant the name of Rama. And so it came to pass. The time was 10:30 am.[14] As the women of Tiruvayyaru trickled in, in ones and twos and began singing softly, the unwanted girl child of Vakil Subba Rao passed away, a ripe old woman, secure in her devotion to Tyagaraja.

A telegram was sent to Banni Bai informing her of the demise. When she came the next morning she found long queues snaking their way to Nagarathnamma's door. Inside, she found Nagarathnamma's body dressed in the traditional red sari and seated in her usual reclining chair. Two bowls of *kumkum* and *vibhuti* had been placed by her side and the people were helping themselves from these as they would do at a temple.[15] It was customary in the temple of Srirangam and a few other shrines, Tiruvarur included, that when a Devadasi died, her last raiment would be gifted by the shrine to which she was attached and the flame for lighting her pyre would be sent from the temple kitchen. But Nagarathnamma was no ordinary Devadasi. Her patron saint sent his vehicle to carry her on her last journey. At 11:00 am, the chariot in which Tyagaraja's portrait was usually taken out in procession was brought to the house. Amidst the chanting of Rama's name, the body was placed in the chariot and the procession set out for Tyagaraja's Samadhi with CV Rajagopalachariar leading it. Thousands, including many women, lined the streets and sang "Raghupati Raghava Raja Ram" as the cortege passed. Garlands were heaped on the body by the mourners.[16]

There was considerable debate as to where Nagarathnamma ought to be buried. She herself in her will had identified a spot on the banks of the river, to the eastern end of the Samadhi land and facing the shrine, but a group of people felt that this was very far and difficult to access. The orthodox elements objected to the idea of a woman and a Devadasi at that, being buried in the grounds where many *sanyasis* had been interred. As the procession reached the Samadhi, tension mounted and the police and the Boy Scouts had to be called in to maintain order. The shopkeepers of the town downed shutters in protest against the move to bury Nagarathnamma in any place other than the Samadhi land. That clinched the issue and a grave was dug close to the banks of the river exactly as Tyagaraja would have wished. When it was completed a few drops of rain fell as though in benediction. As the men looked up at the sky, they noticed an eagle circling the spot.[17] This was considered a good augury. As her mortal remains were lowered into the pit, speeches, praising her, were made by CV Rajagopalachariar and leaders of the merchant community.

It was the first and last time that the historic burial ground of Tiruvayyaru was receiving the body of a woman. As the earth closed in on Nagarathnamma, there was a spontaneous outpouring of grief. Meals were not cooked in most homes that day. In Madras, the Sri Tyagabrahma Mahotsava Sabha met to pass a condolence resolution. Musiri Subramania Iyer stated that her dynamic presence would be missed in future Tyagaraja *Aradhanas*.[18]

For days afterwards, CV Rajagopalachariar harboured the doubt that miscreants may desecrate Nagarathnamma's grave. He repaired every evening to the spot and remained there till late at night, keeping a vigil. After a few days a *brindavanam* was built over the grave. The first anniversary of Nagarathnamma's death was observed as per her wishes with the feeding of the poor, with Banni Bai supervising the proceedings.

Then one day, a *sanyasi* who had lived close to a Hanuman temple in Tiruvayyaru called on Banni Bai. Very little was known of this man, except that he was once a railway employee having last worked as stationmaster in the temple town of Sholinghur. He desired to erect a statue of Nagarathnamma over her Samadhi. A life-size stone image of the lady was soon ready. She was depicted in a seated posture, with her hands folded in obeisance to Tyagaraja. This was installed over the grave facing the Samadhi and a small structure was erected over it. On the day of the installation, Banni Bai and her sister were present and ceremoniously offered worship to the statue.[19] And there Nagarathnamma remains, ever watching over the Samadhi of her mentor.

Banni Bai later wrote the biography of Nagarathnamma and composed songs on her, which were to be used for performing a *Harikatha* on her life. It was the story of how in an art form, where women were largely considered inferior and if belonging to the Devadasi community equated with prostitutes, the greatest musical personality, Tyagaraja, chose to fulfil himself and perpetuate his own memory through the sacrifices of a woman.

Incredible though it may seem, the Samadhi and the sub-shrine to Nagarathnamma remained devoid of electric supply for ten long years. It was with great difficulty that devotees managed to visit the place in the evenings, except when the *Aradhana* was in progress, when of course the place was a blaze of light. None of the musicians came forward to do anything about it and it was again left to a woman to make it possible. Kolar Rajam, a Devadasi, funded the electric wiring and illumination of the Samadhi in 1962, in memory of her beloved consort *mridangam* maestro Palani Subramania Pillai, who passed away that year.

The original trustees of the Nagarathnamma Trust passed away, one after the other and the Trust passed into the hands of others who ran it their own way. It is now said that most of the properties bequeathed by her to the Trust, both moveable and immoveable are no longer in its possession and today it only retains ownership of the Samadhi premises and the surrounding land. Certainly, the numerous charities that she stipulated to be performed in temples of Madras and Mysore are no longer being observed. The valuable pictures of Gods and Goddesses covered in gold leaf that she left behind at the Samadhi no longer exist. Her portrait however hangs close to the sanctum and reminds visitors of her greatness. Her *puja* is looked after at the shrine.

The *Aradhana* has however become a grand affair with television coverage adding to the glamour. Indeed, the story of the *Aradhana* and the way it has developed over the years after Nagarathnamma's death would make for fascinating reading. Suffice to say, it does not in any way represent the spirit of piety that Malaikottai Govindasami Pillai, Soolamangalam Vaidyanatha Bhagavatar and Bangalore Nagarathnamma brought to its observance. Even the direct line of sight that the statue of Nagarathnamma enjoys on ordinary days, to the Samadhi of Tyagaraja is obscured during the *Aradhana* with a screen being put up in front of her shrine. By 1990, Nagarathnamma was a distant memory though she remained fresh in the thoughts of those whose lives she touched. Replying that year to a letter from Janaki Subramaniam, Banni Bai, by then a respected senior citizen in the world of arts, wrote regretfully that she did not even have a photograph of Nagarathnamma in her possession. Even the biography of Nagarathnamma which she had penned was not with her and it was with great difficulty that she managed to obtain a photocopy and pass on to Janaki. Recording a *Harikatha* on *Rukmini Kalyanam* for the archival centre, Sampradaya, Banni Bai stated that the life of Nagarathnamma should serve as an inspiration and that while it was being rapidly forgotten, she was sure someday it would be revived. She herself passed away a few years ago, her wish that a *Harikatha* on the life of Nagarathnamma be performed, being fulfilled by her disciple Gowri Rajagopal.[20]

The 50th death anniversary of Nagarathnamma passed by unnoticed in 2002. It would appear that everyone had forgotten the sacrifices the woman had made to ensure that Tyagaraja's Samadhi became a worthy memorial to him. It was in that year that I made up my mind to pen a biography of Nagarathnamma. A precis of her life appeared in *www.sangeetham.com,* the website I, along with Sanjay Subrahmanyan, ran at that time. I had first read her story in 1984 when T Sankaran had written about her in the *Sruti* magazine. Even then, when I was a freshman in college, it made a deep impression on me. It was however only when I delivered a talk on Bangalore Nagarathnamma's life at

The Tag Centre under the auspices of the South India Heritage Series organised by Ramu Endowments in 2005, that I once again began seriously thinking about a biography of this remarkable woman.

The task of getting any information about her, beyond what lay in the published biographical accounts of T Sankaran and Mysore Vasudevachar appeared near impossible. As I set about collecting information several incidents happened that made me feel that I was being guided about my work by an unseen hand. I was given a copy of Banni Bai's biography of Nagarathnamma by my good friend and fellow contributing editor of *Sruti*, Lakshmi Devnath. A copy of Nagarathnamma's will was left with me by Manna Srinivasan, *Sruti's* Roving Editor. I had heard about a chapter on Nagarathnamma in one of DV Gundappa's books and was searching for it everywhere. One day Swami Gautamanandji Maharaj of the Sri Ramakrishna Math called for me after he had read my book *Carnatic Summer*. During the conversation Maharaj enquired if I was working on any other book. I mentioned this biography of Nagarathnamma's. Maharaj immediately brought out the book of Gundappa's, that I was looking for and finding that I did not read Kannada got the librarian of the Math, Bhooma Padmanabhan to translate it for me. It was through this article that I came to know about Justice Narahari Rao and the important role he played in Nagarathnamma's life.

The next task was to find out more about Justice Rao. A chance mention of his name to my friend PV Laxminarayana brought forth the reply that he was related to the descendants of Justice Rao and he arranged for a meeting with them in Bangalore. I was thus able to obtain a handwritten manuscript written by their kinsman on the life of Justice Rao. The finding of Nagarathnamma's eyrie, Mount Joy was an adventure by itself and many a taxi driver of Bangalore wearied at the task of identifying the place. Finally I managed to locate it and it was the happiest moment in my life when I saw the inscription carved by Justice Rao over the temple arch. It appeared to assure me that my quest for Nagarathnamma would be successful. I have since made many visits to this hillock and prayed at the shrine where once Nagarathnamma too must have worshipped. I was however unable to obtain any information on Nagarathnamma's other patron, CS Rajarathna Mudaliar.

It was well-known danseuse and writer Lakshmi Viswanathan who first alerted me to the story of Nagarathnamma challenging the Tiruvarur Kondi family over their right to dance at the Tyagaraja temple. Shortly after this I did an interview of PR Thilagam, the last of the Kondi line for the *Sruti* magazine and she did confirm to me the veracity of the story.

The Tamil Nadu Archives was a storehouse of information on the *Radhika Santwanamu* episode in Nagarathnamma's life. It was however from Indira Menon's book, *The Madras Quartet* that I first came to know of the book and Nagarathnamma's role in publishing it. Subsequently, the two-volume *Women's Writing in India* compiled by Susie Tharu and K Lalitha gave me valuable information on the file numbers in which the Archives contained information on the *Radhika Santwanamu*. Similarly, the books by Kay Jordan and Priyadarshini Vijaishri on the Devadasi system showed me the way to Government files on the subject. I can never forget the thrill I experienced when turning over a page in a file, I saw Nagarathnamma's signature in English. A very valuable and helpful contact I obtained through Dr Priyadarshini Vijaishri was Mehboob Basha of the Ambedkar University, Lucknow. He gave me the pages of the 1929 *Grihalakshmi* issue in which the debate between Nagarathnamma and V Saraswathi features.

Among those whom I interviewed for this book, two are sadly no more. One was music historian TS Parthasarathy and the other was singer T Muktha. I benefited immensely from my conversations with Tiruvayyaru Chellam Iyer, who though disagreeing with my analysis of

Nagarathnamma's contribution to the *Aradhana,* gave me several papers pertaining to the time when the Katchis conducted the Aradhana. Chellam Iyer even now represents the interests of the erstwhile Chinna Katchi and is fighting to establish the rights of that group to worship at the Samadhi. It was also he who told me about the existence of Seethapathi, Nagarathnamma's assistant who still lives at Tiruvayyaru. I met this remarkable nonagenarian thanks to the efforts of Dr R Kausalya, retired Principal of the Maharajah's College, Tiruvayyaru who not only managed to locate him but also got him to stay at her warm and hospitable house in Tillaisthanam, till I managed to come down and interview him. During lunch I could not help noticing that while I, in my forties, refused ghee and fried vegetables, Seethapathi ate everything with relish. I must also thank Dr Kausalya for introducing me to Nagarathnamma's coachman Krishnan. My interview of him as he bathed under a village tap was a unique experience. I am also indebted to Dr Kausalya for her mentioning Janaki Subramaniam to me. However it was KV Ramanathan, ever my mentor and the editor-in-chief of *Sruti* who managed to locate her and give me an introduction to her. I spent a happy afternoon with lunch thrown in, chatting with Janaki and Nagarathnamma emerged a better-defined personality at the end of it. The highpoint of that afternoon was my connecting Saguna Bai and Janaki over the phone. I had earlier met Saguna Bai, thanks to my friend Sujatha Shankar. It was a moving experience watching the two women picking up the threads after so many years, now laughing, now shedding tears over the joys and sorrows that life had dealt them.

It was however my Saturday afternoon sessions with my friend VAK Ranga Rao that I enjoyed the most. VAK translated the preface to the *Radhika Santwanamu* into English and his being one of the few people around today, who had met Nagarathnamma and interacted with her, succeeded in bringing her to life for me. VAK wanted me to digitise a few songs sung by Nagarathnamma and enclose them in a CD, along with this book, but paucity of time has not allowed me to fulfil his wishes. It was also through VAK that I met Gopalakrishna Yachendra, the younger son of the last Rajah of Venkatagiri.

T Sankaran, in his article on Bangalore Nagarathnamma mentioned that the March 1949 issue of *Grihalakshmi* contained a detailed account of Nagarathnamma's life. I located a copy of this magazine at the Amarajeevi Potti Sriramulu Library and thanks to the kindness of Y Ramakrishnan, obtained a photocopy of it. My friend Sujatha Lakshminarayan translated it for me into English. Had it not been for Mr Ramakrishnan and Sujatha, this book would have lost out on some valuable information. Similarly, I am indebted to Dr N Ramanathan, retired Professor and Head of the Department of Music, Madras University, for providing me with the only review of a Nagarathnamma concert, written by Bhatkhande himself. I must also thank Dr Premeela Gurumurthy, the present Head of the Department of Music, Madras University for the interest she took in this book and Dr S Samanthakamani, Head of the Telugu Department, Madras University, for loaning me her personal copy of the 1950 edition of the *Radhika Santwanamu*. Many thanks also to eminent scholar BM Sundaram for the nuggets of information he gave me. I must also thank *The Hindu* and in particular K Rajendrababu, its librarian, who gave me many news clippings related to Nagarathnamma. Thanks are also due to Sivakumar of *Dinamani Kadir*, who gave me the information regarding Nagarathnamma's Tamil work.

Then there were a few others, all of them very important, as far as I am concerned, who by continuously listening to my 'finds' about Nagarathnamma, whether it interested them or not, kept my enthusiasm high. On this list would be Sanjay Subrahmanyan and his wife Aarthi, Prasanna Ramaswami, '*Sruti*' Janaki and Sushila Ravindranath. All credit for the title of this book must go to S Muthiah, the well-known historian of Madras and my mentor, who gave this title to an article I wrote on Nagarathnamma for the *Madras Musings*.

On the home front, I think my in-laws kind of resigned themselves to a son-in-law who was eternally steeped to the gills in Devadasis and spoke of little else. My parents wisely chose not to investigate too deeply. Avinash and Abhinav, my sons, I think must be the only pre-teens to know all about the Devadasi system and be as familiar with Nagarathnamma as their friends are with current-day film stars! And as for Sarada, the light of my life, as always everything that I do is dedicated to her in full measure. For which wife would tolerate 'another woman' in her husband's life for so many years?

As I am always fighting for the preservation of old buildings, I cannot resist putting in a bit about the buildings associated with Nagarathnamma. There is practically nothing left. According to DV Gundappa, the house, in which she lived when she first came to Bangalore, was near the Kalikamba Temple in Nagarathpet. Today, finding it is impossible. 'Bangalore', the house that Justice Narahari Rao built her on Mount Joy has vanished, though the temple she worshipped in, survives almost intact, barring the addition of a *gopuram* in front. Nagarathnamma's house in Srinivasa Iyer Street, George Town, Madras still stands though it has changed considerably, externally. Rather aptly, given her learning and erudition, the house is today called Saraswathi Nilayam. The market that Nagarathnamma built for the Nandikeswara Temple in Tiruvottiyur is unrecognisable, given that the area is a warren of shops today. In Tiruvayyaru too, there is nothing that commemorates her, what with the house where she lived, Tyagabrahma Nilayam having been sold by the Trust. The Tuesday Ghat Chattram still stands, with its Maratha period wall paintings slowly peeling away and the carvings on the exterior, crumbling, owing to years of neglect. The temples at which she regularly worshipped, the Ekambareswara Swami temple of George Town and the Prasanna Seetharama Anjaneya

Swami temple in Thatha Muthiappan street survive even now. Of course the Tyagaraja Samadhi, with which she was most intimately associated, has since expanded to comprise a Valmiki Mandapam built by the collections of a postal department employee, Srirangam Sundaram Iyer, who dreamt of all the songs of Tyagaraja being inscribed on marble slabs around the Samadhi. This he completed by means of public donations over a period of five years from 1953 to 1958.

As for the written works of Nagarathnamma, none barring her *shloka* on Tyagaraja survive. Her edition of the *Radhika Santwanamu* was republished in 1950 and has since been in print. However, the *Panchikarana Bhautika Viveka Vilakkam, Madya Panam* and the *Devadasi Prabhodha Chandrodayam* are not traceable. Perhaps they are gathering dust in some library.

What then is the legacy of Nagarathnamma? From an under-privileged background, she rose by sheer dint of hard work and talent and made it big in life. Despite earning enormous amounts of wealth, she chose not to rest on her laurels and continued involving herself in one passion after another. If it was not the *Radhika Santwanamu*, it was the fight against the Anti-Nautch lobby. Once that was over, it was the Tyagaraja *Aradhana*, where she not only created a temple for the composer but did not rest till musicians united in the observance of the annual rite. When this was done, she dedicated herself to collecting funds for the improvement of the area and till the very end, she was involved in the propagation of Tyagaraja's songs. She had any number of patrons and yet she never took the easy way out by subsuming her personality to theirs. She retained an individual identity and stood up to be counted in a male-dominated society. She encouraged women to come to the fore, fought for their rights and established their equality with men in the music field, without once consciously being aware that she was leading such a movement. Coming from a community that was considered backward, she did not wallow in misery and seek help. On the other hand, she prided herself on her background and forced the world at large to recognise her and take pride in being associated with her. Finally, from the status of a vilified Devadasi she rose to become a venerated saint. Perhaps there is a lesson in her life for all of us.

A summer day is drawing to a close. The monsoons in Nagarathnamma's Mysore have been plentiful and so the river in Tyagaraja's Tiruvayyaru is in full flow. Children are swinging from banyan roots and jumping into the water, though adults keep admonishing them that the water is not fit to bathe in for the first few days after it is released. The house where Tyagaraja lived has been demolished in order to make way for a 'memorial befitting the saint', whatever that means. Perhaps a monstrosity will emerge, all granite, marble and mosaic. Nagarathnamma would have protested, had she been around. There is talk of a *tambura*-shaped hall to be built, facing the Samadhi. This is in direct contravention to the old lady's wishes. But then who is to fight her battle?

It is dusk as I walk into the Samadhi compound in Tiruvayyaru. Tyagaraja's Samadhi is still locked and I walk around it. Cheek by jowl with it, a 'modern' public lavatory has been constructed and as is customary in our country even the surroundings are treated as an extension of the toilet. Nagarathnamma would have never allowed this to happen. Perhaps they do not make people like her anymore. I, like everyone else, walk through the human refuse, complaining about it, but not thinking of doing anything constructive. As I turn the corner, Nagarathnamma's Samadhi comes into full view. I walk across and peer in through the locked doors at the statue. The lines of writer Malan, as once recited by scholar Sujatha Vijayaraghavan come to mind:

*Kings worshipped him*
*Musicians sold his songs and survived*
*Was it not a courtesan who built him a temple?*

# References

1 Ramanujachari, C; p 578.

2 Nagarathnam, Bangalore; Last Will and Testament; 4th January 1949.

3 Information given by maestro Madurai GS Mani.

4 Information given by PR Thilagam.

5 Letter from Bangalore Nagarathnamma dated 11th August 1951; courtesy Sri KN Sundaram.

6 Grihalakshmi; p 5-64.

7 Interview with Janaki Subramaniam; Bangalore; July 2007.

8 The Hindu; January 26th, 1951.

9 Interview with Seethapathi, assistant to Bangalore Nagarathnamma at Tiruvayyaru, May 2006.

10 The Hindu; 1st February, 1951.

11 Jackson, William J; p 152

12 Interview with Mr Gopalakrishna Yachendra, younger son of the last Rajah of Venkatagiri in Chennai; June 2007.

13 Information given by AR Sundaram; Chennai; May 2007.


14 Bai, C Banni; p 18.

15 Ibid; p 16.

16 The Hindu; 20th May 1952.

17 Bai, C Banni; p 19.

18 The Hindu; 21st May 1952.

19 Bai, C Banni; p 20.

20 Information given by Dr Premeela Gurumurthy.

# Glossary of Terms

Abhinaya – Art of depicting emotions mostly using facial expressions and hand movements.

Alapana – (also *ragalapana*). Elaboration of ragas. This is extempore music and a lot depends on the creativity of the artiste.

Amavasya – New moon day.

Aradhana – An annual worship; obeisance.

Ardra Darshanam – A festival dedicated to Nataraja (Siva as the cosmic dancer) which falls in the month of *Margazhi* (Dec/Jan).

Ashtottaram – A hymn containing 108 names of a deity.

Ashram – Hermitage

Bai – When used in connection with the arts in North India, this term usually signified a courtesan.

Bhagavatar – One who sings the name of God, also denotes a male singer.

Bhajan – The singing, mostly in chorus, of the name of God.

Bhajana Mandiram – A place where *bhajan*s are rendered regularly.

Bhakti – Devotion

Bharatanatyam – South Indian classical dance, formerly known as *Dasi Attam* or *Sadir*.

Brahmotsavam – Annual festival in a temple.

Chattram – Rest house for the public.

Choultry – See *Chattram*.

Dasa Koota – A sect whose members were devotees of Hari or Vishnu and who sustained the *Bhakti* movement.

Dasi Attam – The dance of the Dasis. See *Bharatanatyam*, also *Sadir*.

Devaranama – Devotional songs in Kannada.

Dewan – Prime Minister of a princely state in pre-independent India.

Dharma – Righteousness; duty.

Dubash – Agents who knew two languages and who could therefore translate from one to the other.

Durbar – A king's court.

Gopuram – Temple spire.

Harikatha – Literally the story of Hari or Vishnu. This is an art form where the main performer recites a puranic or historic story using songs, *shloka*s and verses to illustrate the tale. He/She is usually accompanied by a singer, a violinist, a *mridangist* and sometimes a harmonist and a chorus.

Hartal – A protest/strike.

Idli – Steamed South Indian rice cake, a popular breakfast dish.

Jalatarangam – A method of percussion using porcelain cups filled with water. The cups are struck using thin bamboo sticks.

Janmashtami – The festival of Krishna's birth, usually celebrated in the month of *Avani* (Aug/Sep).

Jati- Group or caste.

Javali – Originally connoting lewd love poetry, *Javali*s are today a genre by themselves and can be best defined as semi-classical love songs.

Kalpana Swaras – (also *Swarakalpana*) Extempore strings of notes sung to a *tala* and dovetailing with a particular line in the lyric.

Kannadiga – A person whose mother tongue is Kannada.

Kathakalakshepam – See *Harikatha*.

Kirtana – A musical form akin to the *Kriti*.

Kriti – The three-part song that forms the bulk of Carnatic repertoire.

Kumbha Harati – The rite of waving a camphor flame placed on a brass pot in front of a deity and signifying the climax of the worship.

Kumkum – Vermilion powder which women place on their forehead as an auspicious symbol.

Kutchery – The concert.

Laya – Rhythm

Linga – The phallus, worshipped as a representation of Shiva.

Mandapam – Pavilion.

Manipravalam – A song which has Sanskrit and at least one other language in it.

Mantra – Hymn

Mridangam – South Indian drum that is a vital component of Carnatic concerts. Shaped like two bottomless flowerpots joined at the rim, it is made of jack wood. It has two faces, both made of hide. The one that always faces the audience is called the *valantalai* and has a round circle made of a black paste comprising boiled rice and fine iron filings with other elements added to it. This gives the *mridangam* its tone. The other face called the *toppi*, is made of buffalo hide and is the face with the greater diameter. Sixteen braces of leather connect the two and by adjusting the tension of these, the pitch of the instrument can be raised and lowered.

Mutt – A religious institution.

Nabob – Corruption of Nawab and indicating the early Englishmen who became rich in India.

Nautch – An Anglo-Indian term for Indian dance.

Navaratri – Festival of Nine Nights, observed in September/October.

Pallavi – Single line of lyrics which is used for extrapolation and rendition as part of a suite comprising *Ragam* (which is the *alapana*), *Tanam* and *Pallavi*. This is often referred to as the RTP suite. Such Pallavis are often set to complicated talas and are a test of the musician's calibre. The refrain of a *kriti* is also called *pallavi*.

Pancharatnam – Five gems.

Pandal – A temporary pavilion generally covered with thatch.

Pottu – A disc of gold worn around the neck as a symbol of marriage. For Devadasis this was the symbol of dedication to a deity.

Prabandam – One of the four original forms of South Indian music. The term also denotes verses from hymns.

Puja – Worship

Puranas – Mythological tales.

Ragalapana – See *Alapana*.

Ragamalika – A song set to different ragas.

Rama Natakam – An opera based on the Ramayana composed by Arunachala Kavi.

Rudraksha – The dark berries of *Elaeocarpus ganitrus*, used to make Shaivite prayer beads.

Sabha – Literally a gathering. But now denotes an organised body that holds concerts.

Sadir – The old name for classical South Indian dance.

Samadhi – In the context of this book, a memorial to a saint.

Sambar – A popular tamarind and lentils-based South Indian gravy.

Sangeetha Vidwan – Musician

Sangita Sahitya Kavita Visarada – One who is an expert in music, prose and poetry.

Sanyasi – One who has renounced the world.

Sastras – Scriptures

Satyagraha – A form of non-violent resistance developed by Mahatma Gandhi.

Shraddha – Annual ceremony for the dead.

Shringara – Eroticism

Shloka/Sloka – Sanskrit hymns that are usually sung in various ragas as part of extempore music in the latter phase of a concert. These are sung without rhythm.

Sri Vidya – An elaborate form of Devi worship.

Swamigal – A holy personage. Tyagaraja is often referred to thus.

Swarabath – A stringed instrument now no longer in use.

Swarakalpana – see *Kalpana Swaras*.

Tambura – Stringed instrument strummed for maintaining the pitch/drone.

Tahsildar – A sub-district level Government functionary in charge of a portion of a district called a *taluk* or *tahsil*.

Tali – Pendant of gold worn around the neck by women as a symbol of marriage.

Tavil – The main percussion instrument for *nagaswaram* performances.

Tiruppavai – A set of thirty verses composed by the Vaishnavite saint Andal. These are usually sung early in the morning during the month of *Margazhi* (Dec/Jan).

Tiruppugazh – Tamil verses composed by Arunagirinathar of the 14th century AD.

Tulasi – Indian basil.

Upanyasam – Religious discoursing.

Vakil – Indian lawyer.

Varnam – A type of song that has three parts like the *kriti*, but has more *swara*s or notes and less of lyrics. There are simple *varnam*s that are taught to beginners and more complicated ones that advanced practitioners of the art learn. It is usually the practice to begin a performance with a *varnam* as it settles the voice. *Varnam*s are usually rendered at a brisk pace and this also helps the concert begin in a lively fashion.

Vibhuti – Sacred ash.

Vidwan – A learned person. In this context a musician.

Vairamudi – Stylised diamond-studded headgear for idols.

Yakshagana – Ethnic theatre of the Mysore region.

Zamindari – Vast estates. The head was referred to as *Zamindar* and his wife as the *Zamindarini*.

Zenana – Women's quarters in a royal household.

# Index